Endorser

I was new to faith, and one of the more youthful saints worshipping at All Saints, Marple when God called Wendy to Beirut. I was shocked that God and God's church would risk someone so young, attractive and full of potential to the little-known dangers of Lebanon. Reading Wendy's story today, fifty years after her call, makes me ask a different question: *What if Wendy hadn't listened to God?* It's a question all Christians must ask, and the answer is rarely easy for those who trust enough to obey.

Rev. Dr Dennis Bailey, PhD
South Africa

The tapestry Wendy creates is far more than a personal recollection of a journey of service in Lebanon in response to God's call. That story is interwoven with vivid descriptions of Lebanon's troubled beauty, glimpses into nearby contexts and freeze-frames of a defining period of collective trauma in Lebanon. Rich cultural insights (from surprises and frustrations encountered in the education system to the overwhelming hospitality and loyalty of family-like friends) bring further colour. And the golden thread, running clearly through every page, is God's sovereignty and His care for His people, even in the midst of chaos, suffering and heartbreak. The events depicted in this tapestry may be decades old, but the message is thoroughly current. The Middle East region remains highly volatile, and millions know nothing of God's love and truth. There remains an urgent need for gospel workers who, like Wendy, will step out in faith, filled with Christ's love, delighted to share not only the gospel of God but also their lives (1 Thessalonians 2:8).

Stephen
Alumnus of Miss Radcliffe's Eastwood College Kindergarten, 1975
Now serving in a regional mission leadership role

Eye-opening, inspiring, enriching, humbling are just some of the ways to describe this book. Wendy's call to work in Lebanon as a teacher in the 1970s, her preparations and overland journey to that country, and the eventful years that followed are vividly brought to us, drawn from the letters she wrote home that were faithfully cherished by her mother. We are given an insight not just into the place, but even more into the people she got to know and love, and the children with whom she longed to share the message of God's saving grace. And running as a constant theme throughout the whole is the mercy, protection, guidance and daily sustaining from the Lord which Wendy experienced in the most demanding and frightening situations. Wendy has given us her personal story and her insights into how God brought her through every setback. Her daily dependence on the Lord is a challenge and inspiration to the reader.

Hazel Bolton, MA(Cantab)

This is a life story told with warmth and conviction. Wendy heard God's call to the Middle East at the age of eleven. After training as a teacher, she went to Lebanon to work in a Christian school. She found a country of great beauty with mountains, cedars, vineyards and flowers. But war was approaching, with killing, destruction and danger, through which she was sustained by a sense of God's protection and constant presence for many years. Later she married, and she and her husband have continued to work with those in the Middle East.

Sue Ingleby, RGN.Dip.Couns., BACP, Accred.

This is a very readable story of how God calls a young, dedicated teacher to set up a Kindergarten department in a new Christian school in Lebanon prior to the Civil War which began in 1975. The school was in a hotly contested area just outside Beirut and frequently came under attack. Wendy is very honest about the joys and pains of entering into a new culture. But her contextualised approach to teaching clearly makes a deep impression on her young pupils, and makes the gospel very relevant to them in their difficult lives. One of the striking features of the story is the way she is sustained at every stage by the Bible and prayer. On almost every page she shares verses of Scripture that speak to her at crucial times; and she proves the power of prayer by asking her parents and supporting churches back home to pray about very specific issues. Having lived ourselves through some of these difficult times in Beirut, we have learned a lot about how Wendy and others lived through some very hard experiences.

Colin and Anne Chapman
Former mission partners in Lebanon with CMS

Letters from Lebanon

In peace and war,
reaching children
with God's love

Wendy Davies

O&U
Onwards & Upwards

Onwards and Upwards Publishers

4 The Old Smithy
London Road
Rockbeare
EX5 2EA
United Kingdom

www.onwardsandupwards.org

First edition, published in the United Kingdom by Onwards and Upwards Publishers Ltd. (2024).

ISBN: 978-1-78815-793-3
Typeface: Book Antiqua

The views and opinions expressed in this book are the author's own, and do not necessarily represent the views and opinions of Onwards and Upwards Publishers or its staff.

Every effort has been made by the author to obtain the necessary permissions to reproduce copyrighted material. If, however, there have been any omissions or errors, please contact the publisher to have these corrected in future reprints and editions.

About the Author

Wendy Davies was born in Ashton-under-Lyne, Lancashire, shortly after her father, Graham Radcliffe, was demobbed from the RAF at the end of World War II. She had always wanted to work with children and enjoyed teaching Sunday school classes long before she trained as a primary teacher. Her life call was to work with Arab peoples and share God's love, especially with the children.

In 1973, following two visits to Morocco to help with Easter holiday clubs for expat children, the opportunity arose to help start a new bilingual Christian school in Lebanon. After much prayer and deliberation, aged twenty-six, she responded to the invitation and found herself in the midst of a totally different culture which she grew to love. No sooner was the school becoming established than Lebanon plunged into a devastating civil war which lasted until the early 1990s. With the passage of the years of war and the multiple displacements, the families of the children she taught are doubtless now scattered around the world. Only eternity will reveal their heart responses to the message of Jesus and God's love which was shared in school day by day.

Back in England, Wendy taught in Gloucester and Cheltenham and never lost her love of Arabic-speaking people. In 1992 she married Ian Davies and together they work to support Arab believers where they suffer for their faith in the Middle East and North Africa.

To contact the author, please write to:

Wendy Davies
c/o Onwards and Upwards Publishers
4 The Old Smithy, London Road
Rockbeare
EX5 2EA

Letters from Lebanon

Contents

PREFACE v

ACKNOWLEDGEMENTS vi

DEDICATION vii

INTRODUCTION 1

1. Faith, Hope and Glory 5
2. The Invitation and Call 15
3. Borderlines and Boxes 21
4. Lebanon and the New School 32
5. A Benevolent Dragon 48
6. Life with the Lebanese 61
7. The First Christmas 77
8. Amine's Vision 87
9. To Sydney and Back 94
10. Visiting 107
11. Hospital, Holidays and Home Again! 112
12. A Growing Challenge 123
13. Unsettling Times 139
14. Out of Egypt I Called My Son 147
15. Peace that Passes Understanding 158
16. Shooting Permitting 176
17. Walking in the Midst of Trouble 193
18. Blue Peter and Bible College 212
19. Return to Lebanon 226
20. Damascene Adventure 239
21. Hammana 249
22. Disappointments and Miracles 269
23. The End of the Beginning 284

EPILOGUE 300

APPENDIX 303

Letters from Lebanon

Preface

It is nearly fifty years since my feet first stood on Lebanese soil. Following those footsteps has been at times exciting and at times painful, as I have sought to understand the complexities of the life I encountered there and God's loving and glorious purposes running through it all.

It is not my intention to present a closely worded explanation of the history or politics of the Middle East. This has been excellently reported elsewhere. Nor do I wish to place any rationale or logic upon the sequence of events or my involvement. Rather, I invite the reader to walk with me through my letters, diaries and other memories and share in my attempt to *"remember how the LORD your God led you all the way"*[1].

Praise to His name!

April 2023

---

[1] Deuteronomy 8:2

Acknowledgements

The book you hold in your hands has taken twenty-five years to write, but the letters and memories upon which it is based go back much further than that – a lifetime, in fact. There are a number of important people I wish to acknowledge who have helped to bring it to fruition.

The challenge to write came from my mother, who kept all the letters I wrote when working in Lebanon during the 1970s. In their memory, I thank both my late parents for the sacrifice they made in allowing me to follow God's call on my life as a young teacher and for supporting me in prayer throughout. I also thank the late Edith Bowyer and the saints of All Saints Church, Marple for their prayers and generosity to me during that period.

My early mentor in the writing process was the late Margaret Potts, who sat with me on a regular basis as we sifted through my letters and photos. I am grateful for her eye for detail and listening ear as I started to put the memories into words. I also acknowledge the late Linda Gay, who deciphered my handwriting, gave affirmative feedback and typed the whole manuscript to the end of chapter 9. Nearly twenty years elapsed before I was able to write again, and I was greatly encouraged by the provision of a 'writing retreat' in the nearby home of Lorna and Jeremy Shearman whilst they were visiting friends in the States. From chapter 10 onwards, I acknowledge the help of Alison Pascoe, who has given hours of work typing the remainder of the book.

I am also indebted to my precious proofreading friends – Moira Johnson, Ann Grüneberg, Phil Hall, Hazel Bolton and the late Frances Briscoe – all of whom have given their time and language skills to the process. My husband, Ian, has aided and abetted in numerous ways, not least in his desire to affirm me through the ups and downs of revisiting the memories, but also when he was travelling in the Middle East and I had the house to myself!

Throughout the publishing process I acknowledge the help of the team at Onwards and Upwards and thank them for their creative skills, their attention to detail and their friendly support at every stage.

To the precious children of Lebanon, the Khoury family and all the staff with whom I lived and worked from 1973 to 1980.

To God be the glory!

Letters from Lebanon

Introduction

T he noise was deafening – crashes, bangs, booms and explosions from far and near – would it ever cease? Night after night, day after day, merciless, godless – but was it? Suddenly, the unexpected happened, pulsating through my entire brain and body as I lay huddled, cocooned within my sleeping bag. What was it? What was happening to me? Why was *I* in the midst of all this senselessness? It was senseless to be here, and yet my songs of praise were drowning the explosions. Does the wrath of men really praise Him? The more they shoot and shell and murder and destroy, the greater God becomes. Only *He* brings sense into the madness; only *He* brings order into the chaos; only *He* arrests the powers of destruction abroad in this land. And this majestic Being arrests *me*, filling me with spiritual power to live and move and to have my being here in this senseless country. As I pondered the reality of these things, such deep joy filled my whole being and I laughed out loud…

The following Sunday, November 16th, 1975, in the safety of our church building in Beirut, as I sat in those familiar pews, something of the meaning and purpose of being in the centre of God's will for my life started to shift into focus in my mind. What had been happening that night? How was God revealing Himself to me? What was I doing, seemingly trapped in a land that knew only the language of mortar, tank and machine gunfire? As the preacher spoke, I ferreted in my handbag and pulled out a letter from my parents. It was one of the few that had got through, postmarked September 28th, 1975. I started to scribble on the back of the envelope.

This is what I wrote: "Somehow the Lord is bringing me to a climax hitherto unreached as far as my identification with these people and this beleaguered country of Lebanon is concerned. He is able to keep His own: a source of courage in time of fear, strength in weakness and comfort in pain. Many outside have prayed. The church worldwide has had Beirut on its heart, and in this way both the Lord and His people are with us wherever we are. There is no heroism in just sticking it out for the sake of it. Nehemiah's words, *'The joy of the Lord is my strength'*[1], become so real when senseless men are taking their revenge in gunfire and explosions and

---

[1]   Nehemiah 8:10

you find yourself huddled down in the basement of the building with a family of mice scuttling around. In praising Him and acknowledging His control over events while in the midst of them, there comes an overwhelming sense of peace and security, because He is entirely trustworthy and honours His Word: *'Trust in the LORD ... dwell in the land and enjoy safe pasture.'*[2]"

My scribbles continued. "Truly, His ways are higher than the ways of men. To me, when it seems that men's actions are so illogical and unreasonable, so negative and destructive, the Lord proves so abundantly that He is entirely other than men. He is a rational Being, and He is in control of what to me seems so senseless. Multiplying it all together, could it possibly be that all these negatives will produce something positive in the calculations of my Heavenly Father? I simply have to place myself in a position of commitment to Him. Then He brings His own reward – *joy* – the joy that brings forth even more praise in the midst of pain and suffering. This is the joy that Christ prayed for His followers, just before His final hour came, for those who would obey Him and abide in His love. It is the reward, not of frantic activity in His service, but of patient waiting and suffering. It is the blessing only the Holy Spirit can bring to God's children."

As the sermon drew to a close, I reflected that this was perhaps a pivotal moment in my life; a subconscious realisation that God's Holy Spirit was being poured afresh into my life and being for a purpose. *"...if indeed we share in his sufferings in order that we may also share in his glory."*[3] I could only reply with Paul, *"I consider that our present sufferings are not worth comparing with the glory that will be revealed in us."*[4]

Why then was I here in war-torn Lebanon, over two thousand miles from my comfortable home in northern England? It was certainly not for career advancement or to fulfil any personal ambition. God's hand had been upon my life from my earliest memories, and I had trusted Him to lead me throughout my earthly life. I truly believed it was He who had set within my heart the desire, even the passion, to identify with Arabic-speaking peoples from an early age. *"Remember how the LORD your God led you all the way in the desert these forty years, to humble you and to test you in*

---

2   Psalm 37:3
3   Romans 8:17b
4   Romans 8:18

order to know what was in your heart..."[5] *"Be careful to follow every command I am giving you today, so that you may live and increase and may enter and possess the land that the LORD promised..."*[6]

And so there follows a personal account of God's call upon my life, as I reflect upon the early stirrings, my Christian upbringing in the face of many struggles and all the ways in which the Lord has led me. My prayer is now, as it was then, "Lord God, may Your greater *glory* be my supreme concern."

To God be the glory, great things He has done.

---

[5] Deuteronomy 8:2
[6] Deuteronomy 8:1

Letters from Lebanon

CHAPTER ONE

Faith, Hope and Glory

It was on January 1st, 1999 that my husband and I went to visit a dear lady who had dedicated her life to serving the Lord through her village church. Her mind was failing then, but I reminded her of the significant part she had played in my life just over forty years earlier. She was my Sunday school teacher for some time and loved to share the books of Christian writers with us as awards for good attendance. One such book was to sow a seed in my life. I still have the original hardback copy that was presented to me in September 1958 with Edith Bowyer's writing inside:

To Wendy, with much love and very happy memories of our Sunday afternoons together.

From her sincere friend and teacher

E. Bowyer

I was nearly twelve. This was the beginning of what has become a lifelong desire to identify with Arab peoples, to live and dwell amongst them and to share with them all that I am: my skills, my talents, my emotions and my Christian faith. My faith? I cannot remember not believing in Jesus, my Friend and Saviour. He was the One to whom I could talk when I could talk to no one else.

I did not have an unhappy childhood, but it was not a carefree one. My earliest memory relates to an incident when I managed to lock my mother out of the main house by means of a small bolt on the hall side of the kitchen door. I must have stood up on my little wooden chair. The front door too was bolted on the inside, and so I was a self-inflicted prisoner in

My parents, Dorothy and Graham
Radcliffe, 1945.

my own house! I recall reaching up to the letterbox, standing on tiptoe in the hall and my mother speaking reassuring words to me: a clever ploy to distract my attention as a neighbour was breaking a panel of glass in the back sitting-room window in order to rescue me! I must have been pretty frightened, really, as I couldn't understand what was expected of me to undo the bolt; I was hungry and wet, and this all seemed quite bewildering. I was barely two years old. My mother was a trained Norland nurse, who prided herself on getting all matters to do with the health and hygiene of babies and young children absolutely perfect, but unbeknown to me at that time, she was struggling with a chronic post-natal depression and life was far from carefree for her.

These were the early post-war years, when rationing was mandatory. We were allowed four eggs per week: one per adult and two for the baby. On one occasion, they were wrapped by the grocer in a brown paper bag and rather trustingly placed by my mother at the front of the large pram in which I was sitting. I have no idea why I decided that particular afternoon to wriggle down through my reins and explore the contents of the brown bag with my toes. Having finished playing, I then handed my mother the brown bag complete with egg dripping through, saying, "Ta!" with a satisfied grin on my face. What a sticky mess! That was the end of the week's egg ration!

I was always falling over, never quite sure whether I was left- or right-footed and acquiring multiple cuts and bruises. Imagine being an angel in a Christmas play aged five or six, wearing a huge bandage around my knee! I was an only child until that age and had few close friends. Jesus was real to me. I enjoyed the local Sunday school and my mother would tell me Bible stories and taught me to pray. If I misunderstood or felt penalised by the harsh realities of life, Jesus was always on my side, and I knew His forgiveness when I felt hurt and guilty. And it was Jesus who gave me the courage to sort myself out, pick myself up, get to school again the next day and do my best to carry on. When life was unhappy through illness in the home, I would retire to my room with its bright red carpet, sit on the bed or by the two-bar electric fire and look out of the window onto Manchester Road and watch the trolley buses trundle by, asking God to protect and care for our family and give us the strength to go on, for by this time my little baby sister was in a cot in the corner of the room.

My father had to travel on business from time to time, mainly to Germany. It was hard when he was away, but how I looked forward to his return, bringing me

Aged four, 1951.
I always loved flowers!

(sometimes late at night) some little trinket or other from his travels, which I cherished greatly! On one occasion, it was a little tortoise made from a walnut shell. I took it to school clutched in my hot, sticky hand and showed it off in the playground at break-time, telling the other children that it was a real tortoise! Another time, he brought an exquisite little box covered in tiny shells and velour-lined, in which to keep my silver threepenny pieces and other treasures. It had "Hamburg" inscribed on the inside of one of the shells. Maybe this is how it would feel when Jesus returns again, this time not as a babe but in all His glory.

I simply loved that word 'glory'. I think I first discovered it towards the end of the Lord's Prayer that we all recited at church. *"For thine is the kingdom, and the power, and the glory, for ever. Amen."*[1] I even wanted my parents to call my little sister 'Glory' because I thought it was such a beautiful word. And it was my hope that one day, when my life here came to an end, I should see Jesus as He really is, full of grace and truth and glorious majesty. This was the greatest of joys to look forward to. Maybe Jesus would even come again before I died – equally glorious – no more suffering or unhappiness. Why I took life so seriously at such a young age was probably related to my mother's emotional illness; nevertheless, I knew within my heart that Jesus loved me and was guiding me through all the joys and jolts of life.

[1] Matthew 6:13 (AV)

Our house in Marple.

It was when I was about eleven or twelve that my father had a *serious* talk with me. This was not altogether a surprise to my sensitive spirit. It made me feel very grown-up to have him confide in me in this way, though I was aware it brought him sadness. He loved my mother dearly, but he was weakened by the demands of her illness, along with the daily trek to the office in Manchester and a growing family. He wanted me to understand that my mother's depression was chronic, that she needed plenty of rest and quiet in the house, and that even on the few occasions when she appeared to be happy and relaxed, she was still 'poorly' – I remember that word so well – still struggling to cope with life.

The implications of this were many and varied. My mother's needs always had to come first, and so, as the eldest, I often had to bear practical responsibilities, along with my father, to ensure the smooth running of the household. On top of the school day, there would be the uncertainty as to how *well* my mother would be. Perhaps she had had a better day; but perhaps not, in which case there would be the verbal barrage of criticism to face up to, usually revolving around the less than perfect state of our bedrooms or toy cupboards. These were difficult times, and life seemed unfair because her standards were somehow unattainable. Then there would be the practical tasks of cooking, washing and ironing, but on such days one could never quite measure up and the atmosphere would be full of judgement and failure. No, life was far from carefree during childhood and adolescence.

It was about that time that Edith awarded me the book for good attendance at Sunday school. It was *Star of Light* by Patricia M. St John. She was a missionary nurse who worked for many years in Morocco, and the story was based upon her life and work with the Moroccan people. I read it again and again, fascinated by the descriptions and the *carefreeness* of a life given entirely to working with the Arabic-speaking people of that land and especially the children. I longed to be trained as a teacher and to be able to give myself in that way. Both my father's mother and my mother's grandmother had been teachers, as well as two great aunts, and they all encouraged me to pursue teaching as a career. Increasingly, as I went through my years of adolescence, I knew that God had a purpose.

In June 1961, when I was fourteen, the Billy Graham Evangelistic Association held meetings at Maine Road Stadium, the home of Manchester City Football Club. Both my parents were involved as counsellors, having themselves come to personal Christian faith some years previously. One evening, towards the end of the meeting, sobbing and yet fully resolved, I made my way forward with the music of *Just as I am, without one plea*[2] playing in the background. Perhaps now I was beginning to understand more fully about the suffering Servant of God, the Lord Jesus Christ Himself. The prophet Isaiah portrayed Him as a tender shoot, unattractive to others and familiar with misunderstanding, rejection and suffering. I knew now why Jesus could be so close to me; why He could draw alongside when I felt weakened and frustrated, when I seemed to be so adept at getting 'the wrong end of the stick'. When He went to the Cross, *"He took up our pain [my weaknesses] and bore our suffering [my sadnesses]. ... he was pierced for our transgressions [my wrongdoings], he was crushed for our iniquities [my failings]; the punishment that brought us peace was upon him, and by his wounds we are healed."*[3] My glorious Friend Jesus was none other than my wounded Healer who would empower me by His Holy Spirit for the whole of my life. I now understood more fully that Jesus had died on the Cross to completely remove all my sin and shame, including the shame of a childhood that was full of care and responsibility. I confessed it all and rededicated my life, my very self, to the Lord Jesus Christ, to serve Him wherever He led.

Edith Bowyer,
my Sunday school teacher.

---

[2] Charlotte Elliott (1789-1871)
[3] Isaiah 53:4-5

The day I left Clarendon School, with my sister and brother, July 1965.

There was an undeniable motivation within me to train and explore all avenues for teaching overseas. I even had the opportunity to meet Patricia St John in person when she was in North Wales looking after her aunt for a short while. Miss Swain, Patricia's aunt, now retired, had been the headmistress of Clarendon School, Abergele in North Wales – a Christian boarding school which I had attended as a boarder for my sixth form years. They were two wonderful, mind-stretching, eye-opening and spiritually enriching years. I did not attain academic excellence, but I found freedom to discover and express myself in a safe, loving and prayerful environment that I shall always recall with gratitude.

Shortly after my arrival at Clarendon, I became aware of the need for a Sunday school teacher at St Margaret's Church, Bodelwyddan, 'the Marble Church' as it was commonly known. Patricia had instigated the children's work with a few local families the previous summer when staying with her aunt. I gained invaluable experience – just imagine being taken in school uniform Sunday by Sunday in term-time to teach these little ones, dutifully wearing my straw boater perched flat on the top of my head, at only seventeen years of age! Pat Moss, with whom I worked, was a friend of Patricia and a member of staff who had a real heart for mission and outreach. She would always stop her Morris estate car halfway down the Clarendon drive on the way to Bodelwyddan for us to have a short time of prayer together, asking that God would go with us, bring His Word to life and use us in the lives of these families.

In the early days, we used the church itself for the Sunday school. I would carefully prop up my visual aids against the marble font for storytelling, and the four-, five- and six-year-olds would sit around me in a circle, whilst Pat taught the older juniors in another part of the church. How those Welsh children could sing and how they responded! It was not long before the numbers grew so much that the vicar arranged for us to move into the church hall and more girls from Clarendon and another staff member became involved. At least then we could remove our boaters!

At the close of every term, straight after early breakfast, we would sit in the dining room for the reading of Psalm 121, followed by prayers and the singing together of a short chorus which affirmed our trust in the shielding power of our heavenly Father:

Decorating the sand pulpit, Perranporth, CSSM, August 1968.

> *Kept by the power of God,*
> *Kept by the power of God;*
> *Day by day, come what may,*
> *Kept by the power of God.*[4]

Then there was the rush for the coach to take us to Abergele station *en route* for home and holidays. On my last day at Clarendon, my father had gamely volunteered to collect me by car, along with my accumulated belongings. Having waved off the coach, and others, I walked down the office passage with Miss Haughton, who was to head up the school the following autumn. "Do please pray for me and all of us here, Wendy. I feel as if I shall be walking in footsteps far larger than my own." And the Lord surely honoured her humility, enabled her to plough her own furrow and lead the school forward, knowing that the 'government' was still firmly upon His shoulder.[5]

During the summer after I left school, I joined a team of people at the seaside town of Perranporth, Cornwall, using my experience and growing love of sharing Bible stories with young children at the CSSM[6] beach mission. This was run by Scripture Union, whose Bible reading notes I had found helpful for many years.

As for Psalm 121 and that lovely old chorus, *Kept by the power of God*, the truth of these words became inbuilt into my subconscious, to be

4   CSSM chorus based upon 1 Peter 1:5
5   Isaiah 9:6
6   Children's Special Service Mission

recalled and experienced through the eventful, painful and sometimes dangerous years to come. *"The LORD will keep you from all harm – he will watch over your life; the LORD will watch over your coming and going both now and for evermore."*[7]

I was able to spend two wonderful Easter vacations based in Tangier where Patricia still worked, helping some other expatriate Christian teachers run a Bible club for the English-speaking children on the hospital compound. Once again, I gained invaluable experience and insight on these trips. I drove all over the country the French way: honking my horn and giving way to anything that appeared on the right. I just loved the life; the people, the smells, the food, the flowers, the markets, the climate and the sea. Standing on the rooftops of Tangier watching the sun set in the west over the Straits of Gibraltar was magnificent, and even more so over the pink-washed walls of the houses of Marrakesh with the Atlas Mountains in the background.

I visited schools, bookshops and hospitals. I went way up into the Rif Mountains with Patricia and shared the *Wordless Book*[8] with lone Christian believers who dwelt in tents in the mountain villages. One lady had not had a visit for two years, and yet God had kept her faith alive in Him and she was full of joy. One day, I shall meet her again in that glorious home of heaven represented by the gold page of the *Wordless Book*. The little mission-run school in Tangier was delightful, and I admired those who worked there, attended their daily act of worship and watched the children playing on their rooftop playground. Could this sort of life ever be for *me*?

One day, I decided to have a chat with Patricia. By this time, I had spent four years teacher training in Cheltenham and acquired a degree in Theology and Education, specialising in early years and the basic skills. I was well into my second year of teaching in the pre-prep department of a Christian preparatory school in Hoylake on the Wirral. Robin, my eight-year-old brother, was well settled into life at the school and was one of the youngest boarders. Unbeknown to me, my father had asked him to address me formally as Miss Radcliffe during school time. As soon as we got into

---

[7]   Psalm 121:7,8

[8]   First used by Charles Spurgeon in 1866, the *Wordless Book* is used worldwide to explain God's plan of salvation. It had only three pages – black, red and white. Spurgeon told of an old unnamed minister who put the three pages together to remind himself of his sinfulness, of Christ's blood poured out for him, and of the "whiter-than-snow" cleansing provided for him. Later a gold page was added front and back, depicting the love of God and the glories of His heavenly home.

the car to come home for the holidays, he would return immediately to calling me Wen, one of my pet names in the family!

Patricia explained that even if I were to find a teaching post in Morocco, e.g. through the British Council, I would not be able to have any public contact with the missionaries because Christians were not allowed to meet together for any purpose or witness to their faith. I accepted this as a 'not God's timing just yet' answer to my prayer and geared my thoughts in other directions.

There was a postal strike in Britain at that time, but we were able to use the telephone. This was great faith-training for future experiences. An opportunity arose for an interview at a senior comprehensive school in Wallasey to be a Religious Education (RE) teacher working primarily with the lower ability pupils under a Christian headteacher and Christian head of department. I went to the interview and was offered the job. My mother was sedated in hospital at the time. "Just do whatever you feel God is leading you into," she said. I accepted the job, and as this was a state school, I was able to complete my probationary year in my third year of teaching! And so, for just a couple of years, my life went in quite a different direction.

I entered into an aspect of life I had never really experienced before. Many of these teenagers were emotionally damaged, sexually abused and exceedingly tough to deal with. But the opportunities for opening up God's Word and sharing Christian truth with them were immense. This was faith at the cutting edge. These were girls who needed to be loved and to have their dignity as human beings restored. "My work's in an awful state," became, "I like doing RE and making my work neat, miss." We worked a Biblically based syllabus both for school and examination RE, and it was a great joy to see fourteen-year-olds thumbing through their Good News Bibles, copying the Annie Vallotton drawings and discovering therein characters who were as human and sometimes as desperate as they were. Perhaps the stories of the patriarchs were the most well loved: Abraham, Isaac, Jacob and Esau, and, of course, Joseph. But they also devoured Mark's Gospel in episodes of the life of the 'Man who was Different', Jesus Christ, who had power to bring new life by His Spirit.

My task was not to evangelise or nurture, but to educate and inform. It became an exhausting and demanding job, especially as I not only taught the low-ability teenagers but also a fourth-year GCE course in addition to CSE and sixth form RE discussion groups. I was thoroughly engrossed in the work and responding to the challenge of being a Christian teacher in the RE field at a time when this was viewed as something of a 'Cinderella' subject in secondary schools.

There were a number of Christian teachers on the staff and we supported each other in friendship and 'edification in the spirit'. These were *heady* days. I was stimulated mentally, theologically and spiritually. I can still recall the feeling of utter exhaustion as I walked down the corridor for period eight of a non-stop teaching day, clutching a pile of exercise books that I had only just finished marking, saying to myself, "You must walk in with a smile on your face and be prepared to face up to whatever is going on in the classroom." A fourth-year girl who was rarely in school accosted me in the corridor one day to tell me she had become a Christian. "Miss, it's time you started telling the girls to be Christians – that's your job!" Yes, they were exciting days, and I prayed for aptitude combined with gentleness, astuteness and discernment, not to mention daily protection.

Some of the younger adolescents were in such need of adult love and affection that they would do seemingly anything to gain attention and vent their feelings. It was not uncommon, when faced with the words of God in written form, for girls to spew out obscenities, take a black permanent marker to their work and scrawl all over it, or even take a penknife and cut their arms till the blood blotched over their work, the desk and the floor as well. One lunch hour, I walked to the RE room to pick up a book, only to discover a group of girls huddled around a homemade *ouija* board on one of the desks. That demanded an instant response: tear up the letters and put them in the bin, and open all the windows to let the evil spirits out. After all, I had to teach in that room during the afternoon!

My head of department had worked previously as a Home Economics and Needlecraft teacher at an American missionary school in Freetown, Sierra Leone. She was gentle, firm, full of humour and practical good sense. We became firm Christian friends. It was she who encouraged me to respond positively to a letter I received quite unexpectedly in November 1972, early in my second year at Wallasey.

14

CHAPTER TWO

The Invitation and Call

The writer of this letter was the aunt of the writer of *Star of Light*, which had had such an impact upon me some fourteen years before. Patricia's aunt had now retired from her post as headmistress of the Christian boarding school in North Wales that I had attended during my sixth form years, but was still living in a small apartment on the premises. Miss Haughton was now the head. As the contents and the timing of this letter have had such a major effect on my life and my unspoken desire to teach overseas, I make no apology for recording it here in full.

CLARENDON SCHOOL, ABERGELE, DENBIGHSHIRE

6th November 1972

Dear Wendy,

I am wondering whether you might be interested in the following:

My niece, Hazel St John, is now in this country on deputation work. She returns to Lebanon, D.V., to open a new big school outside Beirut and is praying to be given some staff from England to live with her and work with a team of English and Lebanese Christian teachers. It is a great opportunity in Christian education. She is particularly anxious to find two well-qualified teachers to launch and take charge of the Nursery and Kindergarten Department, and Miss Haughton, when talking with me last evening, said that she thought you might find it an attractive proposition.

My niece would so gladly meet you, when up here in December, to give you all particulars if you are interested. It would be a job with plenty of

Miss Swain and Miss Haughton at
Clarendon, July 1965.

scope and she is anxious to get the equipment, books etc. that would be the ones chosen by whomever would be in charge.

It would be a two-year contract in the first place, with fares paid. The salary scale is according to the Lebanese Government, to which Independent Schools have to conform. That is not as high as Burnham[1] but costs are considerably lower in Lebanon than in England and accommodation would be provided free of charge.

I think it should be a very interesting, stimulating piece of work for any keen young Christian with initiative and a real concern for Christian team work. It would be from September next. Will you pray about it and let me know if you are interested and I would then put you in touch with Miss St John. I do not want to raise her hopes if you have already quite other plans or would not care to go abroad.

With love,

Yours always affectionately,

E.G.R. Swain

My first reactions were of shock and bewilderment. *Care to go abroad?* Of course I wanted to go abroad, but I was now embarked upon a totally different type of teaching career. Mrs Mary Whitehouse had become involved in a campaign to save RE in our schools, and I was very committed to that, knowing first-hand what immense opportunities there were. And yet, had I not been thrilled to the core of my being by what I had experienced of life in Morocco with Arabic-speaking people? Had I not prayed for an opportunity to teach overseas and already pushed a few appropriate doors? Had I not only recently revisited Morocco and shared with my pupils in Wallasey some of my insights and experience of Arab Christian believers trusting in God and maintaining their faith in Him in

[1] the national pay scale for teachers

16

spite of opposition and persecution? Had I not actually met and stayed with the Palestinian wife of an English missionary in Fez who had a cousin in Beirut? And so the list of pros could go on. I had never met Hazel St John, but if she were the sister of Patricia, equally dedicated to Christian work with Arabs overseas, then surely I could be comfortable with

My parents in the 1970s.

that. It was certainly beginning to look as though God were answering my prayer in the affirmative – September 1973 is the timing, but not Morocco, try Lebanon! But I needed to be one hundred per cent sure from God's Word.

Half term was later that year, and I had planned to visit a friend from Birkenhead who was a Parish Worker in Sheffield at Christchurch, Fulwood. I decided to go ahead and take advantage of the break. That particular Sunday was designated to be a special Gift Day, not a Missionary Sunday, and Rev. Michael Baughen was the visiting preacher. Though the church was pleasantly full, I felt as though he were preaching God's specific words to me from God's Word. I was riveted to the seat as Joshua 1:1-9 was read from the lectern.

Underlined in my RSV[2] Bible are the words of the Lord's specific instructions to Joshua: *"...arise, go over this Jordan ... Every place that the sole of your foot will tread upon I have given to you, as I promised to Moses."*[3] In case I needed to be even more specific, even more than one hundred per cent sure this opportunity to teach near Beirut was for me, the words continue: *"From the wilderness and this <u>Lebanon</u> ... I will not fail you or forsake you."*[4] The preacher emphasised that here was God's clear call and commission to Joshua, Moses' successor.

Here was God's command and accompanying promise right from the start that His presence would always be with me to uphold, provide and sustain. Here was a 'taster' to encourage me that something of that godly *carefreeness* I had so admired and desired in Patricia's life could be for me,

---

2   Revised Standard Version (RSV)
3   Joshua 1:2-3
4   Joshua 1:4-5 (emphasis added)

if I would obey. Her life spoke to me of someone who had found that God's will was *"good, pleasing and perfect"*[5], and in obeying His call she had discovered true freedom of living.

Even so, I struggled with intense feelings of the sheer impossibility of it all. Would my father accept this as God's clear call upon my life and be prepared to take full responsibility for my mother and the rest of the family? By this time, she was out of hospital, my sister was away in the States on a student exchange programme at Pennsylvania State University and my nine-year-old brother was boarding at Kingsmead School, Hoylake, where I had spent my first two years of teaching. Could I teach young ones again after having immersed myself in secondary education? I had no experience in teaching English as a foreign or as a second language and had only just scraped through O level English Language myself. Furthermore, I had no knowledge whatsoever of the Arabic language. Surprisingly, I was protected at that moment from any disturbing thoughts about the implications of living and working in a totally different culture. My concern was more in terms of my teaching inexperience than anything else. This was surely a once-in-a-lifetime opportunity to go overseas to an Arabic-speaking country. Dare I take the plunge?

The preacher moved on into Joshua 3 for the reassurance from God's Word which spoke directly into my situation: *"This day I will begin to exalt you in the sight of all Israel, that they may know that, as I was with Moses, so I will be with you. ... command the priests who bear the ark of the covenant ... '...stand still in the Jordan.' ... when the soles of the feet of the priests ... shall rest in the waters of the Jordan, the waters shall be stopped from flowing ... and the people [shall pass] over opposite Jericho."*[6] The struggle with my feelings was over. It was as if the Lord were saying to me, "Have I not prepared you for this moment? Have I not now given you the opportunity to fulfil your heart's desire? Have I not now called you, given you My Word to never fail you nor forsake you? Now I will honour My Name in your willingness to get your feet wet for Me. You do not even have to swim across the difficulties and uncertainties. [I can't swim anyway!] Just stand still and dip your feet in the water and you will see Me acting on your behalf for the honour of My Name and My people whom you wish to serve."

How very many times, in the eventful years to come in Lebanon, did I return to those words of call and commission, of promise and reassurance?

---

[5] Romans 12:2
[6] Joshua 3:7,8,13,16

18

But for the present, I was no longer in any doubt. In the margin of Joshua 1, I wrote "19.11.72", and later in the evening on my return to Birkenhead, having written a reply to Miss Swain, I made a note at the foot of her letter to me: "Replied 19.11.72". God was clearly at work.

There followed an interesting first meeting with Hazel, Patricia's sister, just before spending a shared Christmas at home with my parents, other friends and relatives. I was full of questions and desperately wanted to get a clear picture of the children with whom I would be working. Hazel explained that some would know English, as there were families with one parent British or North American and the other Lebanese, but the majority would know only their mother tongue of Arabic. We talked about textbooks and resources, and agreed that by grouping the children within their age bands and teaching all subjects – Arabic, English, mathematics, creative activities, music, PE and Scripture – across the ability range rather than by 'streaming', we could be a truly bilingual school based upon child-centred teaching and learning. Each child could then be allowed to develop at his or her own rate, and we would be able to give equal weighting of importance to both the English and Arabic curricula.

I was encouraged by Hazel's willingness to provide funding for books, equipment, constructional toys and other educational resources, and indeed found it exciting to be asked to plan the provision of all this from scratch for a brand-new school. She promised to pray daily that I would know peace in a growing assurance of God's will for me and for the school. She wrote in December 1972, "I know He can provide for us too, even while He knows how I'd love that provision to come through you *if* that is His way." What an encouragement this was to me.

Two other English teachers, Margaret and Kirstene, who already had experience of working in Lebanon, had agreed to head up the English curriculum in the junior and secondary parts of this new all-age Christian school, and we were to share living accommodation along with Hazel in a good-sized flat on the fifth floor of the school building. The family who owned the school lived on the two floors above. This too was reassuring.

My parents were encouraging, and so were members of my home church in Marple, Cheshire. My former Sunday school teacher, Edith Bowyer, offered to type up and distribute prayer / news letters for me on a regular basis. My grandmother, recently widowed, whom I loved dearly, wrote, "You are being shown the Way." My head of department in Wallasey, Gwyneth Darbyshire, and some of the pupils continued to

Gwyneth, my head of department at Wallasey.

uphold and encourage me, along with girls and leaders from the Crusader Class in West Kirby with which I was involved. By the end of January 1973, in spite of all the uncertainties surrounding leaving the security of my home country and immediate family, I had God's inner peace and assurance about the whole matter.

Hazel was an excellent correspondent and plied me with regular missives about visa and work permits, medical checks and immunisations, insurance and travel arrangements. Then there was the challenge of purchasing and packing English and mathematics teaching materials along with educational games, puzzles, constructional toys (Lego pieces scattered all over my suitcase took up no space at all!), creative materials and sundry other teaching resources, and finding a suitable way of getting them to Beirut. Many were praying that these details, as well as some political disturbances resulting in the Lebanese / Syrian border being closed in Lebanon in May 1973, would be resolved.

By June 5th, we had the solution. I, along with the two other Christian teachers, was to travel overland in a Bedford Bedouin van with Mr and Mrs Habermann of Romsey House Theological College, Cambridge. The Channel crossing was booked for 8 am on September 1st, and the journey was expected to take ten days. The new school was to open on October 3rd. We all prayed that everything would be ready in time and that the northern Lebanese / Syrian border would soon be reopened. It was, by mid August, not long before my father valiantly agreed to drive me down to Cambridge, his trusty Volvo packed solid with my belongings and all the equipment I had gathered together. There were nine boxes full of all manner of educational resources and two large suitcases. This was to be the journey of a lifetime for me.

CHAPTER THREE

Borderlines and Boxes

Having taken two Sea-legs[1] the night before, I found it extremely difficult to wake up at 2 am on Saturday, September 1st, 1973. However, we were at Ramsgate with the van fully packed by 6.30 am and eventually boarded the hovercraft at about eight o'clock. It was rather an inauspicious start. I was only thankful that we did not attempt breakfast until we had disembarked at Calais, for by this time it was a beautiful, sunny day. The crossing had been somewhat choppy and reminded me of the Big Dipper in Blackpool! The van was chock-a-block with food, enough to feed an army. Our host and hostess, the Habermanns, were extremely organised – and 'dab hands' with the tin opener.

We set off after breakfast through France to the border with Belgium, joining the E5 *autobahn* at Ostend. Belgium seemed remarkably flat and not very impressive, but the Sea-legs were still at work and I fell asleep for most of the morning until we stopped for lunch just north of Brussels. After lunch, we drove over the border into Germany, through Aachen and wooded countryside to Cologne, where we stopped for the night at a campsite at Limburg just north of Frankfurt. Kirstene had been unable to travel with us because her father had sadly died very suddenly; so Margaret and I were able to stretch out in the van and the Habermanns pitched their tent. Before retiring, we explored Limburg, especially admiring the narrow streets and the *schloss* on the hill, floodlit by night. It was really quite warm, and we slept with the soothing sound of the river flowing by the campsite. I had warm, happy memories of my father's business trips to Germany. Much to his disappointment, I had failed

---

[1] Sea-legs are antihistamine tablets, now discontinued in the UK. They can help prevent travel sickness for up to 24 hours and can cause drowsiness.

Ready for the trip of a lifetime,
September 1973.

miserably in my attempts to learn German, but that did not detract from the memories of those little treasures that he would bring back, often late at night. After four hundred and seventy miles of mainly lorry-free driving on the *autobahn*, I was thankful for a good shower on site and an uneventful first day of our journey.

We left Limburg after breakfast on the Sunday morning, *en route* for Frankfurt and Munich, driving once again on the *autobahn* through rolling hills and mixed forests. As we approached the Bavarian capital, the terrain became flatter, with fields and fields of maize and a hazy outline of the German Alps in the distance. We took a ring road around Munich and then the *autobahn* to Salzburg. It seemed as if Bavaria merged into Austria as we crossed the border, with the Alps towering ahead of us. The views were forested, with pretty chalets dotted here and there, and window boxes overflowing with geraniums of multiple colours. We bought fresh rolls and milk that evening near our campsite outside Salzburg and fell asleep after three hundred and ninety miles of driving, marvelling at the beautiful sunset.

The next morning, we drove on through the Alps, catching a brief glimpse of a glacier in the distance. There were little churches with painted black steeples and plastered houses with window boxes and overhanging chalet-style wooden roofs. The grass was so very green and smooth like a carpet. After lunch at Graz, we motored on to the Yugoslav border, where we encountered considerable officialdom at the border crossing of Sentilj. Our passports were stamped for the first time, and there was some delay as vehicles were routinely searched. The customs men must have been exhausted after searching the boot of the car in front of us, and we were just waved on! Was someone praying, I wondered.

There was a brand new road as we drove southwards, that belied the fact that the first town over the border, Maribor, showed signs of squalor and neglect. The farming was primitive: millet, maize and melons growing together in the same field and very simple farming methods. We saw two scraggy oxen yoked together, for example, and cows being led along on

22

leads. It was still warm (eighty degrees Fahrenheit) when we decided to camp for the night at Novska, between Zagreb and Belgrade. The road by this time had become more rutted, so we were glad to get out of the 'saddle' for a while.

The campsite at Novska seemed to be quite popular, as there was a queue to enter, with young lads taking the opportunity of earning a few pence by jumping up on the bumper and thence the bonnet to clean the windscreens. I shall never forget the washing facilities at this particular campsite. The doorless 'loos' were of the perch-and-puff, hole-in-the-floor style – and fairly filthy, as there was no running water to flush. The stench was indescribable. The showers were positioned immediately in front of the loos, and as they constantly dripped, wading through the floods to 'spend a penny' was a risky and somewhat public business. Our passports had been removed as soon as we entered the site, so we were stuck with it! Another three hundred and forty miles had passed by nightfall.

On Tuesday, September 4th, we recovered our dignity and our passports, and continued along the E94 *autobahn* towards Belgrade – a straight, rather uninteresting road surrounded by flat agricultural countryside. The ground was more parched here. We passed through an area of forestation in the mid morning, stopping for coffee by a campsite with small wooden huts literally made out of barrels pinned down with roofs over them! Belgrade itself was surprisingly modern: a newish city with high-rise blocks of flats. South from the capital, the roads deteriorated as we approached Nis; however, we were impressed by a spectacular drive through a beautiful gorge which brought us nearly to the Bulgarian border, praying hard! It was well after 6 pm and the sun was setting when we arrived. By the time we had paid the princely sum of two pounds sterling for our visas, exchanged currency and had our passports stamped, it was quite dark as we passed through customs itself. The officials were in a good mood; they took a cursory glance inside the van and waved us on. We were through. Praise the Lord!

Where were we to stay the night after all this delay and the darkness gathering apace? After an abortive attempt at camping at a site fairly near the border, we drove on sixteen miles to Slivnitsa and into the first campsite that would have us. Though we could see not a single soul on this site, it was late and we needed to stop. The state of the washing facilities once again defied description, and here there were no showers at all. The facilities were a little more private than at Novska but boasted holes in the ceiling immediately above each 'loo'. Very strategic planning, we thought, and saved bothering with flushing in the wet season! We were just glad it did not rain, and so full of praise to have got through the second Communist border uneventfully, that anything would do.

Whilst having our evening meal, we had an interesting experience. A young Bulgarian came to the back of the van and introduced himself in perfect textbook English. He said he had been learning English for two years by himself using the BBC World Service programmes in order to perfect his pronunciation. He wondered if we had any English magazines or booklets that he would be willing to pay for, more than their cost price, in order to improve his English. I listened in prayerful silence as Mr Habermann replied again and again very firmly, "No." The British were not allowed at that time to bring literature into Bulgaria, and this man was remarkably persistent.

"*Radio Times?*"

"No."

"*Daily Mail?*"

"No."

"*Financial Times?*"

"No."

And so it went on. We were relieved when he finally gave up and walked off into the darkness. After praise and prayer together, we turned wearily to bed. I hardly noticed the cracked and broken washbasin that allowed the cold water to run right through so that my feet were washed at the same time as my hands! Another four hundred and fifteen miles on the speedometer and our clocks went forward by one hour. Praise God, those boxes full of educational equipment were firmly in His care and protection.

Wednesday, September 5th dawned early, or so it seemed, and we were thankful to move on our way to the Turkish border. However, our Bulgarian adventures were not yet over. The people themselves were desperately keen to impress tourists. They were equally keen to be seen to be ruling their country with the iron rod of Soviet socialism. There seemed to be police at every corner waiting to pounce and fine on the spot, especially at roundabouts. We were very nearly fined as we came round a smallish roundabout on the outskirts of the capital, Sofia, simply because the outside wheels of the van strayed onto the centre white lines for a few metres!

Propaganda posters abounded along the roadside. There were huge billboards declaring, "Long live the Communist Party of Bulgaria and the Soviet Union," and a great deal of emphasis upon friendship and comradeship with the Soviet Union. Even the lamp-posts in the dusty towns had peace slogans stuck onto them. Large bizarre and severely crude angular illustrations carried 'work for the socialist state' type slogans, with men and women depicted swinging their arms around, carrying welding tools and sickles. There were large posters of Lenin, Marx, Kosygin and Brezhnev, endlessly reminding the people of what was reputedly the first anti-fascist uprising in the world in September 1923, fifty years ago to the month.

I felt frighteningly bombarded by all this crude visual imagery. Was the poverty and filth we had experienced in this People's Republic of Bulgaria that was founded in 1946, the year of my own birth, all that could be said of the progress of a Soviet socialist state? We saw a little agriculture but primitive in method. Tobacco was grown and the leaves hung out to dry. It was so polluted industrially around Sofia that we were glad to get out of the town and back onto the open road again. I remember only people scurrying, Lowry-style, all wearing grey. Even the oranges on the fruit carts were grey. We saw a few sheep and cows, but even the sheep seemed to be regulated!

As we travelled eastwards towards Plovdiv, there was fruit growing in abundance: apples, tomatoes and huge vineyards, plus more tobacco. We actually stopped in Plovdiv to buy fruit and, for under fifty pence, bought two kilos each of grapes, peaches and pears along with one kilo of tomatoes. We were served most pleasantly with everything in bags. As we continued along the roadside, there were peasant women amidst the donkeys, fruit-picking. We saw still more propaganda posters and then something beautiful I shall never forget. The roses, for which Bulgaria is famed, were planted and blooming in sandy islands down the middle of the road as we approached the customs post and the Turkish border. The Bulgarian official took a cursory glance in the portable toilet compartment at the rear of the van and we were through, out and away from the tension of police surveillance at every corner and the mighty weight of Communist oppression.

We had a longish wait at the Turkish border. There was a great deal of military presence. Above the border post was a patrol tower guarded by armed soldiers. Again, we prayed for ease of passage into Turkey with all

Travelling through Turkey,
September 1973.

our boxes and baggage. After much form-filling and submitting of lists of such items as electrical goods, we were allowed through. Another merciful escape from wholesale searching through the contents of the van! Passports were stamped and we drove on to Edirne, where we fell with pleasure into the BP Mocamp, a huge, well-organised caravan and camp site. What a contrast from our previous experiences: fresh hot water, sparkling clean showers and 'loos'. I stood under the shower for simply ages and let the warm water, for the first time in several days, tumble down through every strand of my hair and pulsate through every cell in my body, as if in a jacuzzi. It was wonderful to feel so totally clean and reinvigorated for the rest of the journey. Another two hundred and forty-five miles since daybreak, another hour on the clock, and we were about to enter the next phase of our journey: from Communist Europe to Muslim Asia.

"We'll praise Him for all that is past and trust Him for all that's to come."[2]

Our conversation at breakfast the following morning was tinged with shock and not a little humour. "We were aroused to become aware of a hand poking amongst our underwear, which was hung up at the foot of the sleeping bags in the tent." One of the Habermanns must have screamed at this point and the hand disappeared! One or two of the surrounding tents had indeed been slashed during the night in spite of the Turkish guard supposedly on night patrol. It seems the thieves were looking for money. They had pilfered approximately one hundred and eighty pounds sterling in Deutschmarks from some young Czech people who had escaped from Eastern Europe and were heading for Istanbul. Mercifully for us, our money and passports were locked in the front of the van and there was nothing of value in the tent. Nevertheless, I had fallen in love with Turkey almost immediately after we crossed the border. There was something familiar about it, scattered as it was with mosques and minarets, Asian but with a strong Western influence. How very different

[2] Joseph Hart (1712-1768)

from the so-called free, peaceful country ruled by the emancipated Bulgarian National Communist Party and dominated by the USSR.

We drove on down the E5 routeway through to Istanbul. The countryside was flat, burnt and barren, apart from a few scattered fields of sunflowers bending their heads in the wind. It was pleasantly cooler, but still with no rain since leaving home. Giant watermelons along with honeydew melons were stacked up high for sale by the roadside. The road was straight, but dipped and humped quite alarmingly at times. We passed through Turkish villages, typically Muslim, and again it struck me what an interesting cultural bridge we were traversing as we approached the Euro-Asian border. Turkey at this time was a military pseudo-American buffer state backed by NATO – anti-Christian, pro-Muslim and exceedingly fearful of the possibility of Communist domination. The Sea of Marmara is separated from the Black Sea by a narrow inlet, the Bosphorus, on which Istanbul is situated.

We passed through Corlu, which was impressively clean and bristling with life, impressive indeed contrasted with the filth and dust bowls of the towns in Bulgaria. By midday, the van was duly loaded on the 'drive on / drive off' ferry that crossed the Bosphorus from Thrace (European Turkey) to Anatolia (Asian Turkey). The water was smooth as a millpond, as we wandered around on the twenty-five-minute ferry crossing, mingling with local travellers. We had driven through Istanbul and past the great mosque of Hagia Sophia, once the Christian cathedral of Constantinople. Now I could photograph it from the ferry with its shining dome and tall minarets receding into the distance.

The next stage of our journey took us down the busy main road to Izmir. We were heading for the Koru camp, which was operated by the German equivalent of our Automobile Association. We found it a few miles west of Bolu, but not before stocking up on our fresh fruit at the roadside. We purchased four kilos of large juicy apples with a wonderfully firm texture and two kilos of huge peaches, all for the equivalent of sixty pence. Koru camp was superb. We were completely on our own in the midst of pine woods and mountains. There was gas for cooking and plenty of hot and cold water once again. For once, there were no border anxieties, no risk of being searched and our boxes and luggage scrutinised. Another two hundred and ninety-five miles of our journey had safely passed.

Friday, September 7th was a day of mixed impressions and very varied countryside, which flashed by as we drove eastwards across the country.

There were the special military police with white flat-cap helmets, appearing like jack-in-the-boxes in towns and along the roadsides. There were the shiny minarets like rockets about to be launched from their mosques in every town and village. What a contrast in vegetation from forest to desert as we approached Ataturk's capital, Ankara, a modern university city with high-rise blocks arising out of the desert!

As we travelled on eastwards, there were more scrubland, dried-up lakes and barren reddish-brown mountains. Sunflowers were growing in field after field, and there were just a few vineyards with children selling grapes by the roadside. Sheep and goats flocked together with shepherds, who waved cheerfully as we passed by. Donkeys were heavily laden and often two would be yoked together, pulling a cart piled high with produce. Women were winnowing the corn, and their menfolk were organising the donkeys as they trailed round and round the threshing floor. Little villages in the sand almost blended into their background, but a spark of the colour of modern living was evident with the BP, Shell or Mobil petrol station situated along the main road. The mosque, as always, was the hub of village life. And so we arrived at Nevsehir, a few miles off the main tarmac road, in order to reach one of our now favourite BP Mocamps. We were not disappointed, either with the campsite or the glorious sunset, which was a great photo opportunity after a further three hundred and twenty-five miles on the road.

Nevsehir was a growing town, largely as a result of the invasion of tourists who were coming to explore the Cappadocia region of central Turkey. A great deal of building of houses and hotels was evident. By now, hot showers were commonplace, and we gratefully drove into Cappadocia to be proper tourists ourselves the following morning, cameras slung around our necks, feeling quite clean and civilised. This is the part of Turkey that is appropriately described as a volcanic moonscape! The volcanic lava / soil has undergone erosion, breaking up into amazing shapes such as towers, columns, cones, pyramids and crazy-shaped spires rising up in their thousands. These rocks are riddled with openings large and small, leading to churches, monasteries and underground cities where the first-century Christians took refuge. They are decorated with re-markably well-preserved paintings in bright colours depicting saints and episodes from the Bible. We crawled around the rock churches at Goreme and drove through Uchisar, which overlooks the entire eroded basin; then on to Avcilar, where fairy chimneys emerge. Locals were selling onyx and alabaster from small shops and factories in the caverns. I still have a small onyx vase which I bought for my grandmother as a reminder of our half-day of sightseeing. What a fascinating part of God's creation!

Avcilar, Turkey, September 1973.

After lunch, we returned to our south-east-bound route at Nigde and were nearly mobbed when small Turkish children surrounded the van and bounced on the bumpers back and front! We then travelled on through mountainous scenery and many tortuous Z-bends to the road that led to Adana and the glorious southern coast of Turkey. It was magnificent scenery, yet littered with overturned trucks which told a tale of reckless driving. Once again, just as at the borders in Europe, we were aware of the Lord's protection over us during these last seven days of our journey. *"Thus far the LORD has helped us."*[3]

We encountered some coniferous forest in the south, along with vineyards, apples and marrows in the flatter parts. From time to time, small whirlwinds of dust raced across the fields, known locally as 'wind devils', but by the time we reached Adana, we were immersed in luxuriant vegetation and palm trees surrounding the Motel Enar campsite. The facilities were excellent and there were glimpses of the Mediterranean humidity with which I should later become so familiar. Only two hundred miles on the speedometer that day due to our sightseeing foray into Cappadocia during the morning, but it was a worthwhile and memorable experience.

Adana is the fourth largest city in Turkey: busy, industrialised and polluted. It is situated in the heart of the cotton-growing region. First thing in the morning, it rained for about forty-five minutes, which did nothing more than settle the dust. In any case, we were up early that morning, having been awakened at five o'clock by the call of the *muezzin* from the mosque. We proceeded along the excellent E5 routeway down to Antakya, the Biblically familiar Antioch-in-Syria, where the followers of The Way were first nicknamed Christians. From here, there were some exciting views of the Mediterranean Sea. The route from Antakya to the Syrian

[3] 1 Samuel 7:12

border took us on a twisty mountainous road with superb views over terraced valleys and little scattered farming villages. The terrain was rich red, rough and stony; a little tobacco was being grown and bracken was pushing up amongst the stones. About midday, we arrived at Yayladagi at the border. This should have been the easiest crossing of all, but a totally unexpected hitch was about to change our plans completely.

The border post was quiet, secluded and surrounded by forest. We presented ourselves and our passports as usual: three British and one German. Mr Habermann, a German national, still travelled on his German passport even though he had married a British lady some years previously. Yes, the three British could pass through into Syria, but not the German gentleman. Special permission had to be obtained from Damascus, the capital, and this could take up to a fortnight! This was a retaliatory ruling on Syria's part as since the terrorist incidents at the Munich Olympics the year before, the German government had not allowed Arabs to enter Germany. As Kika was our driver, we had no option but to sit and wait. It seemed unbelievable that we should have come this far with our full van of boxes and luggage and be stuck on the border with Syria, barely a day's drive from our destination. There was clearly no way of making contact with Hazel St John in Lebanon – or anyone else, for that matter!

The Turkish officials were very friendly, plied us with melon and watermelon, and insisted that we camp on their side of the border. There was nothing for it but to accept the delay and pray for an early resolution of the dilemma. Walking around the border post and accepting Turkish hospitality, we witnessed a Muslim circumcision ceremony in a clearing in the pinewoods. All this helped to pass the afternoon and we turned in early. No hot showers on this occasion!

Early at daybreak, just ten days after leaving home, miracle of miracles, the Istanbul to Beirut bus came trundling over the border. After a great deal of handshaking and general palaver over payment of fares, Margaret and I found ourselves on the bus. We were seated halfway down on the right facing the front, and I was delighted to have the window seat. We had nothing but our overnight luggage and were heading for Beirut city centre. It was a glorious, exciting and yet nightmarish journey, driving with a busload of Turks and Arabs right down the western coast of Syria and across the border into Lebanon. At the border post, our passports were collected up and disappeared from view. Not long after, duly stamped on

Martyrs Square, downtown.
Servis cars in foreground.

the precious page that carried our entry visas, we had the official permission to enter Lebanon.

From the border, we drove on south through Tripoli, passing the salt flats and down the narrow coastal strip through Byblos, Jounieh and on into Beirut. We finally arrived in the early evening, hungry and exhausted, still needing to find the school in Kafarshima! It was nearly dark; there were neon lights blaring on cinema billboards and cars zooming around Martyrs Square. Margaret had seen all this before, but for me – what a welcome to Lebanon!

CHAPTER FOUR

Lebanon and the New School

We arrived in downtown Beirut as the light was fading. There was the bronze statue erected as a memorial to the martyrs of Lebanese independence, November 22nd, 1943. There were the covered markets or souks that I was familiar with from the old town of Tangier, and narrow streets with stone archways flanking either side, leading down to the port area. Down the streets were tall houses with red-tiled roofs, green-painted wrought iron doorways and balconies, typical of the Lebanese architecture of the period. The balconies were overflowing with palms, geraniums and vivid purple bougainvilleas. Around the square which formed the heart of the old city of Beirut were barrow-boys and others peddling their wares – anything from bananas and citrus fruits to toys made in China, feather dusters and cans of Coca Cola and 7UP.

I was aware of none of this specifically that first evening, only the hustle and bustle and the imperative to reach Kafarshima before it grew much darker. Buses and taxis raced each other around the square, honking at every opportunity, and people were shouting and dashing in all directions. My only thought was, "If in doubt, ask a policeman." *"Ou est le taxi pour Kafarshima?"* The whistle-blowing, uniformed gentleman we approached was most probably a traffic warden, but at least he looked official. He understood neither our French nor English nor "Kafarshima", but helpfully gesticulated towards a lock-up sweet shop and tobacconist where we were handed a phone. In vain, we dialled every number we knew for Hazel, the Khoury family and the school. Each time the numbers rang out, our hopes were raised, only to be dashed as the line was terminated by an infuriatingly high-pitched *ping, ping, ping* sound.

There was nothing for it but to make our way to the taxi stand at the top of the square, asking repeatedly for a cab to Kafarshima. No-one seemed to respond, and we were beginning to wonder whether the place even existed! Eventually, amidst the chaos and hopelessness, one driver nodded: *"Na'am, Kafarshima, beit Khoury,*

Kafarshima village, summer 1974.

tfaddalu." Thankfully, we were bundled into the back seat of a Mercedes-Benz taxi, along with our sleeping bags and overnight cases. To this day, I cannot remember how we convinced him to take us the seven miles south of the capital at night and with no cash to pay for it! I think he must have been one of God's special messengers sent in time of extreme necessity. This was to be the first of many evidences of His grace and heavenly provision for our needs in Lebanon.

We drew up the drive of what was to become my home and workplace for the next couple of years or so. The gate was locked, the dog was barking, and it took a little while before Jusef the caretaker realised we were friend, not foe, and slowly pulled back the gate. By this time, Hazel and others were out on the balconies at the rear of the building, and I thankfully hailed the one familiar figure:

"Hazel, we're here."

"Come up to the fifth floor," she shouted back.

And so we arrived with neither boxes nor baggage and made our way up to the fifth floor in the lift. It was enough just to realise we were in the right place; the surroundings could be assimilated the next day. There was Hazel, a tall lady in a white dress, standing in front of a double-doored sitting room which had a shining chandelier in the centre!

Meanwhile, back at the Syrian border, Mr and Mrs Habermann camped alone, no doubt thankful that Margaret and I were on our way to Lebanon. Next morning, the German Interpol came over the border, and after a deal of interceding and negotiating with officials in Damascus, the Habermanns were permitted to pass through and drive on south to the Lebanese border. From there, they were able to travel south to Beirut and the school in Kafarshima. Perhaps somewhat recklessly, Hazel and a couple of the Khoury family had motored up to the border to collect the boxes and luggage and commiserate with the Habermanns. It was about a five- or six-hour journey, but they must have missed each other on the way. We were united by the evening, thankful for all God's protective mercies every step of the way. The Habermanns finally left Lebanon the following Saturday – mission accomplished successfully, praise God, but not without adventure.

Lebanon, to me, was a complete enigma; on the face of it, so European, and yet distinctly Middle Eastern, bound together by the language of Arabic, the influence of the family and the people's faith in God. It was clearly the place to which God had called me; of that I had no doubt. Indeed, I had only to turn back in my Bible to the first and third chapters of Joshua to be reminded of that Sunday in Sheffield when God's Spirit of call and equipping had come upon me so directly. But I also now had to learn how to *feel God's heart* for the Lebanese people of whatever racial or religious origin, Christian, Muslim and Druse alike.

The drive across Europe, though an adventure in itself, had also served to underline in my experience how God is in control, overruling and timing events, protecting and providing all the way. The ten days on the road helped me to acclimatise gently to the subtle yet distinct change in cultural norms of behaviour that I was about to experience in Lebanon. During our evening prayer and Bible study times on the campsites with Mr and Mrs Habermann, we had looked at these cross-cultural issues. I was beginning to realise that God's way is the way of humility and love, self-giving love.

"Many of the things you see will be different from those with which you are familiar in England," Mrs Habermann warned. "Many of the ways in which the Lebanese people behave will be very different, towards one another and especially within the family. Don't react in a critical or biased way. Be open, and be willing to take cultural divergence seriously." Indeed, the times would come when, though I was the one ostensibly in authority, I would feel as if my hands, figuratively speaking, were tied behind my back and I simply had no familiarity at all with the way in which people were thinking and feeling. Her godly advice was to watch, listen, absorb, receive and, most of all, to be attentive to God's Word. I clearly had a great deal to learn about bearing responsibility with a servant spirit in this culture.

The journey across Europe, though exciting, had taken its toll on my resistance to infection. After barely three days in Lebanon, I went down with diarrhoea and sickness. Hazel announced that this was not at all unusual for those new in the country, and so I felt strangely encouraged! It may be called 'Beirut tummy' by the expatriates, but the dizziness and stomach pains reminded me all too clearly of a duodenal ulcer I had suffered some six years before. My fears proved to be unfounded, and by early October, I was not only adjusted but was really beginning to enjoy the Lebanese food. Olive oil is plentiful and so are vegetables such as aubergines, squash and baby marrows that can be stuffed with a rice and meat mixture. I loved the plentiful supply of fruit. There were small sweet bananas, many varieties of grapes and big, bulbous tomatoes. I was also beginning to anticipate a favourite Lebanese salad known as *tabbouli*: a nutritious mixture of cracked wheat soaked in oil and lemon, chopped mint, parsley and tomatoes, and served in long, crispy cos lettuce leaves. Of the meat dishes, I was a little more wary, due perhaps to my vegetarian tendencies and love of cheese and dairy produce, and especially so when I first encountered a dish which included raw meat, *kibbeh nayeh*. It was certainly not my first choice!

Once my constitution had adjusted to the food and water, there was still the heat. Late September was the time for the *sirocco* winds from the desert lands of Iraq and Saudi Arabia to pass through Lebanon, raising the humidity to ninety per cent and causing the atmosphere to become completely airless and stifling, day and night. We simply had to close the shutters to prevent them from swinging about and causing damage, and also to keep the sand out. This did not improve the atmosphere at all. Far more disconcerting than the hot winds in those early days in Lebanon were the mosquitoes! The nearest I had ever been to this particular delight were midges on the Isle of Skye in the early evening, humming around the ears and biting, ruining early evening walks. This was nothing in comparison to my first encounter with Lebanese mosquitoes. At its worst, I had barely a square inch of skin on arms or legs that was not thoroughly bitten. Horrid little bloodsuckers! I looked like someone with an advanced case of chickenpox. People were not very sympathetic in their diagnosis: should you have fair skin and red hair in the family (I have both), you are more appetising to the mosquitoes!

My first line of counterattack, especially for protection at night, was to burn the mosquito coils, but the smoke made me cough. Consequently, I gave that up pretty soon and invested in a more high-tech weapon: an electric mosquito killer! Subsequent letters home included bulletins in the

Khoury family and Sam,
summer 1974.

battle to overcome the worst effects of living in mosquito territory. At the beginning of October, I wrote to my parents, "You can just about see my legs through the bites now, and it's cooler. I've taken to wearing slacks because my legs look so scarred." By the middle of the month, I wrote again, "Mosquito bites still going strong – approximately twenty-five bites on each leg, arms not too bad!" At the end of the month, I decided to step up a gear and seek advice.

The doctor at the *pharmacie* in Kafarshima advised five antibiotic injections, as the scars were becoming reinfected and a number of the bites were septic, showing no signs of healing. My right foot and ankle, furthermore, were the size of a football. I was a little wary and decided to contact the doctor at the Christian Medical Hospital in Beirut with whom we were registered. He suggested a cream, 'Cicatrin aminoacetic acid cream', to put on the septic bites and then to cover with a gauze dressing. There was also another cream to stop the itching and irritation. Within days of using the cream, the bites became far less angry and thankfully started to heal, and my right ankle reduced to its normal size. By mid November, I was glad to be able to report in letters home, "I still have the scars and am obviously susceptible to bites on the legs from any creature who feels like it! But we have now won the fight." The weather by now was cooler in any case and less favourable to the spread of the mosquitoes. To those readers who do not suffer from fair skin or red hair, kindly do not tell me that mosquitoes are part of God's good and perfect creation. I'm sure they crept in after the Fall!

Apart from the mosquitoes, everyone else was friendly and welcoming. The Lebanese family who owned the school building that was also our home, the Khoury family, were particularly kind. Mr Michele Khoury owned the eight-storey building with its large rooms and plenty of garden. It was situated in the southern suburbs of Beirut on the old road to the Crusader town of Sidon. The village behind was Kafarshima, a developing area just near the new big buildings of the Lebanese university.

His eldest son, Amine, aged twenty-one, had approached Hazel some eighteen months before, requesting help with a new all-age Christian school he hoped to start in this building. The pre-school, kindergarten and junior school were to be co-educational, and the senior school 'girls only', at least at first.

Eastwood College, 1973.

Hazel had been praying about her next assignment in Lebanon after some months on home leave, and this opportunity was a very real answer to her prayer. Hence her desire to find Christian English teachers to work alongside her on a contract basis and to share the accommodation on the fifth floor of the building. Amine was still at the American University of Beirut at this stage and needed someone experienced to launch the school in conjunction with a school committee of local Protestant evangelical Christians. His vision for the school in this part of Lebanon deserves a chapter in itself.[1] One could only admire his desire to create a school that would be a lighthouse for the teaching of the Bible and the way of salvation through Christ. Our prayer was that this place would be a means not only for gaining a bilingual Arabic / English education of excellence, but also of winning children and their families for the Lord. We wanted to reach out to the neighbourhood around in close co-operation with the local evangelical church that had a lively youth group and young people's work. The school was to be known as Eastwood College.

Mrs Khoury, whom we came to know affectionately as Madame, and the six children, aged now between fourteen and twenty-one, had come to know the Lord in the previous few years, largely through the witness of Joy Jones, a former Lebanon Evangelical Mission (LEM) worker. Joy lived in Kafarshima in her retirement, ran the Sunday school for the evangelical church and did a great deal of visiting. She would come to the school regularly, and many of the village children knew and welcomed her. She was also tutoring Madame a little in English whilst spending time with her in prayer and Bible study. We too were helping Madame to practise her English, as we were able to have our midday meal with the family each

[1] See chapter 8.

Hazel St John.

day until the term actually started. This was an excellent introduction to Lebanese cuisine and our first taste of the Lebanese hospitality that is such a hallmark of the culture. Madame was also willing to launder our sheets and towels in her washing machine, and for that, the midday meal, hot water, electricity and help with washing the floors of our large flat, we paid a nominal sum of thirty Lebanese lira per week, approximately five pounds sterling.

Hazel's welcome too was warm and genuine. She had returned by air considerably earlier than Margaret, Kirstene and me. From late June onwards, she was working in the office, admitting students, employing Lebanese staff and helping with the preparations for the opening of the new school. At first, there was a tendency to be discouraged, as so few were applying; so Hazel set a target for prayer that there would be at least a hundred students registered by October. Some friends of hers who spent the whole summer in the village were particularly faithful in prayer. Their four-year-old son, Bernard, prayed every day about the matter. He would frequently ask how many more students had registered and was as pleased as the rest of us to watch the Lord answering prayer and the numbers creeping up, eventually to well over a hundred.

We four were to share accommodation on the fifth floor of the building, and the Khoury family were above on the sixth and seventh floors. It was a good-sized flat, and we each had rooms with our own balconies. There were two bathrooms, a large sitting and dining room, plus a kitchen and a maid's room with a long balcony for drying out the washing and a chute for disposing of the rubbish! There was plenty of space, and Hazel had been eagerly anticipating some companions to share it. "To me," she wrote in a letter to friends, "the coming of these three to share in the work and to live together here was the greatest joy and relief of the whole summer, and I can't be grateful enough to God for bringing them." To me personally, there was a card in my room – "To welcome you, Wendy, with much love and much thankfulness at your coming. Hazel" – and a reminder that we are safe and provided for when we acknowledge and embrace the strong name of the Lord. I cherish that card.

Hazel was able and willing to introduce us to many longstanding friends who worked with the Lebanon Evangelical Mission, and all were reassuringly welcoming. She herself had been with the mission in Lebanon since 1939. She also arranged for a church family picnic of the Christian and Missionary Alliance International Church that met in Abdel Aziz Street in Ras Beirut. This was to be held in the garden at Eastwood one Saturday before school opened and proved to be an excellent opportunity to get to know the English-speaking families better. We came to appreciate the Bible teaching and ministry of Pastor Harry Taylor and his wife Miriam, and worshipped there regularly at the Sunday morning English service.

As Hazel had been living in the village since late June, she had become very involved with all the preparations for the new school. The whole Khoury family had been involved too. Madame had been busy on her sewing machine on the seventh floor and had produced well over a hundred simple uniforms; bright orange crepe nylon overtops with small black and white check collars, pockets and buttons down the back for the pre-school and kindergarten children (three- to five-year-olds). For the junior boys, she had made turquoise nylon jackets with zip fronts and two large pockets, and turquoise wrap-around pinafores for both junior and senior girls. All were easily washable and liked by both parents and children.

Madame's brother, Amine's uncle, was a carpenter by trade. He took on the mammoth task of constructing all the school furniture. There were metal-framed tables and chairs of all shapes and sizes with different coloured Formica tops for each classroom, and greenboards and pinboards for the walls of each room. The pre-school had small, low square and circular tables, some in orange and some in white. The kindergarten tables were slightly higher, with yellow and blue Formica tops, and there were yellow-topped individual desks with a shelf underneath for the first- and second-year juniors. The teachers' tables were a good-sized rectangular shape with similar Formica tops in brown; all very easy to wipe over and keep clean. The chairs were colour-matched and the appropriate height for the tables and desks. Mr Feghali also made wooden easels with low-edged shelves to contain paint pots for the pre-school and kindergarten, and open locker cubicles and shelf units with castors for the children's lunch boxes

My first kindergarten class, with
Mona, May 1974.

and our mathematical equipment. All these, along with the lockable cupboards for each teacher's equipment, were substantially built to equip the classrooms.

This was an exciting time, as we saw four large, empty rooms begin to look like classrooms. I began to unpack the nine boxes full of educational equipment that we had brought through Europe in the van and distribute the contents around the department. One last purchase was the piano that I found on a trip with Amine to a piano workshop in downtown Beirut, the very area where we had been tipped off the Istanbul / Beirut bus on September 10th! This part of Beirut was a veritable hubbub of all forms of crafts and manufacturing. Here I later discovered an excellent stationery shop, Star Stationers, from which we could purchase essential expendable craft items such as plasticine, powder paint, and coloured tissue and sticky paper. From here, too, I could order exercise books with plain paper for the little ones to write in and large sheets of newsprint for painting and drawing. Once my trunk, sent on in advance from Manchester, had arrived at the docks, I was able to unpack a few more items, including a long-armed stapler for making big books. I had purchased this at the last minute as an essential piece of equipment, along with my own copy of the Hamlyn Children's Bible that had always been a real favourite of mine.

Quite a deal of the work of altering the inside of the building had been effected by the time we arrived, and Mr Khoury and the younger sons had joined the workmen in indoor alterations and in transforming the big citrus garden into basketball, volleyball and tennis courts. Also busily involved were Jusef the caretaker, his wife Asia and their four children, Ishaq, Samir, Rosa and Hanna. They were Assyriac by birth and spoke Arabic as an adopted tongue. They were employed by the Khourys and lived in a small apartment on the ground floor, adjacent to the Lower Junior classrooms and near to the large gate at the head of the school drive. Ishaq was already doing well at a French school nearby, but the other three were registered with us for free. It was to be a joy to have them and give them equal educational opportunities, the same as all the others who could afford to pay. The two youngest, Rosa in the kindergarten and Hanna in the pre-school, simply soaked up the experiences of being in the Lower Junior department and opened their hearts to the Word of God. Their parents were hardworking and loyal to all our endeavours. It was Asia who washed through our flat on the fifth floor every week and cleaned for Madame upstairs, and Jusef who cleaned and was general factotum on the ground floor, balcony, garden and playground.

Nevertheless, in spite of all combined efforts, the alterations seemed to go very slowly. The finishing of the concrete laying of the tennis court intended for the younger ones' playground was hailed with great delight. Both the pre-school and the kindergarten classrooms were large and fronted a wide balcony with fibreglass roof. The children would be able to go straight out through large glazed double doors, down a few steps, through a stretch of grass and onto their playground. Junior 1 (six- and seven-year-olds) and Junior 2 (seven- and eight-year-olds) had smaller rooms at the back of the building, with high windows and linking doors. As the number of the children we were recruiting was heavily weighted in the pre-school and kindergarten classes in this first year of the new school, this proved to be an appropriate distribution of space.

There was one last room, perhaps the most important, which had two toilets, one small and one standard size, a row of washbasins and a drinking font. The plumber never seemed to have quite completed his task satisfactorily. I do not think I have ever prayed for a plumber so hard before. If one 'loo' were out of action, the prospect of four classes full of children going out for playtime was unthinkable!

The first floor had been converted into a school hall, staff room and administrative offices. To have a well-presented office for greeting prospective parents and other visitors was, I discovered, a vital part of the overall impression the school gives as an educational establishment. From this floor upwards to the fourth floor, the glazed panels at the front of the building had been moved right out to the edge of the original balconies to allow for more internal space in the hall and the classrooms on the floors above.

For this first year, we were to let out the rooms on the second and fourth floors to the British Community School and share the playground and the hall. This was to work well and be of great help financially in that

41

first year, when simply everything had to be purchased from scratch, from a doll's pram for the pre-school home corner to a stick of chalk and waste paper bins. Amine was horrified to behold the sheer quantity of equipment that the British Community School brought into the building. This made it all the more difficult to refuse the demands of his newly appointed English teachers, including me! I do recall Miss Hammond, their headteacher, seeking to reassure Amine that they too had very little when first starting in Beirut, but this was small comfort for a harassed school director.

There was one item we all required for craft work and displays, which required not a little tenacity and linguistic courage to acquire. It had not taken us long to realise that the factory behind us was extremely noisy because it kept us awake at times; our bedrooms were at the back of the school building. This factory, we discovered, specialised in the manufacture of cardboard boxes and other packing materials, chiefly for the food industry. Cardboard and paper offcuts – just what we needed! One afternoon, Margaret and I set off up the narrow footpath through the olive grove and onto the little road above us that led into the rest of the village. I do not remember the exact details of the conversation except the mixture of pidgin English, polite compliments and gesticulations until we finally emerged staggering under the weight of one hundred sheets of white card, seventy centimetres by one metre, for about three pence each. This was even more beneficial than we had hoped for, extremely good value for money, and a good source of paper and card for years to come! Furthermore, we had communicated our requirements and thoroughly enjoyed the whole affair. Arabic is a difficult language for the Westerner to acquire, but we were encouraged.

Although Amine was heavily involved with preparations for the new school on the business side, not one of the Khoury tribe was at this stage interested in teaching on the staff or indeed qualified to do so. So with the complete agreement of the school committee members, we prayed for ten Lebanese staff of evangelical Christian commitment to join us for that first crucial year. In my department, we had need of two pre-school teachers, preferably one mother-tongue English-speaking and the other Arabic. In the kindergarten, we needed an Arabic teacher, as I was able to take the English. We also needed two Lebanese teachers to cover Arabic, mathematics, science, creative activities, Scripture, music and physical education in Juniors 1 and 2; a total of five. I was timetabled to teach the English in the junior classes. The two young junior teachers had already been appointed when I arrived, as they were newly qualified from the Christian Teacher Training College in Beirut. One was clearly more competent than the other, but both were keen to make a go of their first teaching post.

We had hoped that I should be able to teach all the English in the kindergarten and Juniors 1 and 2, but as the registrations came in and numbers built up at the lower end of the school, it was becoming obvious that the pre-school and kindergarten would be the largest classes. We attempted to close the roll at twenty-five in each class, but it was nigh impossible to keep to that figure. Ultimately, the numbers in those classes settled at around twenty-seven or twenty-eight with about fifteen in Junior 1 and ten in Junior 2, some eighty plus altogether out of a total opening figure for the entire school of a hundred and thirty-four: well over half in my department! So keen were families to register their little ones in the pre-school for mornings only, that we had to make an easily verifiable ruling for the lower age limit: they must be consistently out of nappies. Even so, the youngest child checked in at two years and seven months!

I knew I should not be able to teach English to three complete classes, kindergarten and Juniors 1 and 2, yet the parents had been promised a pure Anglo-Saxon English teacher! We made this dilemma a matter of urgent prayer. I was the oldest staff member in the department, with only four years' teaching experience, none of which was in teaching English as a foreign language. It seemed a big responsibility! Our prayers were answered in the form of a Lebanese lady of mature years with whom I knew I could work from the minute we met.

I cannot remember how she found out about our need, only that Hazel and I were able to interview Mona in Amine's office just a few days before we were due to open. She wore a cheerful yellow suit and had an air of solid experience and reliability. Though an Arabic-mother-tongue speaker, her English was fluent and clearly enunciated. She had taught previously under an English headmistress and enjoyed it. She was more than happy to discuss more direct, communicative methods of teaching English rather than rote learning from the book alone, and she was fully committed to the Christian basis of the school. She readily agreed to joining in our daily act of Christian worship to which all the parents subscribed on registration regardless of their religious faith or persuasion. Mona was clearly God's provision for me and also for the children. She was competently bilingual, and though she taught only English, she had a wealth of knowledge of the

Arabic language and history. She was more than happy to interpret for me and to put parents at ease when discussing their children's educational progress. Mona was to become a real friend and associate in the work. Her coming was a clear sign to me personally that God would provide the staff support I should need in the unknown days ahead.

In spite of all the busyness of the preparation for the opening of the new school, opportunities arose for us to travel at weekends and taste a little of the beauty of Lebanon, the country to which I had been so clearly called. I wrote to Edith, my former Sunday school teacher who had volunteered to circulate prayer and news letters for me, "Lebanon truly is a beautiful country, and I should love you to visit one day. It is only the size of North Wales and yet it is a land of such contrasts, from the Mediterranean coast where you can bask in the sunshine to the heights of the cedars in the snow-covered mountains. It is also a mixture of old and new, from the archaeological discoveries at Biblical places like Tyre and Sidon to the high-rise blocks of offices and apartments which fill the Beirut skyline."

There was a further important matter that involved some travelling around the country. Our work permits that should have come through before we left England had failed to materialise. Our six-month visas of August 1973 stated, "Visa holder must not take up employment in Lebanon." This meant we would have to drive to the Syrian border at Masna'a, purchase new visas that would allow us to 'travail' and then re-enter the country. Political uncertainties around that time, due to the Yom Kippur War which involved Israel, Egypt and Syria, delayed us from making the journey, but we did actually make our way with Amine on October 9th. All was peaceful in Lebanon except for the fact that *en route* we spotted a couple of Israeli bombers flying over the Beka'a Valley. We simply walked over the border into no-man's-land, waited around for the new visas to be stamped in our passports and returned to the school.

The visas lasted for one calendar month; so we now had till November 8th to sort out the work permits that had been granted in principle back in August. How long it would be before they materialised was anyone's guess. The Arabic reply when questioned is *"bukra"*, which literally means 'tomorrow or the next day, or the day after, or even the day after that'! I was beginning to learn the lessons of patience and passive acceptance, especially when applied to all matters bureaucratic and in connection with Lebanese government offices.

We had a refreshing change that day, and it was great to experience a little more of the country as we drove out on the Damascus Road, through the Lebanon mountains and across the fertile Beka'a Valley, from where can be seen the snow-capped peaks and slopes of Mount Hermon sparkling in the sun. Some have said that this could be the spot where Jesus took His disciples on the occasion of His transfiguration. I could well imagine the scene: as if the sun shone right through His body and His glory was revealed to them in all its splendour. Their eyes would have been dazzled as the brightness of the light was reflected back from the glistening white snow. No wonder Peter, James and John fell face down to the ground in awe and astonishment. What a privilege to behold Jesus in this way and to hear the voice from the cloud, saying, *"This is my Son, whom I love; with him I am well pleased. Listen to him!"*[2]

Hazel had taken us for trips into the mountains to the south of Kafarshima. I loved the steep-sided valleys, with the scent of the umbrella pines and village potters quietly moulding their pots, displaying their wares by the side of the road. The cedars at Barouk are majestic. It was wonderful to stand in rooms lined with sweet-smelling cedar wood in the President's summer palace at Beit Eddine. Lebanon, after all, was the land of the cedars. I read it all avidly in the early chapters of 1 Kings, how the wise and prosperous King Solomon traded with Hiram, King of Tyre. For the building of the Temple, Solomon sent Hiram plentiful amounts of wheat, barley, wine and olive oil in exchange for cedar logs and pine. The logs were hauled down from Mount Lebanon to the sea and floated on rafts along the coast to Israel. This went on year after year for seven years, involving thousands of men, until the Temple was finished. Solomon's palace too was built almost entirely from cedar wood: columns, beams, roof and inner walls. The throne room was lined from floor to ceiling with the fragrant cedar wood. This was not the only time I was to find myself being taken up by the majesty and strength of the cedars or their significance in the history and identity of the land of Lebanon.

We were often stared at as we drove through narrow, steep, twisty village streets with men sitting outside their stores and houses, relaxing with their hubble-bubble pipes. The women were no doubt busy with domestic chores. I did not mind being stared at, for in a strange way I was beginning to feel part of the Lebanese life, even at that early stage of adjustment to a new culture. Mona lived in one such Druze village, a few

[2]   Matthew 17:5

View behind school towards Kafarshima, summer 1974.

miles away from the school. Her family home was set back a little from the road, a little lower than road level, and there were stupendous views across the valley from under the shade-giving vine on top of the flat roof. We went down the coast road to Tyre and Sidon, towns steeped in Old Testament and Roman history. I could not help recalling the story of Elijah and the widow's cruse of oil. Jesus Himself came to Zarapheth, a village above the coast road, where He freed the daughter of a Syro-Phoenician woman from the grip of an evil spirit.

Another of the newly appointed Lebanese teachers lived in the village of Damour on the Sidon Road. Here there were delightful examples of colourful, individually blown items of glassware. Water jugs with tall stems and intricate spouts and handles, for instance, jostled for attention with the citrus fruits, bananas and grapes sold on the different roadside stalls. Visiting the homes of new staff members also opened my eyes to the great Lebanese virtue of hospitality. "But we are *waiting* for your visit," would be the reply when ringing to enquire if a particular time would be convenient for calling.

Most houses had a room specially set aside for receiving visitors, with curtains and shutters drawn to retain what coolness they could. After a few words of conversation, tea or cold drinks would be brought in along with sweet delicious pastries such as *baklava* or expensive chocolates wrapped in silver papers. There would be further pleasant chitchat before we were asked if we would care to drink Arabic coffee, rich and strong, flavoured with cardamom and served in tiny cups. I soon learnt to enjoy not only the coffee but also the emphasis upon receiving visitors and spending time with each other in making relationships.

Making new friendships was important as, in the throes of all this preparation and adjustment to a whole new lifestyle and culture, I was missing those from back home. Friends from the Wirral were particularly faithful at writing in those early days, and I loved receiving their letters. Sometimes I could not help but weep a little; perhaps in gratitude for their care and concern as much as because I was missing them. Kirstene returned from a walk to the Kafarshima post office after school one day clutching a pile of airmail letters, all for the English teachers! "Remember Proverbs 25:25," she said. That night I looked it up in my Bible. Sure enough, His Word was so true and appropriate to the need and the situation – a fact I was to be reminded of time and again in the exciting yet difficult years to come. *"Like cold water to a weary soul is good news from a distant land."*[3] How true this was.

Early in October, I received a letter from one of my former Crusader girls in West Kirby. Crusaders was a Christian movement for children and young people. She was a sixteen-year-old who had aspirations of becoming a teacher and she told me not to feel lonely because they were praying every Sunday for me! It was just so uplifting and reassuring to know that people were supporting me in prayer, particularly during this settling-in period when everything seemed to be so strange.

It was still oppressively hot and humid. The surrounding language was as yet fairly meaningless, though people who knew English tried hard to include me in their conversations. Furthermore, I was about to face the responsibility of eighty young children of whom only a handful spoke English as their mother tongue. I felt excited and somewhat inadequate as I looked at the registers of names I could hardly pronounce on the evening before the school began. *"...I will be with you; I will never leave you or forsake you. Be strong and courageous..."*[4]

---

[3] Proverbs 25:25
[4] Joshua 1:5,6

CHAPTER FIVE

A Benevolent Dragon

School had been busy for a whole week before the grand opening day, as Hazel and Amine received last-minute registrations and the final touches were applied to the building, the grounds and the fleet of new buses. There were six buses that were painted cheerily in orange and white, the school colours. "Eastwood College, Kafarshima, Tel: 431525" was written on both sides and the rear of each bus, in Arabic and English. A big new signboard had appeared at the foot of the school drive, printed with the same information as well as the new school badge depicting an open book and the sun rising in the east behind pine trees.

One bus was directed to pick up children from their homes in the village of Kafarshima. The others were to go north and south, each driver receiving instructions as to the best round trip to take, whom to pick up, at what time, and from which house or building. The children who came in from Beirut, some seven miles away, had a very long trip because there were those to be collected from different parts of the city. They had a very early start too: 6.30 am pickup for 8.15 at the school. I felt sorry for the little ones who came from this great distance. Yet for many who lived in high-rise concrete blocks with small balconies and no play area, to travel daily to a school with a large playground, a more rural atmosphere and cleaner air to breathe made it all worthwhile. I think some of the real 'tinies' sat on their older siblings' knees, ate their sandwiches and went back to sleep! Whatever the truth of the matter, they always seemed to have plenty of energy when they piled out of the buses, rushed with their lunchboxes into the classrooms and then outside to play a little before school started.

Amine had employed bus drivers who were, on the whole, good-humoured and firm with the children. One of the drivers was a keen

Christian believer and later undertook to stay on for half an hour or so on Wednesday mornings to give a direct gospel message in Arabic at Assembly in the Upper Junior section of the school. Having delivered the children, the buses were then lined up at the far end of the school grounds, ready to be marshalled in front of the school, one behind the other, just before home-time at three o'clock.

I myself had hardly been outside the building for at least a week. There were not only the final preparations in the classrooms to attend to, but also parents and members of staff from the Upper School to meet and get to know. Hazel spoke in glowing terms of my competence in English teaching as she introduced me to the parents. Would I ever live up to their expectations? My brief to introduce a child-centred teaching and learning curriculum after the kindergarten style of Professor Froebel was clear to *me*, and this was indeed what I had been asked to do. Communicating this fact to parents, who had themselves been taught by rote and passive acceptance of knowledge gleaned solely from a book, was another matter. This was the practice that was widely accepted throughout the Middle East. I soon came to realise that the traditional educational system forced too much dependence upon studying by rote and memorisation, leaving little place for imaginative and creative thinking.

Furthermore, my task involved inspiring the staff towards child-centred rather than subject-centred teaching in order to give the children in our care the chance to be creative in all subjects; to think and discover facts and concepts for themselves. We wanted them to shine at being and expressing themselves as God created them to be. This would involve providing opportunities for discussion within class in a way that placed value upon every view expressed and led the children on in the development of their cognitive and creative abilities. There was to be no pressure to accept facts subordinately, memorise and reproduce them parrot-fashion in order to gain the accolade of a high mark, merely as an end in itself. Rather, we were seeking to inculcate an excitement in learning and the acquisition of language for receiving and expressing new knowledge. We wanted to create a joyful atmosphere in school and, perhaps most of all, a sense of belonging within a loving Christian environment. If we could introduce such a *living* curriculum, where our students were encouraged to gain confidence in expressing their understanding of a topic in both Arabic and English and this could be seen to be worthy of merit, I truly believed we could deliver a top-quality

49

education. If the children could achieve a basic grounding in the core curricula of Arabic, English and mathematics whilst they were in our department, they should be ready and able to take responsibility for the massive amount of future learning ahead of them in later years.

Keeping each child with other children of the same academic year was crucial, and this some parents found difficult to accept. We could then group them within each age band according to our assessment of each child's developmental level, discuss any special need she or he might have, and teach accordingly, using the resources at our disposal. In those early days, it proved to be remarkably difficult to persuade some of the parents that each child within a class would indeed be expected to work to maximum potential by the teacher concerned. We would not all be working on the same page of the same book, but different groups would be working in the same classroom and the teacher would ensure that each child would be able to progress at his or her own rate of learning. Assessing cognitive developmental needs and providing appropriate learning experiences was the key to achieving our goals. It was a question not of teaching Latin to Johnnie but of teaching Johnnie Latin. I was quite passionate about this. Within the best learning environment we could provide, we must give every child the chance to be creative in all subjects. Rote learning as a key to gaining merit was taboo.

It was within this atmosphere of caring professionalism that I believed we could exercise our greatest privilege: to introduce all the children of whatever religious persuasion to the love of God the Father, the teaching of Jesus Christ and the joy of a life lived in relationship with Him through the power of His Holy Spirit. This was the power by which we as staff sought to live our daily lives, and we had each proven something of that love and power personally. Assemblies and Scripture lessons gave us the opportunity to share something of that love in worship, prayer and storytelling from the Bible.

We eventually opened on October 15th, 1973, the date set by the Lebanese government. I had been in the country for just five weeks! I had twenty-seven children in the kindergarten, with only four who spoke any English at all, and we were some eighty in the entire department of three- to eight-year-olds. A day or two before, Hazel had gathered all the teachers together in the staff room on the first floor of the building. Amine was present to welcome everyone formally and share briefly the vision God had given him for the creation of a Christian school in this part of Lebanon.

What was God's word for this moment, when we were stepping out in faith and obedience together at a very difficult time politically for Lebanon?

Hazel had received a cable from Clarendon School in North Wales with the assurance of prayer and the promise of John 14:27, where Jesus said, *"...my peace I give you. ... Do not let your hearts be troubled and do not be afraid."* Yes, as my emotions rose and fell alarmingly often, depending on how confident I felt at any given moment, it was very good to be reminded that we were not setting sail on this venture alone in the midst of a sea of uncertainties. Jesus was with us in the boat in order to work alongside us as we were committed to working for His glory and according to His call. He would keep our hearts in peace and remove all fear of the unknown future. We had prayed, planned and prepared. The time had come to venture forward in faith. I could not help but recall the promise made to Joshua, and to me just eleven months previously in Sheffield: *"As I was with Moses, so I will be with you; I will never leave you nor forsake you. Be strong and courageous, because you will lead these people..."*[1]

How I came through that first day was in itself a miracle of God's grace. I based myself in the kindergarten room that was large and spacious. The children started arriving from about 7.30 am. The younger the child, the more likely it was that their mother, father, sibling, aunt, uncle, cousin or grandparent would accompany them, in order to ensure their wellbeing in strange surroundings. I understood this and had allowed time that first morning for a general settling-in period before we all gathered together for Assembly at one end of the kindergarten room. It took me a while to make some sense of the register, even though I had tried with Mona's patient help to rehearse the names beforehand as they were largely unfamiliar. There was Nasreen, Samir, Lamia, Rima, Wa'el, Rula, Mahmud, Rania, to name but a few. I also wanted to be sure that we had the spelling in English that the parents preferred.

After an hour or so had passed and my four- and five-year-olds were more or less settled, wearing their name badges and busy with equipment, there were still one or two mothers in a state of high emotion, both in the kindergarten and the pre-school next door. I had no idea what was being said to those children who were in this tearful, unhappy state. I was also pretty sure that any intervention on my part would be ineffectual whilst the parents were still in the room, especially as I did not know the

---

[1] Joshua 1:5,6

Joy and Gladys with pre-school,
May 1974.

language! Eventually, some kind soul told me that these mothers were actually telling their children how much they would miss them. It was no wonder their offspring were so distressed. That was a new management challenge for me that I had not encountered before! I asked the Lebanese pre-school teacher to explain to these parents that we were sure their little ones would be happy with their teachers and that the time would pass very quickly before they would be home again with their families; perhaps the mothers could be brave for the sake of their children… Eventually, nearly all the mothers had left, and we were able to settle the four- to eight-year-olds, some fifty-five children, for a time of welcome and worship, prayer and a story. Never again would we admit all the pre-school and kindergarten children on the same morning!

It was a great joy to have the freedom to lead a Christian act of worship and introduce the children to a God who wished to have a loving relationship with each one of them. We also rejoiced in the freedom to teach Scripture to all, even though at least a third were from a Muslim or Druze background. Though they had assented to this when they registered their children, the parents' attitudes varied and not all were readily in agreement with our Christian basis of faith. The father of one of my five-year-olds, a university professor and a Muslim by birth, remarked, "I like everything about you here except your religion. Personally, I'm an atheist." His Canadian wife was a lovely, gentle person, who later joined Hazel's weekly Bible study for English-speaking parents and expressed real interest in seeking after God. Marwan, their son, had inherited his mother's gentle spirit, and I longed for him, along with so many others, to find a place with us where he felt valued and esteemed. Another of the parents, a Roman Catholic with three boys and a girl in the school, told Hazel that he was delighted they were to study the Bible. Yet another was heard to say, "Now, at last, my children are learning a better way." How we all prayed that they might find in Christ that *Way*.

Assembly was the time in the school day when we prayed together that God would bring stillness and thankfulness into our lives as a school department, staff and pupils together. That first day was just the beginning of what was to become a daily routine. We always started by greeting each other and all the teachers and visitors amongst us, and then moved into an individual, yet corporate, act of prayer:

Transition lining up for Assembly on school balcony, December 1974.

> *When I'm very quiet and still,*
> *I think how loving God must be.*
> *I just say thank you in my heart*
> *For all His love and care for me.*

My head of department at Kingsmead School in Hoylake, Molly Routly, had written these words, and in the early days we ensured that they were translated into Arabic so that all the children understood. We also translated the simple songs that were sung in worship such as *Praise Him, Praise Him, all the little children; He is love, He is love;* and *I have hands that will clap, clap, clap; God has made my hands.* The only musician amongst the staff at that time was Hilda, the Junior 2 class teacher, but she was needed to play the piano upstairs in the hall for the Upper School Assembly. As their time of worship ran concurrently with ours, I had to bob up and down at the piano, playing alternately with the very few chords that I knew on the guitar! Improvisation is a wonderful invention. If in doubt, do your best and make it fun! I was learning fast.

It was a challenge in those early days to present Bible stories in a way that would be attractive to all the children: Muslim, Druze and Christian alike. That first day, we spoke of the wonder of knowing the God who created the world and created it to be *good* and glorifying to His name. We started to learn about the concept of God as a good Father:

> *God is a Father;*
> *He is always there.*
> *Whatever happens,*
> *He still will care.*

Storytelling with Bahia, June 1974.

As usual, the words of the story and the song we sang were translated phrase by phrase, line by line, into Arabic by one of the Lebanese staff, all of whom, to my great relief, were bilingual. Mona was my greatest help as interpreter, as she stood alongside me to the other side of the flannelgraph[2] board. She not only translated the story phrase by phrase as I paused, but gave her words real expression as if she were narrating the story herself. As we moved on into the Old Testament stories, we made abundant use of the flannelgraph pictures that had come in one of the boxes from England, and the other staff were able to take their turn in leading Assembly.

The storytelling with the movable pictures was vivid and exciting. It was wonderful to watch the children becoming quite involved as they listened and participated and we worshipped and prayed together. We taught the Bible as God's Special Book, knowing that the Holy Spirit who inspired its pages would speak to the children's hearts. I had no doubt of the rightness of making Assembly and our meeting with God a focal point of each school day. I had been greatly inspired by Molly during my first two years of teaching at Kingsmead School in Hoylake. She, by this time, was headteacher of an infants' school on the outskirts of Liverpool, and we were able to correspond, share ideas and pray for each other's schools.

"The fear of the LORD is the beginning of knowledge..."[3]

Mid morning playtime that first day was on schedule for ten o'clock, but the 8.30 to 10 am slot in the timetable when I should have been working with the kindergarten had somehow disappeared! So out of the large glazed doors that led onto the balcony, down the steps and off into the playground, with its concrete surface, they all tumbled. Between the balcony and the playground was a patch of rough grass with a couple of small swings and two seesaws. In addition, we had been able to dig out an area that was then filled with clean sand. All these were popular at playtime. Shortly before school opened, Amine had taken me to a car

---

[2] cut-out pictures backed with flannel or felt which adhere lightly to a flannel
    background draped over an easel
[3] Proverbs 1:7

mechanic's workshop, and we had returned with a dozen or so old tyres for rolling in the playground. These too were popular, though we were still short of activity equipment.

Many of the children were hungry by this stage and either tucked into part of the contents of their lunchboxes or went round to the little shop that had been set up by Mr Feghali, Madame Khoury's brother. He had just about completed his work of furniture-building for the school but was still on call to help with maintenance. There they could purchase for a few piastres the most delicious *manoushi*: Arabic bread spread with olive oil and sprinkled with *zaatar*[4] and cooked under a small grill. It was tasty and nutritious. I did succumb myself at times, when the need for nourishment overcame me. He also stocked an attractive array of sweets, biscuits and bottles of Coke, Fanta and 7UP.

The Lower Junior playground had actually been cut out of the huge grove of citrus fruits at the front of the building, and there were still some two-thirds of the trees growing either side of the playground: oranges, lemons, tangerines, grapefruit, as well as pomegranates, quinces and *akedinya*[5]. I enjoyed *akedinya*, a delicious fruit which had a peachy, plumlike flavour. At this time of the year, the citrus fruits, hanging green on the trees, were not a temptation, but later when the tangerines were ripening juicily on the trees, venturing into Mr Khoury's citrus groves was not allowed. He had a small vegetable plot at the bottom of the garden. Exploring amongst the cabbages was likewise taboo!

By 10.20 am, the long-suffering teacher on duty was probably wondering why she had entered the teaching profession in the first place, and thankfully rang the big school bell to signify lining up on the balcony and returning to class. Most playtimes saw a constant stream of children in and out of the bathroom and in and out of the classrooms with various cuts, bruises and tales of woe. We had a special First Aid tin that contained the necessary ointments, potions and bandages, along with a supply of sugary sweet drops and some waterproof dressing strip. This I had bought at Boots (the chemists) in England, in two separate widths, and we found it to be invaluable. It could be cut to the required length and administered lovingly after the wound had been cleansed. The wounded soldier would then receive a sweet and a kiss on the affected area! On very few occasions did we have to rush a child to the local hospital for a stitch or two, and I

[4] thyme
[5] loquat or Japanese plum

was thankful for prayer and protection over these children whilst they were in our care. The benefits of being able to run and play and build friendships with each other in this way far outweighed the discomforts of the cuts and bruises, much as we tried to minimise them.

I am sure that when I was on duty in the playground, I was probably blissfully unaware in those early days of some of the less savoury comments that passed from one to the other, and indeed the content of the tales of woe. I do, however, remember being asked to deal with a persistent offender whose bad language, in Arabic of course, had been understood by every other teacher except me! I could tell by his behaviour that he was fast developing into a real bully, so it was clearly time to act decisively. I took him into the bathroom and literally washed out his mouth with a big bar of soap because the words that came out were so dirty. I then told him to tell all his friends that I would administer more of the same treatment if necessary. To my amazement, it worked and Marwan F. became one of my staunchest allies!

Lining up on the balcony did not come naturally at the beginning. I soon discovered that it was no use at all blowing a whistle as I had done back home. This merely signalled running off in all directions! So we used the bell. I marvel now at the ingenious ways in which those dear children could have you fooled once they had been allowed just the tiniest percentage of freedom! Some of them would take great delight in playing a kind of cat-and-mouse game just as the bell had been rung. There would be the regular check to see what had fallen into pockets that did not belong there and the inevitable rush to the bathroom. We gradually trained the children to conform to lining up in their classes and coming back into school with their teacher, so that we could start the second half of the morning in an orderly fashion. The pre-school children went out to play at different times from the rest of the department. It was certainly safer for them that way!

After a further hour-and-a-half of lessons in which my kindergarten children studied Arabic with their Lebanese teacher and I took the six- and seven-year-olds for English, it was time for lunch. This was a welcome hour and twenty minutes to catch up on the morning and prepare for the afternoon.

School lunch, a simple hot meal, was served in the junior classrooms at twelve noon; so we had ten minutes to tidy up and clear the tables, but most of the children brought their own lunchboxes *full* of food. We tried various ways of supervision and always encouraged the children to eat as much of their lunch as possible, preferably all of it, as we assumed the mothers would know how much their children could eat. It was a long day, especially for those children who left home at 6.30 in the morning.

Jusef the caretaker and his wife Asia near the gate at Eastwood.

The Lebanese sandwiches were either made from French bread rolls or, more often than not, from the flat *khubbiz 'arabi*[6] with a *labneh*[7] or *mortadella*[8] filling and then rolled round and wrapped in greaseproof paper or even newspaper.

It was around this time that we suspected an invasion of mice who had registered for the department without our knowledge. I was not so much concerned as to where they had come from, more as to why they had come in the first place; what was tempting them in and where were they hiding? We embarked upon a grand search, and it did not take too long for the answers to be revealed. Both the piano and the mathematics equipment trolleys were on castors and reasonably easy to move, especially for Yusef, the caretaker, ready with his stick for the kill. Indeed, the first Arabic phrase I used was borne out of necessity and desperation: *"Fie farah Jusef, fie farah hone bil KG.*[9]*"* Under the piano, which was moved less often, were found lunchbox cast-offs, half-eaten and sometimes whole sandwiches; a veritable feast for the mice, and we were nearly fooled again. On this occasion, I decided that the solution was to discuss with one or two mothers a proposed lunchbox menu and send a letter home in Arabic and English with a list of suggestions. Having too much food in their lunchboxes was not only a recipe for breeding mice under the piano, but sadly was encouraging deception and lying.

Actually, to suggest to parents how much food to pack was viewed as somewhat radical, but I was keen that we should teach the children to take responsibility for eating sensibly during the day and to finish the food they had been given. The Arabic translation caused some delay at first, as it had

6   Arabic bread
7   curd cheese
8   Italian pork sausage
9   There's a mouse here, Jusef, in the kindergarten.

to be checked by the senior Arabic teacher for correctness of vocabulary and grammar. I recall a discussion about how to write 'sandwich' in classical Arabic: literally 'two slices of bread with a filling in between'. I think, for the sake of simplicity, we decided to keep the English 'sandwich' in the end! I was beginning to realise something of the richness of the language and the difficulties our children would face as they studied classical Arabic in the later years. Furthermore, in colloquial Arabic, the jots and tittles that indicate the vowels are omitted. This is not the case in written form; all had to be perfectly accurate in order to give a good impression to the parents of the school's standard in Arabic.

Little by little, the challenges of the work were becoming evident. How thankful I was that Christian friends were at prayer. Our task was to build relationships based upon trust and honesty, and this would take time.

After lunch, one of the pre-school teachers was available to help in the kindergarten, as pre-school finished for the very little ones at twelve noon. Gladys was softly spoken and a great help and support. She loved the children and they loved her. She was Armenian but knew Arabic well, and so could provide the comfort of mother tongue during the activity period in the afternoon. I took every opportunity to communicate in English, but this was not an English lesson *per se* and the children were encouraged to speak in Arabic with Gladys and with me in English.

I soon discovered that it was helpful to allow the kindergarten children simply to put their heads on the tables and rest after lunch before embarking on the creative activity period in the afternoon. During this time, we could erect the painting easels, set out the puzzles and constructional toys, the playdough and Plasticine, as well as the home corner for imaginative play. This allowed for numerous opportunities for the children to learn to express themselves through play experiences.

Many of the little ones literally had to be shown how to play, both on their own and within a social group situation. The language opportunities were immense as we interacted within these small groups and encouraged the children to move from one activity to another. We always used an open-ended question wherever possible – "Can you tell me about your painting?" or "What have you made here?" rather than "Is that a car [or a house, or whatever]?" I did not mind if they initially answered me in Arabic. At least it showed an understanding of what I had been asking them in English.

We were always encouraging the children to express their feelings as well – for example, happiness, sadness, anger or frustration – and to learn to do so appropriately. Playdough made from flour, salt and water was a great medium for working out frustration and anger, and far less disruptive to overall harmony in class than thumping people! Even the shy child could find pleasure

Me on fifth-floor balcony.
Eastwood College, December 1973.

in making tissue paper circles into flowers and taking them home for mummy. Some children liked nothing better than to make a three-dimensional model out of small cardboard boxes and toilet rolls, cover it with pasted paper strips and then paint the finished article. Lego was always popular too, and I was glad I had bought the largest set I could find at James Galt's factory in Cheadle and brought it with me in the van across Europe. Constructional toys were good for developing concepts of size, dimension and proportion, in addition to encouraging creative thinking. These were all great outlets for encouraging healthy use of young imaginations and providing plenty of opportunities for both receptive and expressive language.

Later in the afternoon, we would gather together for a story and singing of nursery rhymes. Sometimes, if the hall on the first floor was free, we would troop upstairs for music and movement or simple physical education. I was able to make use of the new, portable cassette tape recorder that Austin Briscoe, on behalf of the congregation at All Saints' Church, Marple, Cheshire, had presented to me as a gift. Storytelling with puppets and simple repetition, along with flannelgraph or storybook pictures, was a great way to familiarise the children with the sounds and meaning of the English language. They loved my finger puppets and wanted to make their own. I found it amazing the way I could communicate in actions and rediscovered action rhymes and jingles I had long since forgotten. One of the favourites was:

Tommy thumb, Tommy thumb,
Where are you?

Here I am, here I am,
How do you do?

It continued with a name for each finger of the hand. It was a great way to provide action, as our hands were hidden behind our backs and then the thumbs or fingers would suddenly appear upon mention of "Here I am, here I am…" We also repeated the simple greeting in English as the thumbs and fingers asked each other, "How do you do?" What gave me so much pleasure was to hear the children singing these little ditties, in perfect English, around the classroom and on the way home on the bus, obviously feeling so good about it.

Just before three o'clock and home time, we would gather our belongings and say a short prayer together before the children ran out to board the waiting buses:

School is over for today;
Done our work and done our play.
As we go, we come to say,
"Thank You, God, for everything. Amen."

That first day felt like a lifetime and yet it had passed. The first week simply flew by with so many little tasks that could only be done once school was underway. By the second week, I found a spare moment to write home to my parents. "In the kindergarten, I feel more settled and there is plenty of space in the room. With only four out of the whole class who speak any English at all, it can be quite tricky to get things across. I've come to the point now that when a child comes and gabbles away in Arabic, I just point to the toilet and hope for the best!"

A new school had been born. God had been good, and I felt, to quote Hazel's words, like "a benevolent dragon".

Chapter Six

Life with the Lebanese

It was October 1973, and through letters home I was keen to be able to reassure my parents that we were not apparently in any danger from the current fighting in neighbouring countries. Life in Lebanon *was* affected though, and we were prepared with contingency plans for evacuating the children out of the classrooms that fronted the Old Sidon Road and the airport into safer rooms at the back of the building. I did not mention this to my parents, and thankfully these plans were not needed at this time.

In order to save petrol in case of oil-rationing, cars were allowed on the roads every alternate day according to their registration numbers. Those with even numbers drove on the even days of the month. Similarly, those with odd numbers drove on the odd days of the month. All public transport was exempt from this ruling. Quite an ingenious plan, I thought! Hazel's VW Beetle had an even-numbered registration, so this particular weekend she could drive on the Saturday but not the Sunday. This meant leaving the car in Kafarshima and going to church in Beirut by *servis* car. These cars were part of the public transport system in the country and operated a *prix fix*[1] system with specified stops. They could, however, be thumbed down virtually anywhere along their designated route.

We soon became accustomed to travelling into town by *servis*. It was simply a case of walking down the school drive to the Old Sidon Road and waiting for a car to come along. This was not too onerous. I do not think I ever had to wait more than twenty minutes by the side of the road. There were often friendly waves and children shouting, "Hi, miss!" as they

[1] French: fixed price

My Carte de Sejour.

passed by. Thumbing down the *servis* car worked by means of an outstretched arm. If the *servis* was full or acting as a taxicab, the driver would lift his head back slightly to signify 'not available'. I soon learnt to do this too, if I was not sure about the driver. It was usually a smoother drive if you chose an older driver!

It cost fifty piastres (then approximately ten pence) to go the seven miles into Martyrs Square in downtown Beirut, and then only another fifteen piastres to take the bus from there along Rue Bliss and into the more westernised part of the capital known as Ras Beirut. This area is built upon the headland of Beirut. (*Ras* means 'head' in Arabic.) The popular Corniche ran all around the headland, and whether walking or driving, the atmosphere was enjoyable for old and young alike. There was a funfair, complete with an enormous revolving wheel, illuminated by gaily coloured lights in the evenings. Market stalls and street vendors would be selling coffee, roasted nuts, hot corn on the cob, *kaak*[2] and sometimes ice-cream. For church, we had to go nearly as far as the gates of the American University compound and then turn up left with the Librairie du Liban on the corner. This was Rue Abdel Aziz, and the International Alliance Church occupied the first floor of an apartment building on the right-hand side.

It was on one of these fifteen-piastre bus rides that I learnt to use one of the Arabic phrases that I was acquiring, chiefly for survival purposes. As I was making my way down the centre aisle to a seat at the rear of the bus, I suddenly felt a marked pinch on my backside from the person behind. Greatly incensed, I delivered the retort, *"Yallah, imshi min hone!"* which was the Arabic equivalent of "Get lost!" His look was one of great surprise, followed by a huge smile and a shrug of the shoulders, as if to say, "OK, I've got the message."

I was reminded of an occasion in Morocco. A group of us had been enjoying the new year festivities down in the souk in Tangier. We were walking back to the mission compound surrounded by happy children chanting repeatedly, "Woolworths, Marks & Spencer, British Home

2   crisp bread with sesame seeds and *zaatar*

Stores!" Eventually our Welsh-speaking friend, Olwen, could stand it no longer. She turned round and spewed out a torrent of Welsh. The children soon disappeared. "What did you say to them?" we asked. "Oh, it was the first half of the Lord's Prayer," she replied!

Most of the *servis* cars were fairly elderly Audis or Mercedes-Benz, though some of the younger drivers sported newer Chevrolets, Buicks and the like. The cars had bench seats front and back, were left-hand drive and were officially licensed to carry six passengers including the driver. I once saw a family of eleven disembark on the way downtown, including a boy who got out of the driver's door before the driver himself! On our return from Martyrs Square to Kafarshima, we stayed until the car was full before the driver set off, but there would be ample entertainment whilst waiting in the back seat. Inevitably, loud Arabic music would be playing over the radio; not altogether the best introduction to oriental melodies! Lebanese sweetmeats such as *baklava* and Arabic newspapers would be peddled alongside the *servis*. I think the drivers who took the cars into the southern suburbs of Beirut were getting to know these English teachers from the new school in Kafarshima. Amazingly, I always felt as if I were in good hands, especially when travelling alone.

One journey, however, lives on in my memory. I was seated in the back of the *servis* on the far right-hand side and we were approaching Hadeth, the village just north of Kafarshima. I think the driver must have been particularly keen to get home that night, as we had driven at breakneck speed the entire journey. The road veered to the right, and we were travelling at such speed, I could feel the car heaving over the edge of the road. As I looked down, my thoughts were only of that glorious place called heaven where Christ had prepared a place for me and *"to all who have longed for his appearing"*[3]. I felt at perfect peace as I prayed in my heart, "I'm in the place of your calling, Lord. I'm ready to meet you now." How we recovered our balance was most certainly a miracle, and as the other passengers were gesticulating and yelling at the driver, I sat quietly in my corner praising the Lord for keeping us safe. *"...who through faith are shielded by God's power..."*[4]

Driving in Tangier and northern Morocco had prepared me a little for the craziness and chaotic nature of Beirut driving, but for the first time in my life, I had no desire to go solo at the wheel. It was about this time that

[3]   2 Timothy 4:8
[4]   1 Peter 1:5

Alliance Church.
Top: Pot-luck meal, 1974.
Bottom: On the balcony, 1979.

Hazel initiated us into some of the vagaries of driving (for survival) in Beirut. It appears that traffic lights had been erected at important crossroads, and one-way streets introduced in heavily built-up areas – for safety reasons, of course. But to no avail! Once a Beiruti driver came along and encountered a red light but no-one driving across the road, he simply put his foot on the throttle and went his way, be it left, right or straight ahead! Indicators on the car were seemingly only for decoration. The same fate fell upon the one-way streets, and a few disused pedestrian crossings with dilapidated lights told their own tale. The not infrequent power cuts added to the chaos, and you can guess the rest: all attempts at enforcing the new rules were abandoned. Instead, hard-worked traffic police risked their lives at the crossroads, frantically blowing their whistles and waving their arms in all directions. Where the traffic lights were functioning correctly at busy junctions with maybe three or four lanes in both directions, not only was lane discipline unheard of, but the sheer volume of traffic revving and horn-honking was enough to scare me into quiet submission as a passenger for the time being. Maybe one day I would summon up the courage, but not at this early stage. I am not sure whether I would ever have the confidence to drive right through red traffic lights!

I appreciated the fellowship and worship in English at the International Alliance Church. The pastor was American, and there were a number of American families who attended, including students from the American University. The 10 am service was in Arabic; needless to say, we went along for the English service at eleven! At first, I missed the liturgy of the Anglican service and regular attendance at Holy Communion, but I grew accustomed to the Alliance service. It was at times meditative and at times exultant, but always prayerful and with the Word of God at the heart of the Biblical message preached.

Once a month, the church held a luncheon fellowship. Each family or group of people would bring a dish of food, and it would all be placed attractively on tables on the balcony outside the church.

School buses leaving school at 3 pm.

This was a great opportunity for chatting with other believers of all nationalities whilst we ate buffet-style after the morning service. I was always amazed at how there always seemed to be a good balance of savoury and sweet dishes. It was tempting to taste a little of all of them! The Americans seemed to combine their savoury and sweet, in any case, and it was commonplace to serve oneself cold meats, salad, jelly and trifle all on one plate. When in Rome…!

It was at the Alliance Church that we became aware of the work of the InterVarsity Fellowship amongst students in the city. There was a student centre where Bible studies were held and Rev. David Penman, the regional secretary, was based. As so many Lebanese seemed to be perpetual students, adding 'credits' to their degree studies one at a time, it was quite normal for undergraduates and postgraduates to blend together for Bible study and fellowship. Margaret, Kirstene and I soon became involved in the Friday evening study that was held in the home of an American couple in town, Al and Dawn Fairbanks, whom we had met at the Alliance Church.

We would leave Kafarshima as soon as possible on Fridays after school, sometimes travelling on the school bus if there were room for us, though personally I preferred to go by *servis* and avoid the scenic circular route round most of the streets between Kafarshima and Beirut. Once was good for the experience and to see where the children lived, but after that the direct route was much to be preferred!

There were a couple of supermarkets in Ras Beirut that we used to patronise regularly. One was Lebanese-owned and quite reasonably priced. Saloum's stocked some of the local foods that we enjoyed, including *laban*[5] and *hummus*[6]. There were always piles of fresh fruit and vegetables stacked high on the pavements outside. The other was a more upmarket American food store which stocked imported goods, including meat and dairy produce in packs, weighed out in grams and kilos. Here we could stretch the 'kitty' to the occasional treat of a box of Kellogg's Cornflakes or a Mars bar each to 'help us work, rest and play', at twice the price it would have been back home! I think we even managed to find a jar of Marmite from time to time at some extortionate price. I particularly enjoyed the cheddar cheese, a familiar staple food in the midst of a vast array of new tastes to acquire.

Al and Dawn lived in a first-floor apartment in one of the older buildings in town, and we would arrive there pretty exhausted, having snatched a *shawarma*[7] or *falafel*[8] sandwich in town after we had completed the shopping. Dawn worked part time as a nurse at the American University Hospital (AUH), and Al was a lecturer at Haigazian, the Armenian college of higher education. Their two little girls were usually well on the way to bed when we arrived for the Bible study, and it was lovely to be made so welcome as we dumped our shopping bags in the hallway and played with Julie and Kirsty for a few moments in their room.

As a good proportion of us spoke no Arabic, the study was conducted in English, usually led by Al but with plenty of opportunity for questions and discussion, and always prayer together towards the end of the evening. I thoroughly enjoyed being involved with Lebanese students and postgraduates in this way. It was a great opportunity to absorb more of God's Word together. I well recall our studies in the Acts of the Apostles, looking at the way in which the Holy Spirit came upon the early church in such power.

One member of the group, Antoine, lived up in the mountain village of Aley, where Amine's uncle and his family had their carpentry business. He very kindly provided a regular lift back to Kafarshima for the three of us, along with the shopping, in his VW Beetle. I think it was Antoine who tried to explain to us that the Lebanese system of driving is loosely based upon the French Highway Code, whereby right of way is accorded to any vehicle approaching from the right. It was enough for me to assimilate simply

[5] strained yoghurt which made a delicious curd cheese
[6] chick peas and tahini pounded to a paste for use as a tasty dip
[7] lamb cooked on a spit
[8] a vegetarian burger

being *driven* on the right at this stage, and I was more than content to sit back and enjoy Antoine's steady hand at the wheel. It was so good to share with, and receive from, Lebanese Christians in this way, as it provided warm Christian fellowship and a refreshing change from the responsibilities of the new school.

I was certainly not finding things easy at the school with my tribe of Arabic-speaking youngsters. The language at this stage seemed to be impenetrable to my

Assembly 'Good Samaritan' story, November 1974.

ear and my understanding. The whole sound system was so different from English, with all the guttural sounds that I could not even pronounce properly. The syntax was also bewilderingly different from English or French. What I loved about the language was its sheer expressiveness; for example, the face and body movements that accompanied the expressions. *"Shu sar?[9]"* was said in such a way that expressed interest at the thought of some exciting tale to be recounted to the listener. *"Shu biddi a'amel?[10]"* by contrast would be uttered more as a rhetorical question and as an expression of resignation because the situation was now out of the speaker's control. There were also the phrases that recurred frequently in my hearing such as *"biddi[11]"* and more particularly, *"Biddi rhuh al hamam.[12]"* Listening and watching my Bible story during Assembly times being translated into Arabic phrase by phrase was very helpful. The Arabic overheard in the playground was quite beyond my comprehension!

I found the climate quite trying, in addition to this bombardment from a foreign tongue. It was still hot and humid, which was oppressive and exhausting. It was one thing to be sitting around on holiday in the Mediterranean sunbathing, but quite another to be working a seven-hour

[9]   What happened?
[10]   What shall I do?
[11]   I want
[12]   I want to go to the bathroom!

day virtually non-stop five days a week. There was no doubt that I was out of practice in teaching such young ones. I had certainly never had responsibility for six teachers and eighty children before. Furthermore, I had no training or experience whatsoever in teaching English to other than English-speaking children! "I would value your prayers for patience and energy," I wrote to my parents, to the churches in Marple and Birkenhead that were upholding me and to other Christian friends back home, many of whom were sending such supportive letters and transporting me back to their world. I even had a letter from one of my GCE girls at the school in Wallasey, now in her fifth year and due to take her mock exams the following month. She said they were finding it hard to accept the new RE teacher even though she was very sweet (!) and were expecting me to walk in and take over the lesson at any minute!

It was good to be reminded of the recent past in a way that boosted my own ego, but I was also very aware that living on memories of past achievements was not really helpful right now. Deep down, I knew the Lord would honour my trust in His call and redirection of my life so dramatically. "He wants me here and here I stay," I wrote home with more confidence than I sometimes felt at this stage.

The Lord answered prayer magnificently. At the end of the second week of school, we had a most unexpected pleasure: a day off! It was the end of the Muslim fast of Ramadan, one of the five pillars of the Islamic faith. The full moon had appeared over Mecca, the Muslim holy city in Saudi Arabia, so it had been declared throughout the Muslim world that the month of Ramadan was concluded and the three days of feasting could begin. It was not until 7.30 that morning that we knew definitely from the radio that the feast had started and we should close school for the day! It had been one of those weeks when every day since Tuesday had felt like Friday. How grateful we were for this welcome day of rest!

On the Tuesday morning, Hazel had woken up with no voice and had had to stay in bed and sleep, so we were without a headteacher. In the middle of the morning, Kirstene, one of the English teachers who shared the flat on the fifth floor, had to lie down because of dizziness and diarrhoea. This meant all her English lessons had to be covered in the senior part of the school. Downstairs on the ground floor, the pre-school teacher was away. I strongly suspected that she was finding the job too difficult and might not return. There were some very young children in her class with overambitious parents, which was all rather threatening. By mid afternoon, Kirstene was in a delirious state, with fever and a temperature of a hundred and three degrees Fahrenheit. As soon as school was over, we rang Dr Manoogian at the Christian Medical Hospital in Beirut, whom Hazel knew well. He gave us instant advice over the phone and prescribed certain tablets for the fever and others for the diarrhoea.

Kindergarten children near the tuck shop, November 1974.

Along we went to the well-stocked *pharmacie* in the village and asked for the prescribed medication. It was not cheap, but by the next day, though she felt weak, Kirstene's fever was greatly reduced and her temperature was down to ninety-nine degrees Fahrenheit.

Meanwhile, school continued. While Hazel was still in bed with no voice, two of the senior girls got themselves stuck in the school lift, which was out of bounds to the children in any case. They panicked and broke the whole door in order to get out, splaying glass all over the landing, just where children would be moving as soon as the school bell rang. But it was worse. The games teacher, who was proving to be somewhat irresponsible, decided to let out her joint class of forty or so junior children, mainly boys, twenty minutes early and take herself off home. The pandemonium was indescribable, as the children went berserk, screaming all over the place. To think this was only the eighth day since the opening of our brand new school!

God had intervened, and we were all so thankful for the unexpected pleasure of a day off. All was quiet now at the paper factory behind the school building and there was far less traffic on the road. How lovely to be able just to relax for the day, to sit and write letters home before going into town for the IVF Bible study.

The following Wednesday was chaotic too. It was nearing the end of October, and we were treated to the first rainfall of the season. The children behaved as if they had never ever seen rain before – and with some reason. It was not a gentle drizzle. There was thunder, lightning and very heavy rain for the whole day. Some of the little ones in the kindergarten spent most of the lunch hour with their noses pressed so hard against the windows that they could not see out because of the condensation! Others were racing around in a near hysterical manner, shouting, *"Fie shitte, ta'a la shuf.[13]"* It would have been an excellent 'direct method' Arabic lesson for me, had I not been so concerned about keeping some semblance of peace and order in the classroom! I had certainly acquired some useful vocabulary that was persistently drilled into my ears as the monsoon-like conditions prevailed for the whole day. I was really quite glad when the school buses drew up at 3 pm!

The rain continued into the night, but the following day was bright and sunny once again and considerably fresher. The country was badly in need of rain, for the soil was parched and the citrus fruits were hanging unripe in the garden. The government supply of drinking water had ceased altogether, and we were drinking a rather expensive factory-purified bottled water. The ordinary water supply had become rather spasmodic too; so the rain was really very welcome.

I wrote home a few days later, "It's now 4.45 pm (2.45 pm your time) and the sun is sinking down behind the sea. It's a marvellous view from our balcony, and I can guarantee that within fifteen minutes it will be pitch dark. I still can't get used to the early sunsets and short dusks." This was why we started and finished the school day on the early side; so that all the children could be home in the daylight hours.

By the beginning of our fourth week, I was feeling greatly encouraged by the progress of the six- and seven-year-olds, whom I taught for one-and-a-half hours every morning after playtime. There was one girl in this class who was an English-mother-tongue speaker. Her mother, Jill, was from Hove, near Brighton, and had been married to Halim, a Lebanese, for many years. Their home was in the next village to Kafarshima on the road north to Beirut, where a number of Hazel's friends from the Lebanon Evangelical Mission lived. There was also a studio for the production of Arabic Christian radio programmes in Hadeth, and we had been introduced to the Lebanese and the expatriates who worked there. Halim ran a small but busy hairdresser's salon from a spare room in their first-floor apartment; so I became a regular client, both for a trim and for a perm every so often. Halim and Jill were to become firm friends, and I was always made welcome in their home. Jill's family were Jehovah's Witnesses, and she was keen to study the Bible with Hazel and some other English-speaking mothers on Friday mornings in our fifth-floor flat at the school. It was not long before God spoke deeply into her heart through His

---

[13] It's raining; come and see.

Word and she found Jesus to be the only Son of God who gave His life for her salvation.

Nerissa, aged six, was a joy to have in the class, and not only because she spoke English so fluently! Her presence in school gave me an opportunity to demonstrate our commitment to providing a learning programme to suit the developmental needs of each child. Whilst the rest of the class were writing short sentences about Jane and Peter from the Ladybird Reading Scheme or a simple news item in English, Nerissa was sitting towards the back of the classroom busily writing for herself in her 'newsbook'. She had her own alphabetically arranged dictionary for collecting useful words to aid in the writing process. Sometimes it was an item of daily news; at other times there would be the latest episode of her story, always delightfully illustrated with neat little coloured drawings. I do not remember having to teach Nerissa to read, only to check her progress regularly and provide more advanced reading material to interest and stimulate her. She had a friend who sat nearby, and they alternately annoyed and spurred each other on. Rita too already knew some English, as her parents travelled regularly to the States. The two of them were a great inspiration to the rest of the class and an enormous encouragement to me.

There was no doubt by this stage in the term that the Junior 1 children were really beginning to try to speak for themselves in English, albeit with a slight northern accent! I wrote home, "I think some of them are beginning to understand quite a lot and are also gaining confidence in saying short sentences. How I wish I'd learnt French at this age." In addition, some of the kindergarten children were beginning to speak short phrases in English. Imagine my sense of thrill when the first four-year-old bounced in one morning saying, "Good morning, Miss Radcliffe." They were also learning to say essential phrases such as "May I go out?" and "Please may I have…?" with real meaning and fluency.

It was wonderful to have these encouragements, as other factors, in connection with the Lebanese system of education being so formal and marks-oriented, were pressing for my attention. Hazel, as the headmistress, was coming under pressure from parents to send home weekly reports on each child's progress, from aged four years upwards. After some discussion on the demands this would make upon my hard-pressed teachers, we settled upon the idea of devising an end-of-term report to be sent home at Christmas. This would show parents exactly what each child had now achieved as far as written work was concerned in the core curricula of Arabic, English and mathematics. Each child would write his or her name in English and Arabic, plus some numbers and a drawing. The older ones would be able to write a short sentence and do a maths calculation. Finally, there would be a short written comment from the class teacher upon the child's progress and attitude in school. Definitely, there were to be no marks! Hazel approved the idea and was more than prepared to try something new.

Nevertheless, the pressure on us to award marks was far from over, and the parents took some convincing. As I listened to their concerns, albeit through a helpful interpreter in some cases, I began to piece together the motives that lay behind their requests. The traditional Lebanese system imposed an expected and exacting standard of attainment for a particular year of a child's schooling. If a child failed to achieve that standard by the end of the school year, then he or she would have *failed* the year. It would be a disgrace upon the whole family for the child to have to *repeat*, not to mention the additional expense of extra school fees. It was this system that led to the demand for homework and marks.

We had actually admitted a ten-year-old boy into Junior 2 who had already failed the academic year twice in his previous school and so was supposedly destined to repeat the Junior 2 work until he had passed. I was determined that we should not encourage this practice that represented a subject- rather than child-centred approach to the children's learning. Rather, we should be seeking to provide appropriate learning experiences across the curriculum to support this child's special needs. There is nothing wrong with homework in itself when it is necessary to reinforce learning that has already taken place in school and is truly the child's own work. But for the parents to be using homework as a teaching tool in itself was for it to become nothing less than memorisation of facts from the book, only to be repeated the next day in school in order to earn high marks. As for sending my four-year-olds with English workbooks to study at home, some of them could not even hold a pencil!

It was mid November, and I wrote home to my long-suffering parents, "I'm secure in the knowledge that God wants me here, but I just pray that He will enable me to have patience and the grace to learn to strike the balance between sticking to the educational principles I believe in and being dogmatic just for the sake of it."

Hazel was still under pressure from some parents who were urging that we should send home half-termly grades for the under-eight-year-olds – all eighty of them! My prayers were answered after discussion with the staff to hear their views on the possibility of holding a parents' evening one day after school, to include displays in all classrooms of the children's work to date. Thankfully, they were keen to give it a try. They realised that we were, as a fee-paying school, accountable to parents to explain our emphasis upon individual learning needs and our commitment to making the whole curriculum available to every child. There was such a good response to the bilingual invitation that went out, that we had to offer *two* parents' evenings from 3 to 5 pm after school. I encouraged the older children to wait for their parents to arrive and then conduct them round the department, showing their work and introducing their teachers. They were then to disappear off into the playground so that the grown-ups could talk!

The response of the parents was nothing short of enthusiastic and really quite overwhelming. Now they could see the sheer volume of written work that had been accomplished, both in the exercise books and displayed on the walls. They could also inspect for themselves the whole range of reading books we had in both Arabic and English, as well as the educational resources and equipment that were available to encourage the development of reading, writing and mathematics skills. To actually invite the parents in to see their children's work in school was obviously something quite revolutionary, and all seemed to be very appreciative. It was good for me too to see the staff being so encouraged, as one by one the parents expressed their satisfaction and renewed confidence in the department, its weird English teacher and her methods!

Battling through all these difficulties caused me to reflect upon my life and work with the people in the light of God's purposes. My first observations of the Lebanese were of a surprisingly independent people on the surface of things, yet with a strong allegiance to each other within the extended family. There seemed to be a naivety about their independence because their concept of nationhood was so different from that with which I was familiar in the West. After all, the Lebanese had only become independent as a republic from the French just thirty years previously. The family or place of birth came first, even though you might no longer be living in that particular town or village. Indeed, the family took priority over everything.

In some respects, I found this attractive. To me, it was a familiar concept, as I was a northerner by birth, from Ashton-under-Lyne, near Manchester. The greater part of my family still lived and worked around that region, and we would defend the advantages of being born and bred in the north of England at any time. I had spent most weekends as a child visiting other family members, particularly my grandparents, both of whom still lived in large Edwardian houses in Ashton. It was not unusual for twelve or more of us – aunts, uncles, cousins and so forth – to be gathered around the table. I was happy to be able to identify my upbringing and family life with that of the family-orientated Lebanese.

It was a joy to be welcomed so unreservedly. I soon learned to appreciate the meaning of the well-used phrase of welcome, *"Ahlan wa sahlan,"* which has its roots deep in the values of the people. *Ahl* means 'family'; *sahl* means 'a valley'. It is a greeting that offers a guest all the good things that a family and a lush, inviting valley can offer, rather like alighting upon an oasis in the desert. I had already noted that hospitality was a foundation of Lebanese values and very much part of their way of life.

Though I respected this general allegiance to the family, I do not think anything could have prepared me for the 'every man for himself' mentality that seemed to prevail in some areas of life in Lebanon and the reckless disregard for the law, such as it was. Expediency seemed to be the name of the game, and Beirut driving was a good example of this. Even the barriers down the centre of the dual carriageways could be ignored if you were in that much of a hurry to escape the traffic jams. The expertise and sheer panache of the drivers was perhaps to their credit! There was certainly no place for a nervous driver here; aggressive self-confidence was ever to the fore. Shortly before we opened the school, I was introduced to Sam, a close friend of Amine's who had a good head for figures. He was the bursar of the school, with the important role of paying our salaries, which may explain why I was careful in my response to the tale of the strawberries. "I know all about growing strawberries," he said one day as we were walking round the school garden. "I can show the children how to look after them, if you like. I am an *expert*."

Far more important than all these struggles to adjust was the constant reminder of the simple fact of God's call. There were times when I wanted desperately to hide in my room, listening to *Dad's Army* or *Many a Slip* on my pocket radio, which was tuned in to the BBC World Service most of the time. This was my opportunity to make contact with the fluency of the English language, relax in the comfort of its familiarity and have a really good laugh. Lying on my bed with a cup of tea to hand, I could even visualise the characters and sometimes predict what would happen next and chuckle in advance. Often, memories of sitting around the TV at home with the family watching an episode of *Dad's Army* would come flooding back. I would be laughing and crying at the same time! It probably did me good.

One day, not long after we had opened the school, the English wife of a Middle East Airlines pilot stayed for a chat after school. She lived in an apartment building in Ba'abda, not too far from our village. It was a lovely spot near the Presidential Palace overlooking the Mediterranean coast, and a number of the MEA families rented flats there. Her four-year-old daughter was one of my very few mother-tongue English speakers and was registered with us because the kindergarten class at the British Community School (BCS) was already full.

Anita's mother was clearly puzzled about what motivated the three of us qualified English teachers to come to work in a Lebanese school, where we were paid less than if we were teaching in England. Why not teach at the BCS who were sharing the building that year? She could not grasp why we should want to teach alongside the Lebanese, nor what a difference it makes to know the call of God upon one's life. That day she enquired about my social life. "Do you have any English-speaking friends?" she asked, in such a way as to imply that I could not possibly make friends amongst the Lebanese. I was shocked and deeply troubled by this patronising, prejudiced attitude. I believe the incident helped me to focus even more on God's purpose for my being there and my willingness to obey.

There was no doubt that I was beginning to come to love these people with whom I had been called to live and work. I really was enjoying their company and appreciating their emphasis upon family, hospitality and, most of all, faith in God. I wrote to my dear former Sunday school teacher, Edith, "I don't think I have ever been so conscious of the prayers of other people so far away until now, and especially the power of simply trusting in Him to give strength to cope and wisdom in dealing with new situations. I know full well that I've made many mistakes already and I've had times of very real doubt and depression, but through it all, there is that deep assurance that it is right for me to be here."

This was a place that seemed so westernised and secular on the surface, yet the Arabic culture and language was full of references to God, even in the simplest greeting. I soon learnt the protocol of Arabic greetings. You ask a Lebanese how he is and, regardless of how he is, he will say *"Al-hamdu lillah"* or *"Nushkur'Allah"* which literally mean "Praise and thanks be to God." If you make an appointment to meet a Lebanese friend, he will no doubt agree to meet but *"insha'Allah"*, in other words, "if God wills". I found a strong, abiding belief in God amongst most of the Lebanese with whom I was able to speak in those early days and particularly amongst my colleagues in the school, friends at church and the IVF Bible study group.

After just two months of living in the country, I commented in a letter home, "I'm so fortunate to have young, enthusiastic staff to work with, mostly very responsible and helpful, especially with my language problems. I can see I shall make real friends amongst the Lebanese."

CHAPTER SEVEN

The First Christmas

The run-up to Christmas and the end of our first term was drawing nearer. How could the time have flown by so quickly? Amine was keen that we should take full advantage of the opportunities that the Christmas season presented in terms of Christian witness to both children and parents. Equally, it would be good for the children to show off the English they had acquired as well as some dancing and singing in Arabic. These matters were to dominate my thinking and praying from mid November onwards. The burden weighed quite heavily upon me. I so wanted any performance, or *haffleh* as it was known in Arabic, to be meaningful to the children and fun to prepare for, not simply a question of what would please the parents and be good propaganda for the school. I also knew that to practise for too long with young children would run the risk of losing their spontaneity; so I was determined that we should not start preparing until the last week of November.

It was good that the teachers were so keen to help, but oh what a responsibility to co-ordinate the whole department and generally keep everyone happy! I still marvel at the wisdom the Lord provided in those early days of adjustment to working in a different language and culture and readjusting to teaching little ones again. 'Friendly', 'loving' and 'firm' were my keywords, not to mention 'patience', 'self-control' and 'gentleness'. Starting a new school was no 'bed of roses', and discouragement appeared to loom around every corner. A tendency towards over-conscientiousness probably made the scene look bleaker to me than it really was at times; yet I was to prove that God is always greater than all our discouragements.

I wrote home and asked for prayer for inspiration for the *haffleh*. Meanwhile, there were some lovely surprises on the horizon. One Wednesday morning, towards the end of November, I was teaching English to the Junior 1 class after Assembly and mid morning playtime, blissfully unaware of the excitement to come. At about 11 am, I was called upstairs to the school office on the first floor to speak to the Vice Ambassador at the British Embassy on the phone! My mind raced as I climbed the stairs. What could this possibly be about? "Would you be willing to speak to a Mr and Mrs Cresswell who are here with me?" he enquired. It did not take me long to recall who these people were: the parents of Carolynne, who had been appointed to my post of RE teacher at Wallasey.

I readily agreed to speak with them. I knew them only slightly, but enough to remember that Mrs Cresswell worked for a small travel agency in West Kirby. "Hello Wendy," – what a joy to hear her voice! – "how are you? Any chance we might be able to meet up with you today whilst we're in Beirut?" It transpired that they were on a fifteen-day P&O cruise of the Greek Islands and the Mediterranean and were stopping in Beirut for just one day! I was delighted that they had taken the trouble to contact me, but what should I do about my classes?

I need not have worried. Hazel happened to be in her office next door, and by the time I put the receiver down, she had virtually arranged for the Cresswells to come to the school for lunch and then for me to go out with them for the afternoon! Hazel herself was free to cover my lessons; so after we had had lunch together on the fifth floor and I had shown Mrs Cresswell around our apartment, we took a taxi out to the Jeita Grotto. What a whirlwind! I could not imagine such a possibility in the midst of a working day in England! Did I perhaps catch a glimpse in Hazel's response of the carefreeness of life that I had so admired in Patricia, her younger sister, in Morocco? I was certainly grateful.

The Jeita caves lie to the north of Beirut, just beyond the mouth of the Dog River, Nahr al-Kalb. I had missed out on a trip to Jeita during our first few days in Lebanon owing to my unfortunate attack of 'Beirut tummy', so was thrilled to have this opportunity. The two-mile road up to the grotto is steep and winding, and leads to a series of caves full of naturally forming stalagmites and stalactites. The water that pours from it is the source of the Dog River. In the winter, the levels rise so high that the lower caverns are flooded. We were able to enjoy a boat ride, a somewhat eerie and yet magnificent experience as we wound our way through the vast network of galleries and ravines and saw the astonishing natural spectacle of rock formations, floodlit in different colours. The upper cavern had been cleverly charted so that we could go through on foot with a guide and scramble to the very heart, where the cave opened up to reveal a large platform wide enough to seat an audience of a thousand. I should have loved to come to a concert or folklore evening here.

Another taxi brought us down from Jeita onto the main road leading back to the Beirut docks and the ship. Mr Cresswell was impressed by the headstrong nature of the driving and the apparent lack of all rules of the highway. I was amazed at the way in which I had learnt to trust myself to the drivers of the *servis* cars and taxis in which we travelled, praying for God's protection. The cruise liner was just like a floating hotel, with approximately six hundred British tourists aboard. How strange it was to see all these white faces! I really felt quite proud to be able to say, "I live here," to some British people who wanted to exchange Lebanese pounds for sterling because they were sailing that night. I wondered, too, just how much the average British tourist really understands of a country and its people when they only visit for one day.

Next day was Lebanese Independence Day and thus the occasion for another welcome day's holiday from school. It simply poured with rain for a whole day, and I was so glad that the Cresswells had not come a day later. That afternoon, I was privileged to have been invited, along with other staff members, to a Greek Orthodox wedding in the village of Kafarshima. The groom was the brother of one of our teachers. We were presented with sugared almonds in a small dish as we entered the church, to signify sweetness and longevity of life. I was moved by the music and singing and the symbolism of the marriage ceremony, as rings of flowers were placed over the heads of the bride and groom.

Independence Day happened to coincide with American Thanksgiving Day that year. On the following Saturday, I had been invited to a Thanksgiving luncheon in the home of Al and Dawn, the couple who hosted and led the Friday evening Bible study group. It was just like Christmas, with turkey and stuffing, peas and rice, followed by delicious desserts. How I appreciated being able to share this special day with an American family. One incident that has left a mark upon my memory was of three-year-old Julie, their elder daughter, becoming overexcited at the meal table and behaving in a manner that my parents would have described as bolshy. I do not recall the exact details of the incident, only that Dawn quietly took her daughter out to the bedroom for a "little chat" in private. On their return a few moments later, all was sweetness and light again. There was no outright embarrassing confrontation and no loss of face. I was impressed. *"A gentle answer turns away wrath, but a harsh word stirs up anger."*[1]

The weather was still warm and pleasant, and the rain at night was freshening to the earth and a welcome release from the humidity. The oranges in the school garden were ripening fast and tasted delicious. To me, there is nothing so sweet to the taste as a Lebanese orange plucked straight from the citrus grove. This created a problem with the more adventurous children, especially as the nightly rain would bring the ripe tangerines off their branches and temptingly near to the edge of the playground. The grapefruits were ripening too, along with quinces and pomegranates.

Hazel took us out one Saturday, way up into the Chouf mountains, passing the President's summer palace at Beiteddine and on up the twisting road to the small village of Barouk. High above the village is a grove of ancient cedar trees, some of which are thought to be well over a thousand years old. Their trunks have huge girths and their height can reach ninety feet or so. I was told that it is now strictly forbidden to fell these trees as well as the other famous cedars further north, a couple of miles from Bcharre. The trees are known locally as *arz ar-rab*[2] and are under the protection of the Patriarch of Lebanon. There is a small chapel amongst the cedars at Bcharre and the whole grove is protected by a fence. The cedars have long tap roots stretching deep into the earth to reach necessary moisture. *"The righteous ... will grow like a cedar of Lebanon; planted in the house of the LORD, they will flourish ... They will still bear fruit in old age, they will stay fresh and green, proclaiming, 'The LORD is upright; he is my Rock...'"*[3] I was able to purchase a small slab of wood with a cedar tree painted at one side and the words of Psalm 92:12 inscribed in Arabic alongside. My mother kept it as a souvenir and a reminder to pray for Lebanon.

I tried to imagine what it must have been like in Old Testament times, when the cedar forests would have covered great swathes of the Mount Lebanon range. I took some quite dramatic photographs as we wandered

---

[1] Proverbs 15:1
[2] God's cedars
[3] Psalm 92:12-15

around the pine forests and the foothills of the cedars at Barouk that day, marvelling at this breathtakingly beautiful spot in His creation. Certainly, these were gifts of encouragement from His hand as we faced the busyness of the Christmas preparations.

Painting of a cedar tree.

By far the greatest gift was the provision of enough spare cash to purchase a BOAC[4] ticket home to visit the family for two weeks over the Christmas vacation. As I wrote home shortly before my twenty-seventh birthday at the end of November, "I'm just so grateful for the opportunity to come home at Christmas, and I'm sure I'll return with a much more settled view of the situation." As I was under the age of twenty-eight, it was still possible to obtain a daytime direct flight, Beirut to London Heathrow, on student preferential terms. Furthermore, I was able to book a seat on the Heathrow to Manchester Ringway flight and to pay for that in sterling on my arrival in London.

As the days went by towards Friday, December 21st, I was so thankful to be able to look forward to the trip home. Quite a few were loading me with cards and parcels to post on my arrival, and others asked me to bring various items back on the plane. I think Hazel was worried I might not come back, but that was the furthest thing from my mind. My heart was settled in God's will and purpose for me in Lebanon. I believe He knew I needed the reassurance and the security of seeing family and friends in the UK in order to reassess the vision and be refreshed to face the rest of the school year ahead.

The Sunday before my birthday dawned fresh and sunny, and it was a pleasant relief after three days of rather wet, dismal and chilly weather. I

[4] British Overseas Airways Corporation (BOAC) was the British state-owned airline operating overseas services until 1974 when it merged with British European Airways (BEA) to form British Airways (BA).

sat writing letters home on my fifth-floor balcony after the Sunday lunch that we had enjoyed at church, basking in the sun. What a lovely view it was from there across to the airport, that was quiet at that moment, and the sea shining the most beautiful blue. The three days of rain in Kafarshima had been rather colder in the mountains. The road to Damascus had been blocked and the mountains were snow-covered. It was an extraordinary vista, with the sun setting behind the sea, casting a pink glow over the snowy caps of the mountains.

Just as I had hoped to be able to concentrate fully upon preparations for Christmas in school, another anxiety was simmering quietly in the background: our work permits. On October 9th, at Masna'a on the Syrian border, we had acquired the appropriate visas that lasted for one calendar month. It was now nearly the end of November and there was no sign of the work permits. Any mention of the matter to Amine elicited the *"bukra*[5]*"* response, usually with the addition of *"insha'Allah*[6]*"*. And surely God was in control. I still recall the wooden seats in the government offices in Beirut, which were strangely worn down just at the spot where we, and no doubt many others before us, would sit... and sit... and sit. After signing for the work permits, our patience was finally rewarded on November 26th when we received our pink cards, complete with photos. The next task was to apply for identity cards from the Security Offices. Mine was due to be ready by December 12th, just a week before I left for England. What a mercy, as otherwise it could have been difficult getting back into the country the following January.

Waiting at the government offices was a little similar to experiencing the British Bank of the Middle East in Ras Beirut, in that it afforded a good opportunity to observe people's comings and goings on both sides of the counter. It was as if a job had to be found for everyone. Offices and banks seemed to be full of dusty desks with piles of paper and people standing or sitting, shouting to each other and waiting for the next document to sign or stamp. It was so different from the sedate, solemn atmosphere in a British bank at home. It took me a while to pluck up the courage to push my way forward to pay in my monthly salary cheque and later draw out money to pay for my ticket home. Once adjusted to the general mayhem though, I soon began to enjoy this totally different way of doing business!

[5] tomorrow
[6] God willing

Friday, November 30th passed uneventfully during the school day. Margaret and Kirstene had made me a birthday cake with one candle that we enjoyed with a cup of tea straight after school, but there was more to come. The crown of the day was a celebratory meal for eight, including friends from the IVF Bible study group, in a Lebanese restaurant up in the mountains, which lasted for over two-and-a-half hours! The views out through arched windows were magnificent, and the decor was typically Lebanese. I could hardly take it all in, especially as the whole event was a complete surprise to me, other than the curious hint of being asked to wear a long skirt that evening for the Bible study – or so I thought! After the delicious food came the arrival of a scrumptious chocolate layer cake, gateau-style, with two candles and "Happy Birthday to Wendy" inscribed on the top in coffee-coloured icing.

As I recovered from the shock and started to cut the cake, the piano accordionist, who had been entertaining us with traditional oriental melodies, struck up with *Happy birthday to you* and everyone joined in, singing in Arabic and English. My first birthday in Lebanon was certainly a memorable experience, and I felt thoroughly loved and spoilt, and thankful to the depths of my being for the joys of Christian friendship across the cultures.

I was touched, too, by all the cards and good wishes I had received from friends and family back home, but most especially by a card from Hazel St John. It was a postcard of a Moroccan potter painstakingly applying intricate and colourful designs to his pots. The words she wrote were from Jeremiah 18:6 – *"Like clay in the hand of the potter, so are you in my hand..."* – and from Ephesians 1:12 – *"...in order that we ... might be for the praise of his glory."* How good to be reminded that all my living and working is ultimately for His praise and glory, as I allow myself to be moulded by the Maker as clay in the Potter's hand. Oh, that I would be willing to be humbled and reshaped according to how He wants me to be! My greatest desire, then as now, was that the Lord would be glorified in our midst.

No sooner had my birthday celebrations died down than the Christmas preparations began in earnest. After much prayer and discussion, it was decided that the older children in the department would attempt a Nativity play in English, allocating the longer parts to those few who were more confident in speaking the language and would be able to give more meaning to the words. I was thankful for every minute of experience I had gained at Kingsmead School in Hoylake in my first two years' teaching and was able to adapt a play that we had used successfully there. Both parents and children responded well, and soon the details of costumes and practices began to fall into place. The pre-school were to dress up as stars and sing their favourite songs: *Away in a manger* and *Twinkle, twinkle, little star*. With the kindergarten, we were hoping to work out a butterfly dance as well as singing some of the easy action songs in English like *Tommy thumb, Tommy thumb* that they so enjoyed. I was glad for Hilda's musical ability and her enthusiasm for organising the dancing and some singing of Arabic songs too. Hazel assured me that all this would please the parents on the day!

I was keen that the children should all be involved in decorating their classrooms, making their own streamers, lanterns and other decorations. We had no shortage of colourful paint, crepe paper and tissue, and I had a stock of shiny glitter and paper to share out. There were the end-of-term reports to get in motion too, as promised for the parents. What a task it was trying to co-ordinate what the Lebanese teachers were preparing with the four different classes and somehow keeping the excitement levels at an acceptable pitch. As the day of the performance – Tuesday afternoon, December 18th – drew nearer, we had practices *ad infinitum*. It was an emotional roller coaster; one minute reaching the heights of joy at the way in which the children were responding, and the next wondering whether we would ever get them into any semblance of order before the day. Yet I was thankful that they were all thoroughly enjoying the preparations, even if the teachers were completely distraught! Over and again, I had to remind myself of the power of prayer and be determined not to allow my joy in the Lord's overruling of every situation to be destroyed.

I must have been fairly exhausted, in any case, by this stage in the term. I received a letter from my former Sunday school teacher, Edith, explaining that she had decided to duplicate part of my letter to her and send it round to those who were praying for me so that "we may be able to pray more specifically for Wendy's needs". What a joy when my encouragement levels were at a low ebb. "To be perfectly honest," I wrote home in mid December, "I have truly never felt so insecure and discouraged about my work, and the thought of two years ahead of me seems unbearable at times. Yet the knowledge and support of people who are praying and the provision of the Lord to come home at Christmas is just about keeping me on track." How I needed those prayers!

Nine days before the day of the Christmas entertainment, I was driving back from Beirut to Kafarshima with Hazel and sitting in the front passenger seat alongside her. The headlights of her VW Beetle were woefully inadequate. It was pitch dark and there were no streetlights on that particular stretch of dual carriageway. Suddenly, without realising what was happening, we had driven right up onto an island in the middle of the road. The bumper took the brunt of the collision; the front bonnet lid shot up and crashed back into the windscreen, cracking the glass. Simultaneously, we ground to a very sudden halt and jolted forward in our seats. As there were no safety belts, it was a miracle that Hazel was not hurt by the steering wheel, but I went flying and crashed my forehead against the cracked windscreen. As I felt my glasses breaking, I just threw myself onto Hazel, shut my eyes and said, "Pray!" And she did, amazingly, as she must have been just as shattered as I was. As we tumbled out of the car, I discovered that only one lens was broken, and we tried to assess the damage. Together, we pulled the bumper back into position and pressed the bonnet down again. But any attempt to drive away was useless because we were sinking into the sand!

Just as we were surveying the scene and wondering what to do next, one of the many cars which were driving along the coast road that night actually stopped and shone its headlights on us. Out poured four young people, all speaking English but from four different nationalities! God had sent His rescue agents from four corners of the globe. They immediately set to work, jacking up the car, piling up under the wheels with stones and then using car mats to give a smooth surface for the tyres. Next, one hopped into the driver's seat and backed off at a tremendous rate, and we were off the island. The entire operation took less than ten minutes. After much handshaking and offering of gratitude, they piled back into their own car and drove off into the night.

Somehow, Hazel managed to drive to the nearest garage, with a strong smell of burning rubber and at a very slow rate because the brakes were jammed solid! I simply cannot recall how we found our way back to the school, but what amazing provision for our rescue! We really felt God's protecting power in response to those who were praying back home. Two Disprin[7] and an early night put me straight, and the bump on the forehead soon settled down.

7 Disprin are pain relief tablets that can be dissolved in water for quick relief of different kinds of pain, including headache and migraine.

So, to the entertainment – we were due to start at 2 pm upstairs in the main school hall. It was 'all hands on deck' preparing the hall. Our classrooms were temporarily converted into dressing rooms, with parents on hand to help with the dressing up. The anticipatory excitement was almost tangible, and I had a real sense that all would be well now that the day had finally arrived. Hazel had suggested that we advertise starting at 1.15 pm on the invitation, to give people time to arrive. I was horrified lest our little ones would not be ready in time. "Just wait and see," she said. "The timing will be just right." And so it was! Just before two o'clock, we took the pre-school upstairs for their 'stars' performance, after which they were able to sit on mats along the front and have a grandstand view of the whole show, which they had not seen before. Next came the kindergarten butterfly dance and singing in Arabic, and finally the Nativity that simply took everyone's breath away.

Nerissa, wearing her mother's royal blue Crimplene mini-dress that had been altered lovingly to fit, announced clearly, "We welcome all the parents to our Christmas play." Jill, her mother, was sitting proudly on the front row along with other parents, feeling scared that Nerissa would forget her lines! Her fears were unfounded, as the little actors and actresses – Joseph, Mary, angels, shepherds, kings – all spoke out their words with real meaning. Nerissa, playing the part of Mary, was particularly sensitive as she spoke about the God of love who had sent His own Son as a Babe to be one of us and live amongst His people. There was a hush over the entire hall. Parents, friends and children alike were clearly moved at the reverence with which these seven- and eight-year-olds performed their parts. Prayers had been answered. This was far more than a mere propaganda exercise. This was worship. God had been glorified in our midst. *Hallelujah! Alhamdulillah!*

Just three days later, I bundled myself into a taxi to make my way to the airport. "One minute," said Amine as he dashed off into the orange groves. He returned with a large bunch of oranges picked straight from the tree, complete with branch and leaves. "For your mother," he said. "She'll be delighted," I replied, as I hastily pushed the whole bunch into my hand luggage. And indeed she was. Three months after the eventful ten-day drive across Europe, I was home again in a matter of ten hours or so!

CHAPTER EIGHT

Amine's Vision

I had never been unhappy at school, despite my problems with O level German and English Literature. My time in the sixth form at Clarendon School in North Wales was a particularly enriching two-year period, emotionally, socially and spiritually. I could not have wanted for more in terms of consistent, prayerful and wise counsel from the staff and a holistic approach to education that was delivered to a high standard with a really personal touch.

Amine Khoury, the eldest of six, had clearly not had such a positive school experience in the village school at Kafarshima. As young as sixteen years, when he was a nominal Christian, he had felt dissatisfied with the school system. His world was sheltered and secure within the confines of the village, and yet he had a sense of discontent with the standard of education the school provided for its pupils, especially in the English studies. He would say to the other students of his own age, "At some point, I am going to take this school and turn it into an ideal school." One of his classmates actually replied, "You must not forget that we are your friends and we will bring our children in the future." Never a word said in jest! Amine, the teenager, was quietly planning all the details of the setting up and running of the ideal school in his mind. His father's eight-storey building should be available for the purpose in due course, as most of the apartments were becoming vacant. He intended to use this building on the Old Sidon Road rent-free, once he had finished school, and then look for someone to run it as headteacher whilst he himself was in training for a university degree.

Thus it was that when he was eighteen and between school and university, Amine started hinting to family members and telling his father about his grandiose plans. Right from the outset, Mr Khoury was antagonistic. Amine was the eldest son and should without doubt study medicine. But Amine knew he was not in any way inclined towards a medical career. Then Mr Khoury tried to convince him to go into his own car sales and servicing business, with the implication that no-one makes a profit from running a school. It was clear from the outset that persuading his father even to agree with his choice of career, let alone back the project financially, was not going to be an easy task. Yet Amine was deeply convinced that starting a school in Kafarshima, staffed in part by English-mother-tongue speakers, was to be his life's goal.

It seems that the Lord too was working out His purposes through this young man's conviction of his vocation in life. There is a verse in Proverbs which says, *"A man's mind plans his way, but the LORD directs his steps,"*[8] and another, *"Many are the plans in a person's heart, but it is the LORD's purpose that prevails."*[9] Just three years after the whole idea of a school began to take shape in his mind and heart, Amine found his place as a true Christian believer in the Kingdom of God and began to seek God's guidance in the whole matter. After his conversion at the age of nineteen, the whole idea took on a new perspective. Even though his father persisted in opposing the plan, Amine became more and more certain that the school in Kafarshima was indeed within the Lord's purpose and would ultimately come to pass.

There was in the village at that time an Australian lady who had at one time worked with the Lebanon Evangelical Mission. She belonged to the Protestant national Church of God and spent her days of active retirement working with the church and visiting around the homes, fully involved in all aspects of life in Kafarshima. Joy had a quiet, gentle personality that endeared her to adults and children alike, and her wise influence was widely felt and appreciated. She had a real ministry in opening up the pages of the Bible in such a way that the young believers could appreciate the wholeness of Biblical truth for each one as they understood God's loving purposes expressed through its pages. Discipling others prayerfully and persistently was her great gift, and she would visit the Khoury household at least once a week for this very purpose.

Though he ceased any mention of his school idea at home with the family, Amine felt confident in discussing the whole matter with Joy. She shared his desire to see a school in the village that offered a truly Christian education and daily act of worship, including Bible teaching for all pupils. Amine also desired that the school should have a high academic standard, especially in terms of the English language teaching, which he felt should

---

[8] Proverbs 16:9 (RSV)
[9] Proverbs 19:21 (RSV)

be taught by English-mother-tongue specialists who shared his Christian faith. He was aware that his contact with Christians outside Kafarshima was very limited, and he certainly had no idea how to recruit English-speaking Christian teachers. Furthermore, who should be the first headteacher? Amine knew full well that he was too young and in-

Hazel St John and Amine Khoury.

experienced to direct the school himself from the outset, but he was keen for the school to start whilst he was still at university and then gain some experience in management before taking full responsibility. Little did he know at that stage of the events beyond his control that were looming in the not too distant future. It is questionable whether the school would ever have been founded had Amine waited until he was older.

So who could help to fulfil his vision? Joy had been in Lebanon as a missionary for many years and was able to mention various names from time to time. On one occasion, when she had called to visit the Khourys for Bible study, she and Amine were praying after lunch about the school. "Do you know Hazel St John?" she asked. Amine replied that he knew her only by sight in the church and had never actually been introduced. "Hazel is leaving the Lebanese Evangelical School for Girls in Beirut next summer," Joy continued. "Would it be worth going to visit her to discuss the project?" Amine received the suggestion gladly but was strangely curious. A myriad of different thoughts raced through his mind. He knew the school in which Hazel had been the longstanding headteacher. He knew she had a fine reputation in Beirut and was well-known and well-loved. Was it not a little strange to think that such a person would ever consider leaving that long-established, prestigious school to come to a little known village outside the capital? He voiced some of these thoughts out loud. "Well, you won't lose anything by simply contacting her," Joy replied to his expression of doubts. "Speak with her; perhaps she could guide us to someone who would be suitable." So Amine consented.

Joy undertook the task of arranging an appointment with Hazel in Beirut. Furthermore, she accompanied Amine one Saturday afternoon in November 1971 for this momentous visit. Hazel received them in her room at the school, and after the usual pleasantries of tea and cakes, Amine explained in his broken English the whole story: how he hoped to start a new Christian school in Kafarshima and how he was looking and praying for the right person to launch the school as headteacher. He shared with her exactly what a venture of faith this was, as he was having such difficulty in convincing his father to release the use of the Khoury building and provide the initial financial support required for equipping the school. "I believe my father will one day see the point of having a Christian school in Kafarshima," Amine concluded.

It was after some further discussion that Hazel declared, "Amine, I must tell you that this is something I was praying for." Amine was shocked and astounded at her response. It was as if she already knew the whole story and had the faith to encourage him and embrace the project immediately. "Can we go and see the place?" "Yes, of course," Amine assented, and without further ado they were on their way to Kafarshima. Hazel drove Amine in her car, and Joy took Hazel's friend and secretary, Nadia Haddad, in hers.

They explored the building together. Amine was able to give Hazel a better idea of his plans: classes, Assembly hall, and even a flat on the fifth floor would be available for live-in accommodation. He explained how he was longing to have a good academic standard for the school with well-qualified Christian teachers from England for the English side of a bilingual curriculum. He knew how much local parents wanted their children to have a good standard of English. In the French schools, the children would be speaking French fluently by the age of eight or nine years because they had French-mother-tongue teachers on the staff. Hazel agreed to reflect and pray over the whole proposal and to keep in contact. Amine was quietly encouraged by her response but never dreamt that she would take such a personal interest. *"May he give you the desire of your heart and make all your plans succeed."*[10]

Hazel kept her word and contacted Amine. She explained that as a member of the Lebanon Evangelical Mission, she would need their permission to be seconded to work in a privately run institution: would Amine please come to Beirut the following Saturday to meet Douglas Anderson, the then acting field leader of the mission, along with Mr Khoury? Perhaps they thought that at twenty years of age he was too young to attempt such a project. Douglas was interested but grimly

[10] Psalm 20:4

90

realistic in his response. If Hazel were to be seconded, either the school must have a board of trustees in whose name it would be registered or it must be connected to a church. This was wise advice and marked a turning point for the whole project. Hazel herself warmly commended the idea of inviting certain key Christian people to create a committee; praying people who would be interested in supporting the school. Mr Khoury continued his opposition, believing that the mission would never second Hazel to the work. Without such an experienced person, the project could never succeed.

Nevertheless, Amine went ahead. Although it took time, he was agreeably surprised at the interest and enthusiasm of those whom he invited to form a school board. Rev. Philip Zacca from the Church of God agreed to chair the committee. Leila Clargy, the leader of the youth group at the village church, joined and also Nadia Haddad – both wise and able Christians. But the mission was still reluctant to give its permission to loan Hazel, in spite of the fact that she was due to relinquish her post at the mission girls' school to a Lebanese Christian teacher in July 1972. This was in line with mission policy of handing over responsibility to the Lebanese. Perhaps there was also not a little concern that if Hazel were to become headteacher of another Christian school in the country, only seven miles from Beirut, there might be a stream of pupils who would be transferred to the new school! These fears proved to be totally unfounded.

The whole process dragged on for eight months, and it was drawing near to the time of Hazel's return to the UK for home assignment. Meanwhile, Amine's father persisted in his opposition and even tried to rent the building out for other uses. This was a testing time for Amine – and for Hazel, who was becoming increasingly convinced that this was indeed the answer to her prayer for guidance for her future service in Lebanon. Amine continued in regular prayer with Joy. "Lord, if You want the school to come into being, then please provide this particular building and please persuade my father to support me financially and allow us the building rent-free." Hazel too was praying, and putting pressure upon the mission to come to a decision. They finally agreed, just one week before she was due to leave for England. It was at that point that Amine hoped his father would agree to the project wholeheartedly, but that was not to be until later. Mr Khoury, though fearful of the responsibility, never lost confidence in his eldest son, but he struggled with perceiving it as a

Christian project inspired by God Himself. *"The one who calls you is faithful, and he will do it."*[11]

Hazel came home with a clear agenda in her mind. She herself would continue to be a full member of the mission, on the same terms as before. Those now to be recruited in England to join the staff would have two-year contracts with the school and be independent of the Lebanon Evangelical Mission. There were three of us who were led by God to respond to Hazel's invitation to join her for those first two years at Eastwood College, as the school came to be known. I felt the least familiar with living and working in an overseas situation, and somewhat overawed by the experience of the other two.

Margaret had already taught with Hazel at the Lebanese Evangelical School for Girls nine years previously, when she had spent two years in Beirut as a young short-term worker. "Margaret is a most versatile person with lots of initiative, and with the prospect of her help I feel altogether more confident than I otherwise would!" wrote Hazel in glowing terms. True, Hazel had simply not had experience of working with junior age children, so a new all-age school which was building from the lower age groups upwards was something of a daunting prospect.

Kirstene had a London degree in English and two years of travelling with Operation Mobilization under her belt. Part of the time with OM was spent working in Beirut, where she had met Hazel the previous year. She had felt God's call to return to Lebanon to teach if the way should open, and to this end was training with the British Council in the teaching of English as a foreign language. Admittedly, I did have the advantage of having twice been out to Morocco to help with the Easter camps on the mission compound in Tangier. Furthermore, I had taken opportunities to travel around the country and absorb the feel of being with Arabic-speaking peoples. But far more importantly, I had the Lord's clear call and command from Joshua 1:9, *"Be strong and courageous. Do not be terrified; do not be discouraged, for the LORD your God will be with you wherever you go."*

Meanwhile, back in Kafarshima, structural alterations affecting the school building were gathering pace. Five of the seven apartments had to be entirely refurbished in order to create a school hall, offices, staff room, library, art room, music room, science laboratories, classrooms, kitchens and toilets. It was a huge undertaking for Amine throughout the year of preparations. He had already started at the Lebanese University studying

[11] 1 Thessalonians 5:24

Law, but when it was definite about Hazel's appointment to be the first headteacher, he knew it was right to shift to the American University and study for a degree in Administration. The school committee were prayerful and supportive, but to Amine and his family fell the bulk of the everyday oversight of the work. Contacts were made with Christian Lebanese teachers. Mr Feghali, Amine's carpenter uncle from Aley, started constructing the furniture, and Madame started sewing the uniforms.

"When you start a school from scratch, you have to create everything. And yet I know it was all His project and for His glory," Amine reflected some time later. "Even my father came into harmony with the whole idea and really put his heart into it." The vision was taking shape. "God moves in a mysterious way His wonders to perform..."[12] "*Many, LORD my God, are the wonders you have done...*"[13] "*Declare his glory among the nations, his marvellous deeds among all peoples.*"[14]

[12] William Cowper (1731-1800)
[13] Psalm 40:5
[14] Psalm 96:3

CHAPTER NINE

To Sydney and Back

The reader would be forgiven for being confused. Was it not at home in England that I spent the Christmas of 1973? Where does 'down under' come into the picture? Allow me to explain further. It was rather an inauspicious start to the new year and an occurrence which caused not a little anxiety and inconvenience.

In addition to visiting family and friends, I had spent some time shopping in Manchester for folks back in Lebanon. An alarming quantity of winter clothes and shoes had been 'ordered' by various friends and colleagues and had to be packed in my one reliable, green-coloured suitcase. After much pushing and sitting upon the case, it eventually shut tight and I encircled it with my father's wartime leather strap. The combination of green and strap made the case easily recognisable at the luggage reclaim at the destination airport.

It had been wonderful to meet with friends again, albeit briefly, and share some of the joys and trials of the first term at Eastwood. I had no doubt as to the rightness of returning to the fray in January. I was sure the days would fly by and it would soon be time to come home again for the long summer vacation. There was a real sense of excitement and anticipation as we landed at Beirut Airport on Friday, January 4th, 1974. Hazel, Margaret and Kirstene were waving from the airport balcony as I boarded the bus accompanied by Randa, a former student of Hazel's at the Lebanese Evangelical School for Girls, for the short ride to the luggage reclaim. Eager porters pushed forward to carry my hand baggage as I made my way into the building. *"La, shukran,[1]"* I said with great

---

[1] No, thank you.

confidence. I was fairly sure I could manage the green case, especially as the others by this time were downstairs and making encouraging gestures on the other side of a large glass panel.

The luggage started to appear. I had checked in early at Manchester Ringway and especially asked for the case to be transferred at Heathrow to the BOAC flight for Beirut. Wherever was it? I waited and waited as one by one the cases were reclaimed. Randa found her case and went on her way through customs. It had been so good talking to her on the plane. She was now looking forward to seeing her family again after a business trip in London. I nervously continued to scan every case, looking for mine.

Ultimately, the horrid truth dawned: my precious green case had simply not come off the plane. The airport officials checked and rechecked, and eventually decided that it was already bound for Bombay! My heart sank as I filled in a long, detailed form in which I had to list the contents of the case and their value.

"I think about seventy pounds," said I without much conviction.

"Why not call it eighty pounds?" said he with a smile.

"Why not say ninety?" said I in reply.

"OK, one hundred pounds," said he with another big smile. The officials promised to cable Manchester, London and Bombay with the details, and would I please ring back the next day when the BOAC flight was due back from Bombay? It was actually the day after, at my fourth attempt, that I discovered just what an adventure my sturdy green case had endured. It had virtually travelled halfway round the world and was now on its way back from Sydney, Australia via Singapore on a Pan Am flight!

For someone like me who had really travelled very little to date, this was the stuff of which dreams are made. I could almost imagine my case covered with brightly coloured stickers standing up on its hind legs with the leather strap holding it together and speaking of all the exotic places it had visited at the airline's expense! I was overwhelmed with relief, largely because it contained so many items for other people.

We did have some fun in school at the expense of my well-travelled green suitcase. The morning after its recovery from the airport, I took it downstairs in the lift, duly unpacked but with the leather strap around once again. I popped it inside the Junior 1 classroom, ready for my lesson with them. Their curiosity aroused, we had a great time talking in simple sentences and asking the suitcase questions about Singapore and Sydney.

What a wealth of language opportunities the incident provided! They all followed this with some writing and drawing in their 'newsbooks', imaginations thoroughly stimulated. Even some of the parents commented on how their children had enjoyed sharing in the experience in this way.

And so my suitcase had been 'down under' and, by God's protecting hand, had returned to its rightful place completely untouched. This came to be symbolic of my own struggles that first year at Eastwood. I too felt at times as if I were going 'down under'. I encountered difficulties and hardships, times when all my usual points of reference were unclear in terms of cultural norms of behaviour and the politics of the country in which I was living. How foolish I had been to say to friends back home that it was only another teaching job, working with children in Beirut rather than Birkenhead. Yet time and again I was conscious, even at the darkest moments, of a greater power taking control, affording patience, wisdom and the ability to cope in entirely new situations. God was reaching out in answer to the prayers of many, and lifting me up as on an eagle's wings to see things from His perspective. "*...those who hope in the LORD will renew their strength. They will soar on wings like eagles...*"[2] "*[The LORD] satisfies your desires with good things, so that your youth is renewed like the eagle's.*"[3] I had simply to praise Him and expect Him to act. "*I believe that I shall see the goodness of the LORD in the land of the living! Wait for the LORD; be strong and let your heart take courage...*"[4] I needed, therefore, to walk closely with the Lord, loving and obeying Him in order to be renewed mentally, emotionally and physically day by day. Yesterday's blessings (and disasters) were for yesterday. Today's challenge is to walk in obedience to Christ this day and experience God's faithfulness and the Holy Spirit's empowering comfort and help.

Almost as soon as I returned to Lebanon, there was a drastic change in the weather for the worse. The rains started, and it literally sheeted down day and night for the first week-and-a-half back at school. Can you imagine the challenge of keeping eighty Lebanese under-eight-year-olds happy indoors for the whole day, day after day after day? On higher ground above Kafarshima and beyond, there was a great deal of snow, in places up to ten feet deep, and many mountain villages were completely cut off. It was reckoned to be the coldest winter since 1938. The rain was certainly

---

[2] Isaiah 40:31a
[3] Psalm 103:5
[4] Psalm 27:13,14 (RSV)

needed after months of drought and increasing water shortage. To make matters worse, in the school building the rather archaic central heating and hot water system was proving to be woefully inadequate, and the children were coming to school wearing layers of jumpers under their uniform. Draughts seemed to creep through every door and window. How glad I was for the woolly clothes I had brought back from England along with my warm winter nighties!

It is amazing how one crisis seems to attract another, and we certainly had more than our fair share. Even on the first day of term, we suffered one of those rare occurrences when a child cut his head above the eye because he had been pushed off the swing, or so he said. This involved a trip to the local hospital and five stitches to repair. The parents had no inhibitions about expressing their feelings just as I was attempting to settle the kindergarten children for a story. At that very moment, the plumber arrived to bleed air out of the stone cold radiator. Before we knew where we were, we were all covered with a fountain of filthy black water! Praise God for a sense of humour – and resilient children. It is a wonder those parents did not despair of us altogether.

Hazel was keen that I should spend more time socialising with the other staff at lunchtime in the staff room on the first floor. The incessant rain was very trying, and the poor teacher on duty was left with three classes to keep occupied indoors. On my return downstairs for afternoon school, I found the whole of the kindergarten room in an uproar, with toys and mathematics equipment scattered all over the place and three other Lebanese teachers standing around watching! I asked the teacher on duty to organise a clear-up as she was on duty, whereupon she blew her whistle with great gusto four or five times. The noise and chaos were mounting and I could control myself no longer. I suggested to the teacher that she should go and have her lunch break, and she beat a hasty retreat! The children tidied up in no time as I went round helping them, and within minutes there was silence in the room as they all put their heads down on the tables, simply shattered! And so was I!

At the other end of the age scale in the department, I had the eight-year-old boys with whom to contend. The wet weather exacerbated matters, as they would insist on tangling with the older boys in the rest of the school, creating miniature war-zones in the passageways and classrooms. Poor Hazel was extremely constrained and not a little embarrassed by this. Neither of us was experienced in dealing with large boys fighting, and Amine was often simply not around as he was still studying at university in Beirut. A combination of earnest prayer and depriving the offenders of all freedom at lunchtime – two at a time were kept in Hazel's office on the first floor – seemed to crack the problem, part of which was evidently caused by not having enough men around who had any authority. Women apparently did not count in the mindset of some of our boys!

My greatest fear was that someone would be badly hurt and we would be held responsible by angry parents. One of the younger ones had earlier rushed onto the balcony, pushing his hand so forcefully upon the glazed door that it went straight through the glass. Mercifully, there was no one standing on the other side and the boy himself was not cut at all. I should think every child in the department was gathering round to see what had happened!

My patience and lack of experience were being fully stretched during that first week of the new term. Just before dinner one day, I went back into the kindergarten classroom to find that one of the Arabic teachers, without mentioning it to me at all, had completely reorganised the room. Whatever the children were doing whilst she was furniture-moving, I just could not imagine! It seemed that the nearer I reached to gaining an understanding of the people and their volatile ways and the more I threw myself in dependence upon the Lord and His Word, the more I experienced the enemy's counterattack. *"Your enemy the devil prowls around like a roaring lion looking for someone to devour. Resist him, standing firm in your faith..."*[5]

The attacks ranged over a number of issues, not the least of which were the appalling weather conditions that seemed to aggravate the discipline problems. "It has literally rained and slushed and sleeted non-stop from Sunday evening to Friday morning. The mountains behind and beyond are thick with snow. When it rains, it simply pours in Lebanon!" I wrote to my parents. Margaret's bedroom was in a corner of the building and the plaster on the walls was completely saturated. No wonder she had such chronic laryngitis and hardly any voice. The letter continued, "Imagine us in the evenings, with the strength of the elements literally rocking our building, huddled round an open Buta-gas stove, marking books and playing Scrabble! As I look back over the week, I truly can give praise for the immediate help and guidance in so many situations." I was learning

[5] 1 Peter 5:8,9

how praising the Lord and expressing confidence in Him was such an effective way of resisting the enemy and all that is negative and discouraging. *"I remain confident of this: I will see the goodness of the LORD in the land of the living."*[6]

It was certainly not all disaster, though these and other incidents did raise serious questions in my mind. How could I continue running the department with the discipline of the older boys, especially at playtime, proving so difficult? What about the parents whose attitude I found so wearing at times? Considering how vulnerable these young children were, could I cope with what, to me, were false accusations and unrealistic aspirations for their little ones? Life was difficult, and I felt woefully inadequate, but the Lord sent two people into my life at that time who raised my spirits enormously. The first was a long-standing friend of Hazel's from the Lebanon Evangelical Mission.

Pauline had worked for many years in rural mountain villages in both Syria and Lebanon. She had asked me to bring two pairs of K-Skips[7] from England. I was wondering how to reach her, when the bad weather conditions provided the solution. Pauline had been unable to return to Marjeyoun in the south of the country because the roads were blocked by snow and so had called in to see us at Kafarshima. The shoes fitted perfectly and she was delighted. Furthermore, we were able to have a real heart-to-heart discussion, and she shared that even after all these years of missionary service, she still found the readjustment difficult when she returned after a spell away.

The second was an English lady who had been appointed to take over in the pre-school from the German girl who, not surprisingly, had left at Christmas. Her name was Joy, and I was most certainly thankful to have her in the department. Just as Mona had been sent to us so wonderfully, so here was yet further provision. I knew Joy from the Alliance Church and had spoken with her a few times after the morning service at the bring-and-share lunches. She was married to Sami, a Lebanese from the village of Rumeineh near Sidon. They had two children, the youngest of whom was in the kindergarten. Joy had never worked in a school before but had experience of little ones in church, not to mention her own family. She was

---

6 Psalm 27:13
7 K-Skips shoes were made in Kendal, near Lancaster, until 2003. They were generally made from brown suede leather, wide-fit ladies' comfortable lace-up shoes.

a mature Christian lady who I knew would be the mother figure that the two- and three-year-olds needed. In addition, she understood and empathised with my inner struggles concerning standards of behaviour and discipline. She and Gladys, her Arabic-speaking assistant, were soon co-operating well, and I knew they could be relied upon.

Joy and Sami opened their home in Beirut to me as a Christian friend as well as a colleague, and I always felt at home there. "Come right in," Joy would say as she opened the door of their sixth-floor apartment in the Ashrafieh district, "and put your feet up. I'll make you a cup of tea." Such homeliness was refreshment to my soul. I warmed to the ring of familiarity in Joy's northern accent. What a precious gift of the Lord to provide me with a Christian friend and colleague just at this difficult time of cultural adjustment, who was almost my own kith and kin. Joy was born and bred in Blackpool and had met husband Sami whilst working at the Norbreck Hydro, now known as the Norbreck Castle Hotel. He was globetrotting at that time, working as a chef in different hotels throughout Europe. They had married in the UK and eventually returned to his home in Lebanon, where he took up the post of Head Chef at the prestigious Phoenicia Hotel in Ras Beirut.

Joy struggled to adjust to her new life in Lebanon, and eventually found her way to the American pastor and his wife at the Alliance Church. It was not long before she came to saving faith in Christ.[8] She and the pastor's wife began praying earnestly for Sami. He had quite a struggle to come to terms with his wife's newfound faith. He saw himself as a Christian already and knew that there were many grey areas in his life that would need to be renounced. Joy's prayers were answered though, and he too came to repentance and faith in Christ. At the time Joy came to Eastwood, Sami was in training for Christian ministry.

One-day holidays were a great source of encouragement too and a real opportunity to gather strength for the days to follow. There were quite a variety of causes to celebrate, including both Muslim and Christian holidays and also such events as Martyrs Day and Independence Day. Margaret and I figured that there was probably a public holiday during term-time on average every fourth week. We always seemed to be more than ready for a day off!

It was on the morning of the Muslim New Year holiday in the third week of term that I made my way up the winding path behind the school

---

[8] Read more in *Edge of Conflict* by Harry and Miriam Taylor, p.117ff.

building to the little hair salon in the village. We still had no regular supply of hot water! It was heavenly to feel the warm water soaking through my greasy hair right through to the scalp. The temperature of the water was somewhat erratic as it gurgled through a narrow pipe that seemed to be attached to a small water heater that reminded me of my grandmother's gas-fired Ascot! The man and his sister who ran the salon were both deaf but were able to communicate with each other in their own way. I took my own shampoo and paid two Lebanese lira (thirty-five pence) for the privilege of a shampoo and set! I loved luxuriating under the warmth of the hair dryer and thoroughly relaxed in the midst of village life. I especially enjoyed watching and admiring the women as they busied themselves with the most intricate of cross-stitch embroidery work or fine cotton crochet. I spoke only a very few words of Arabic, but they could read my smiles.

That afternoon, we had a complete break from the school and spent the time with other friends from the IVF Students' Centre in Beirut. The sun shone for the whole day, and we set off for an invigorating walk along the front by the Mediterranean. There were snow-capped mountains towering in the distance behind high-storey blocks: embassies, offices and cafés. It was still cold and fresh, but by no means so wet and damp as it had previously been.

There were yet further encouragements in terms of the children's progress. One of the girls in Junior 1, who was really gaining confidence in spoken English, was inspired to write on her own, rather than copying a sentence from the blackboard. Even though her tenses were confused, it was such a thrill to commend her in class and witness the shy smile on her face. The kindergarten children too were increasing in their understanding. I was so glad when a very shy boy, Eli, stood listening intently to what I asked and then quietly translated into Arabic for the boy standing next to him. He had clearly understood, but was not yet confident enough to speak in English for himself. I knew so little myself at that time about the development of second language skills, but I was certainly gaining in practical experience.

The joy of language-learning was being reciprocated! Mona, who had to wait in school for her brother to call on his way home from Beirut to pick her up, offered about fifteen minutes a day after school to teach me some colloquial spoken Arabic. To this day, I still refer from time to time to the simple phrase book that she found in the Librairie du Liban for my use.

The children thought it was marvellous when I tried out my odd words and phrases, though one or two of the really lively ones in the kindergarten laughed hilariously when I struggled with the unfamiliar sounds. I was envious of their ability to pronounce the gutturals and rolled 'r's so beautifully. I was envious, too, of Margaret and Kirstene, whose colloquial Arabic was more advanced than mine, both having lived and worked in Beirut previously. They were learning to write the classical Arabic script!

It was not only Mona who was encouraging me in my efforts to communicate in Arabic. One day, I was waiting at the foot of the school drive for a *servis* car to take me into downtown Beirut. It was not long before I was joined by one or two others, one of whom was Hilda, our very able mathematics and music teacher. We sat together in the back seat and I spent the whole journey with Hilda, learning how to count in Arabic! I cannot imagine what the other passengers were thinking, but everyone took it in good part. Hilda was excellent at both mathematics and music, not to mention English. I have not forgotten my lesson to this day: *sifr, wahed, tnayn, tlateh, arba'a, khamseh...*[9] and all the way to twenty. She even showed me how to write the numbers in Arabic on the back of a slip of paper. If only I had the aptitude for language learning that the Lebanese have!

In Assembly times, the teachers were taking their turns to follow up the Christmas story by telling the early part of Jesus' life, spreading the story over four mornings, Monday to Thursday, each week. By the middle of March, we had moved Assembly from the beginning of the day to a mid morning slot just before playtime. Later on, we finally decided to let the children enjoy playtime a little earlier and then settle down for worship and story together just after 10 am. On Fridays, Joy and Gladys brought their 'tinies' from the pre-school into the kindergarten room to share Assembly with us. Sometimes we would act a short play for our 'audience', telling the story that we had enjoyed during the week. On other occasions, I would share a Biblical story with one clear teaching point, such as Dorcas being kind, making clothes for poor children and their mothers, or King David being kind to Mephibosheth ('Mephi', for short) with his crippled legs. As always, we used puppets and flannelgraph pictures to bring the story to life, and one of the bilingual staff would translate phrase by phrase into Arabic. Just occasionally, we would all cram into the Junior 1 room

[9] zero, one, two, three, four, five

that was easier to black out and show a filmstrip of the story. This was viewed as a very special treat and they loved it.

Celebrating birthdays at Assembly was great fun too. After the story and prayer, we would sing to the birthday girl or boy, "Maha, Maha, how old are you today? How old are you today?" And Maha, for example, would answer, "I'm four years old," sometimes in a very quiet, shy voice! The rest of the children would respond by chanting the number of years together: "One, two, three, four!" We would then break into an enthusiastic rendering of *Happy birthday to you* in both Arabic and English. I especially recall Maha's birthday because her parents offered to celebrate in school with great style. They arranged for the Fanta Orange and 7UP bears to come dressed up, singing and dancing for all the children in the class. Unfortunately, the whole experience was somewhat overwhelming for Maha and she burst into tears! Even so, she enjoyed the cake, and so did the rest of the class and their teachers! We warmly encouraged parents to bring cakes and make birthdays special in school, though we did sometimes differ over how many candles there should be on the cake: *four* for the number of years already achieved or *five* to include the year just starting! Birth dates, in any case, were not always correct to the day, but we did our best to keep adequate registers.

On the final day of January, I wrote home to my parents, "I can hardly believe that I've been back for nearly a month. It is truly wonderful the way, despite everything, the Lord is providing just the strength to continue day by day and teaching us that 'Just a closer walk with Him'[10] is the keynote to tackling every situation." I was looking forward to a conference organised by the Navigators, an American Christian group who emphasised the importance of discipling new believers in Biblical truth, working principally on the university and hospital campuses. This was to be their winter conference – a spiritual retreat to be held in the nearby Mirador Hotel in mid February.

The weather was definitely improving, and I appreciated the fresher, sunnier, dryer atmosphere. One Saturday, Hazel took us for a splendid drive into the mountains as far as Beit Meri, where we explored Roman ruins, an old Greek Catholic church and a Maronite monastery, and marvelled at the most wonderful, almost alpine, views across the whole

---

[10] *Just a closer walk with Thee* is a traditional gospel song based upon words from 2 Corinthians 5:7 – *"We live by faith, not by sight."* – and James 4:8a – *"Come near to God and He will come near to you."* Author unknown.

range of the Lebanese mountains sweeping down to the narrow coastal plain and the sea. We could see for miles along the coast north and south of Beirut, with village after village in the mountains still blocked by the snow that covered the whole range. The air was truly breathtaking!

The Navigators' Conference proved to be a real tonic for me. Even though the hotel was only two-and-a-half miles from the school, it was so good to get right away into a different environment, and to be really challenged spiritually. "How it still amazes me that the Lord had to bring me all the way out here in order to begin to teach me more of what truly relying upon Him for everything really means!" was my simply worded comment, in my letter home, on trusting the Lord totally in a cross-cultural context.

A week later, I shared with my parents how I had known a renewed desire to "get to grips with God's Word and to spend time with Him first thing in the mornings and just expect Him to make changes in my life, especially in my basic *attitudes* to those with whom I live and work." The Navigators do place especial emphasis upon daily personal Bible study and committing God's Word to memory. I determined to improve in this matter. My father, bless him, who had been helped by having small memory verse cards from the Navigators when he first started to witness for the Lord, agreed to join in and encourage me. "How are you getting on with learning verses, Dad?" I wrote. "I am trying to collect verses with the dominant theme of God's steadfast love. Here goes, and I promise I'm not looking(!). Psalm 143:8: *'Let me hear in the morning of thy steadfast love, for in thee I put my trust. Teach me the way I should go, for to thee I lift up my soul.'*[11] Okay? It's a super verse to remember in preparing one's heart to meet daily with the Lord."

That earlier comment to my parents about my basic attitude to colleagues, both in the flat and in the school, was a matter about which I needed to be vigilant. Likewise was my renewed expectancy that the Lord would refine my attitudes. This was a matter that would demand faith and willingness. I was reading from the last few chapters of Romans in my daily time with the Lord, searching and expecting, and there it was: chapter 14 and verse 19: *"Let us then pursue what makes for peace and for mutual upbuilding."* I immediately underlined it in my RSV Bible as a way of acknowledging my willingness to obey. No matter how frustrated I might feel about some of the seemingly immature behaviour of one or two

[11] RSV

of the Lebanese staff, I had to recognise that here were fellow Christians, all equal in God's sight. It was my awesome task to help in the upbuilding of *their* Christian lives, and this in turn would be used by God to bring peace and harmony to us all. I recorded my prayer that morning in my journal: "Lord, please change my attitude toward Nawal. I am looking for You to change my attitudes. Give me wisdom to deal with individual situations that crop up, but above all, please give me wisdom to make for peace and mutual upbuilding."

I had also requested prayer from my parents for day-to-day stamina and wisdom in dealing not only with my own class when I was teaching them, but also when the Lebanese teachers took them for Arabic. Both were new to teaching; one was experiencing significant problems with discipline and the other was untrained and needed a great deal of support in the teaching method. Both were genuine Christian believers; one was of Muslim heritage. That evening, I recorded in my journal: "Thank you, Lord, for immediate answers to prayer this very day." Nawal had come to apologise for losing her temper, and the difficult child was absent from school!

The following morning, I read from the first few verses of Romans 15, and again there was the stress upon *attitudes*. I could not run away from it! This time, the focus was less upon myself and more upon Christ. "Okay, Lord," I wrote, "my attitude has to change to those with whom I work closely, and already I can see Your hand in my relationships in the flat and with the teachers in the school. In the pursuing of mutual peace and harmony, please give me more of the *attitude of Christ*." It took a little while for me to start appreciating what I was actually praying for! Romans 15:3 puts it quite succinctly: *"For Christ did not please himself..."*[12] He lived and died for others rather than for Himself. My subsequent readings in Philippians were to challenge me further on this matter. My journal again: "In everything I do, I must not complain or grumble or argue. These things are symptoms of stubbornness. O Lord, I see it in the children I teach and I see it in myself. Keep changing me, Father; keep working on my attitudes; help me to know more of the servant heart of Christ."

Romans 15:5 also made it clear to me that having the attitude of Christ made for harmonious living across the cultures. *"May the God of steadfastness and encouragement grant you to live in such harmony with one another, in accord with Christ Jesus."* I was reminded how different notes in

[12] RSV

music can blend together in such a way as to form a harmonious sound. What did living in such harmony involve? Surely it was acceptance and love of each other as fellow Christians, *"that together you may with one voice glorify the God and Father of our Lord Jesus Christ"*[13], all of which was heavily underlined in my RSV Bible and, by the working of the Holy Spirit, in my heart.

[13] Romans 15:6

CHAPTER TEN

Visiting

When I first arrived in Lebanon, I was informed, amongst other things, that the people had two important national pastimes: one was bird-shooting and the other visiting. Shooting birds held no interest for me whatsoever, and I was troubled at the thought, as it seemed such a dangerous pastime. One of the teachers at the Lebanese Evangelical School for the Blind, whom we met at the Alliance Church, had apparently been blinded as a young teenager by a mishap with a gun when out shooting birds.

Visiting, on the other hand, offered a culturally acceptable opportunity to get beyond the classroom and into the children's homes. There, I was to discover, one could listen and speak on a deeper level about the emotional and spiritual needs of many of the families who were trusting us with their children at the school. "I have been to visit a few of the parents of my children this week, and it really is rewarding. You honour people by visiting, and they always seem to make you welcome. No need to wait to be invited; they are waiting for our visit!" I wrote home at the end of January.

Hazel was a great inspiration and seasoned organiser of 'visits'. After all, she had lived and worked in the country since 1939! It was not unusual for her to arrange up to three after-school visits, starting as soon as school finished at three o'clock. I tried not to appear ungrateful as the best of the *gateaux* or Lebanese sweetmeats that the hostess could offer were brought out, along with cold drinks or tea, to be followed by aromatic Turkish coffee, for the third time that afternoon! Hazel devised an excellent way of explaining my reticence to partake yet again: "Miss Radcliffe has an appetite *mittel asfour*[1]," she would say, by way of excuse, whilst she herself tucked into her third piece of cake for that day.

Visiting was most certainly worthwhile. There was no doubt that after a trip to their homes by one or two of their teachers, the behaviour of some of the most difficult children in school was transformed. It was as if they could accept the authority and norms of school behaviour now that their teachers had been received in their own homes. But the whole question of my use of the time outside of teaching hours was becoming to me a matter of some concern, surrounded as I was by a small close-knit community in the school building. As far as my personality was concerned, my natural inclination was always to act and reflect, expend energy and then withdraw for a while. I was finding it exceedingly difficult to detach from others, living literally on top of the classrooms and within walking distance of many of the homes of the children. How could I escape? The challenge was to work out a way of revitalising myself, conditioned as I was by my upbringing and the underlying beliefs, assumptions and values underpinning it.

I somehow needed to spend time alone, or at least with people who understood my northern upbringing. I had trained myself to be self-reliant and individually responsible for my own decisions. I had been taught from childhood always to back up my decisions with reasoned explanations, and to have a heart open to God's guidance and possible, if not probable, redirection of my own plans! It was impressed upon me that I should always attempt something myself before bothering others, always work and persevere until the matter was conquered, and always be prepared. The day before I was allowed to borrow my mother's 1958 Austin A35, having only recently passed my driving test, my father gave me three rules to be obeyed: never to drive more than a hundred miles without taking a break from behind the wheel; never to pick up a hitchhiker; and to demonstrate to him that I could change a tyre. Furthermore, he stood over me, watching me jack up the car, unscrewing every nut and duly changing the tyre to prove it! Yes, I had learnt how to be resourceful. "If at first you don't succeed," my grandmother would say, "try, try and try again." Having applied this to my own learning for life, I had sought to inculcate similar values in those whom I taught.

In spite of my call and strong desire to live and work with Arabic-speaking peoples, my worldview was, at this time, distinctively Western

---

[1]   like a bird

as I had little to no experience of anything other. I was simply on the verge of exploring the Middle Eastern way of looking at life, as I found it in Lebanon, and seeking to find a balanced way of compromise. I still had much to learn about knowing and experiencing God's grace in daily living as I continued the process of cultural adjustment.

Nawal with Junior 1, May 1974.

One afternoon in early February, when the days were becoming sunnier, we went to visit the home in Kafarshima of one of the newly qualified teachers. I had been concerned that I was not able to spend enough time with Nawal, and I felt that our relationship was not as open as I should have liked. It was good to meet with her mother, a widow, and the rest of the family of six children. I think Nawal was the eldest, and they were all so proud that she had qualified as a teacher and found a job in this new Christian school in the village. What a deal she had to live up to! No wonder she found her first job in a new school with a head of department who spoke only English somewhat stressful. Later I wrote home, "I just continue to pray that the Lord will give wisdom and understanding in my relationship with Nawal, that she may be guided to a greater consistency in her attitude to the children." I am sure this visit gave me insights and greater compassion for this teacher in her inexperience and indeed in mine.

I too needed to let God show me more of His purposes for the school as they unfolded and as I wrestled with making relationships across the cultures and exerted loving authority within such a close-knit community. My deepest desire was that we should build relationships with each other as a staff team that would be beneficial to the children in our care and not damaging.

It was not only Hazel who loved visiting homes as an expression of our concern to make an impact for good in the village, whatever the religious background of the children. To me, as a Westerner, this seemed intrusive, and I had much to learn: how to honour the family as they offer you their

Ibrahim with Transition in the playground, summer 1975.

hospitality and you seek to enter into their world and listen to their concerns. Joy Jones, the Australian missionary who had retired to Kafarshima and was working with the local church, was still active in the village visiting around the homes when the school opened in September 1973. In her gentle, prayerful way, she continued reaching out, listening and sharing the good news of the love of God through Jesus Christ.

There was one particular family whom Joy had nurtured in this way, who brought their two children to the school. Both the children were in need of special attention in order to learn effectively, and I could sense that this would be a test of the effectiveness of the child-centred approach we were keen to introduce. Zubeida, a lively five-year-old, was growing up fast, but her parents wished to keep her with younger children. Ibrahim, a fair-headed four-year-old and really quite babyish in his behaviour, was struggling with his speech and language. In addition, the social aspect of school life was clearly a challenge for him and he would not be parted from his sister.

Checking on Ibrahim in class became a regular task, especially if he started screaming and kicking in fear, and I longed for a breakthrough for this little boy. After prayer with Joy, we went to visit the family in their home high up in the village. The children were clearly loved, accepted and secure in their home environment, and we were received as honoured guests. My heart melted, and I knew that in time our prayerful persistence would be rewarded and that these children would make a real contribution to society. How I wish I could have known then that one day, about a year later, Ibrahim would shock us all by reading right through the first Ladybird book, out loud and in a clear voice, standing by my desk. How he purred with his sense of achievement! His educational and social needs were many and various, but our persistence and the prayers of many had been answered – he now knew he had achieved.

A further opportunity to make a visit arose when a child had been taken into hospital. "One of my class has been in hospital this week and so the kindergarten have made flowers and pictures for him, and this gave me the opportunity to go with Hazel to the Greek Orthodox Hospital one day after school," I wrote to my parents. "[There were] two children in the room plus two mothers, two grandmothers and two or three other women sitting around knitting. The one mother had been with her son, aged five, night and day, just sitting in a chair by his bed for three or four days."

Sometimes visits were more intentional in terms of faith-sharing and learning together from God's Word. One of the children who came to us in the kindergarten was from a cross-cultural family. Mac's mother came originally from South Africa and spoke Afrikaans, Arabic and English, and his father was Arabic-speaking Lebanese. Suzette was delighted with the school and especially so because we held an act of Christian worship every day. I asked my parents to pray for Suzette and her family. "She is South African, married to a Lebanese, and has been here since she married some eight or nine years ago, and has learnt to speak Arabic. She knows a lot about the Lord but has no real assurance, and it's a real joy to study with her."

Visiting this family was a joy, because after tea and cakes she would bring her Afrikaans Bible and Navigator Bible Studies and we would study God's Word together. What a privilege! Suzette was keen to learn, to grow in her knowledge of Biblical truth and to follow Jesus as Saviour and Lord: *"Whoever wants to be my disciple must deny themselves and take up their cross daily and follow me."*[2] If four-year-old Mac appeared in the sitting room, she would speak to him in Arabic, and then turn to me and speak in English about how the Lord was revealing Himself to her through her Bible in Afrikaans. This was possibly the first time I had been exposed to praying one-to-one with someone whose mother tongue differed from mine… and it was a blessing.

As far as the struggle to find time to withdraw and re-energise myself was concerned, I was aware that there would always be a way of escape. *"And God is faithful; he will not let you be tempted beyond what you can bear. But when you are tempted, he will also provide a way out so that you can endure it."*[3]

When in doubt, trust God – and visit!

---

[2] Luke 9:23
[3] 1 Corinthians 10:13

CHAPTER ELEVEN

Hospital, Holidays and Home Again!

T
he spring term was a long one – fourteen weeks in total – and by mid March we were looking forward to Mother's Day and the Easter holidays. The children in kindergarten were making baskets as little gifts for their mothers and decorating them with sticky shapes. The juniors loved making their own cards using flowery wallpaper and their own drawings and an illustrated poem, which they wrote as a group:

> *I want to thank you, mother (or mummy)*
> *For everything you do.*
> *You give me food to eat each day,*
> *You give me clothes to wear at play.*
> *I thank you for your love.*

As always, help from Gladys who worked in the pre-school in the mornings was invaluable, especially with the kindergarten. The highlight of the Mothers' Day preparations was a short trip in one of the school buses a little way into the mountains to pick spring flowers. The freshness of the spring temperatures was invigorating, and the children were thrilled to be out in the fields picking wild cyclamen, red anemones and field poppies to go in their baskets. Sadly, in hot, sticky hands and with much enthusiasm, the flowers wilted and not all made it into the baskets, but it was a great trip out, especially for Beirut children. We even made a large collage picture the next day to commemorate the occasion, with all their little faces peering out of the bus windows!

By this stage in the term and with the warmer weather, I was concerned that we should provide more play equipment in the playground. Old tyres from Amine's father's garage were good for rolling along the ground and climbing through, and there were a couple of swings and two see-saws, all of which were a huge safety risk but did provide necessary physical activity for children who only had balconies for play. Climbing the orange trees surrounding the playground was definitely taboo,

Playing with old tyres, November 1974.

so imagine my thrill when I heard the news that my church in Marple, All Saints, who had already gifted me with a tape recorder, had allocated a further gift of thirty pounds for the school. So what about some sort of metal climbing frame in the playground for the children?

By the end of March, a deal had been struck regarding the price of steel tubing to construct the frame. I wrote to my parents, "The climbing frame is definitely on the move now – the steel has been ordered and I've given a sketch of how I'd like it to be constructed. I've designed it to include a couple of rope ladders, a single rope with knots and a slide down one side. From the other side extends a horizontal ladder for monkey upside-down-type climbing with a vertical support. I just hope it won't be too long before it actually materialises."

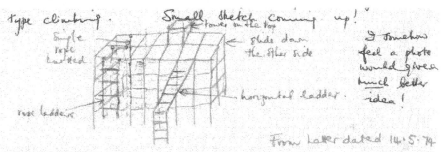

By mid April, I could write, "Work is going ahead on the steel climbing frame. I'll let you know as soon as it's ready and try to get some photos of the children playing on it." Four weeks later, Amine announced the frame was ready and would soon be delivered and erected in the playground – what a joy! Finally, at the end of May, "The climbing frame arrived last Friday and was duly set in concrete. On Monday morning, I was there at 7.15 am as the first busload of children arrived, just to see their faces and

All Saints climbing frame.
Top: 1974. Bottom: 1979.

watch them exploring its possibilities. My little boy with special needs – Ibrahim, five years old, who struggles to manipulate a pencil – was right on the top in seconds and scrambling up and down with great confidence! It really is a success and they just love it. You can imagine the first day when about fifty children all tried to climb up at the same time!" There was just one salutary note from the friends at All Saints: "May the Lord keep safe those who use it!"

We never ceased to be grateful for the prayerful support of friends back in England, and were increasingly conscious of the Lord's overall planning, protection and provision for us in the new school. Attacks on our work came in various guises and tested our willingness to depend on Him at all times. Towards the end of March, not only did we hear the somewhat unsettling news of the military flare-up on the Golan Heights and Mount Hermon, but the extreme left-wing element in the Students' Union of the American University went on strike and started stirring up a violent protest against the authorities. We never knew when there would be demonstrations, and it was most unsettling for the children going home in the school buses at such differing times each day. In Kafarshima itself, we were unaffected; it was not until Margaret, Kirstene and I started going into Beirut after school for the twice-weekly practices for the American University Choir's Easter Musicale in the chapel that we encountered road blockages and a strong military presence. I had never sung Brahms' *Requiem* before, and was thrilled with the opportunity in such an auspicious setting – this was a far cry from singing with the children in school, and the top 'A's were somewhat challenging! But the performance was not to be. The student strikes escalated, classes were suspended and the Musicale cancelled. However, another adventure was in store for me.

It was Palm Sunday, the very day we would have been singing in the university chapel, and I found myself in hospital. In the bed next to me was Margaret, who had contracted infective hepatitis at the beginning of March. The previous Friday after school, feeling fine, I had made my way up the straggling pathway behind the building and onto the path that led to the hairdresser's and a little grocery shop, intending to buy fruit and eggs. Whilst there, my head started to weigh heavily, and I was thankful to get back safely, take a couple of painkillers and sleep. The letter to my parents records what happened next. "At about 10.30 pm, I woke with an absolutely thumping head – I don't think I've ever had a headache like it – almost as if someone were hitting me with a pick-axe in all directions in every corner of my head (do heads have corners?), yet I felt no pain anywhere else in my body." A couple more painkillers brought relief, but only until 6 am the next morning, when the thumping resumed. More painkillers along with toast and marmalade saw me through the morning, and thankfully it was Saturday with no school, but by midafternoon my temperature had soared, the headache had returned and vomiting had begun.

By Sunday morning, Palm Sunday, we were on our way to the Christian Medical Centre (CMC) in Ashrafieh, the Armenian quarter of Beirut. I shall never forget the journey as we drove past Palm Sunday parades – children wearing their best clothes walking through the streets to their church, carrying giant-sized candles elaborately supported on sticks festooned with lilies and palm branches. As they reached the church, the candles were lit to celebrate the triumphal entry of Christ into Jerusalem. Ours was the last vehicle to be allowed through before all traffic was blocked because of the parades! On reflection, this experience was a reminder to me of my total dependence on God and that my times are in His hand. *"The LORD is God, and he has made his light shine upon us. With boughs in hand, join in the festal procession up to the horns of the altar."*[1]

The nursing at CMC was exemplary in every respect. Anti-vomiting injections were administered along with all the routine checks and a diet of fluids until the headache subsided and I began to feel my normal self. This kept me out of school for the remaining four days of the term. Some of the nurses were linked with the Navigators, whose conference I had

[1]   Psalm 118:27

View of Amman from the OM
Girls' Home.

appreciated so much earlier in the year, as indeed were the couple with whom I was able to stay as I convalesced and resumed a normal diet. Hazel and Kirstene could not have been kinder or more reassuring, and I was full of gratitude.

The diagnosis? On my medical insurance form, the doctor simply stated I had a viral infection that had necessitated hospital treatment. Maybe such a viral infection is not quite so simple as it sounds. Very soon after my diagnosis, we heard that a former teacher in Beirut, who was known to both Hazel and Margaret, had suffered a very sad loss. Her little four-year-old daughter had died quite suddenly from a massive viral infection that went inexplicably to the brain. This was a sobering thought for me, as I remembered this family in their grief and doubled my sense of awe and gratitude at my own recovery.

"...I know that through your prayers and God's provision of the Spirit of Jesus Christ what has happened to me will turn out for my deliverance."[2] Even the children at school, led by one of the Lebanese teachers, had prayed for me when I was in hospital and then thanked Jesus when I was discharged just before Easter and the school holidays.

For a little while, Margaret, Kirstene and I had been discussing the possibility of a trip to Amman, Jordan, passing through Damascus. The Easter break would be ideal. Margaret was unable to come, but another friend, Pam, who worked with the Lebanon InterVarsity Fellowship (LIVF), was able to join Kirstene and me in the *servis* car. To be able to stay in the Operation Mobilisation (OM) Girls' House in Amman was perfect, and we were glad of a warm welcome on arrival. After a lengthy ride through Syria and a fairly gruelling search procedure at the Jordanian border, we were eventually ushered through to the Foreign Visitors' Office for visa checks and body searches. The *servis* driver was extremely helpful, heaving our luggage out of the boot and keeping a watchful eye over us as the search progressed. How I prayed that all would be well, especially when I recalled that my *Scripture Union Daily Notes* were tucked in my

[2] Philippians 1:19

Bible and open at the page for that day. Hopefully, they would not notice the photo of the Dome of the Rock in Jerusalem on the front cover. Sleeping bags were prodded and cases rooted through. "He was particularly interested in my Bible," I wrote to my parents, "which he went through most diligently, only upside-down! He also had a good look at my letter-writing equipment, tipping out all the letters in the process!"

We eventually reached Amman early in the evening, three of us huddled together on the back seat of an American Coronet car, passing a large United Nations Relief and Works Agency (UNRWA) camp. Some of these camps had been set up after the 1948 Palestine War and others following the six-day war of 1967 for Palestinians fleeing from the West Bank. We took a taxi to Jebel Amman, one of the seven hills, "a city more as I remembered Morocco, with little flat-roofed houses stretching, as it were, one above the other up the hillsides upon which Amman is built," I continued in my letter home. It was a memorable experience to see the sights: Mount Nebo from where Moses viewed the Promised Land; driving down the King's Highway to Petra, rose-red city half as old as time; the desert of Wadi Rum where much of Lawrence of Arabia was filmed. I even dipped my finger in the Dead Sea and took photos of Pam reading a newspaper as she floated. It was also a joy to meet Jordanian believers who live, work and witness in a country far less westernised than Lebanon, sharing their joys and struggles. The ride back to Beirut took seven-and-a-half hours, with several stops at borders for yet more visas and stamps in our passports. Nearly every vehicle we passed on the road up to Damascus was an army truck, bus or Land Rover, and every town and village was crawling with troops. Passing through the Golan Heights and snow-covered Mount Hermon was utterly depressing, as the surrounding low land leading across to the road was covered with tanks, tank traps and army troops at the ready, and there were even tanks on the horizon. We were thankful to be safely back in Lebanon!

It was now clear to me that after the time in hospital and recovery from the viral infection, I needed to reassess my use of time during the school day. Being on the spot from 7.45 in the morning to three in the afternoon, and being unable to escape to the staff room even in the lunch hour, was no longer realistic. Numbers were up again for the summer term, peaking at a total of ninety-five three- to eight-year-olds in the Lower Junior department. Parents would literally appear at any time with their concerns and expect my full attention! I would also need time to deal with the increased administration and to help new teachers settle in. Furthermore, preparations for the next academic year were underway, as new parents were already coming to register their little ones. It was becoming evident that three new classes would be needed – a second pre-school class for three-year-olds, a second kindergarten class for four- and five-year-olds, and a separate class for five- and six-year-olds which we would name 'Transition'.

I had a serious chat with Hazel over a cup of tea before the new term began. Right now we needed adequate help for supervision of the children during the lunch hour, and for the following year I would need a lighter teaching timetable. Hazel listened, and I was reassured that she would take heed of my concerns.

The summer term started well and the children settled quickly. They certainly had not forgotten their English! Rita, aged four-and-a-half, said without thinking one day, "Nesreen is eating her sandwiches on the balcony." Apart from the fact that Rita was telling tales, this was notable as the first whole sentence I had heard from one so young. I wrote to praying friends, "...do pray that Eastwood won't just be known as a successful school in the teaching of English, but that there will be a real lasting work of God's Spirit in the individual lives of many studying and teaching here."

Prayers had already been answered for help in the lunch hour. Bahia, a former pupil of Hazel's when she taught in Beirut, was already teaching Arabic to the kindergarten during the mornings. On hearing of the need, Bahia volunteered to stay for the full day and travel home in the school bus that went into Beirut. This not only gave me a thirty-minute break at midday but also an extra pair of hands in the afternoons. Bahia proved to be a huge asset to the staff team. She was keen to learn how to teach the Arabic sounds using activity-based methods, and constructed lively and attractive sound-picture matching cards similar to my own English teaching materials. The children loved her storytelling and sat rapt at the end of the school day, listening to her stories and singing little songs in Arabic. Bahia had come to faith in Jesus when she was a teenager at school, but her parents had arranged a marriage to a strict Muslim and life was far from easy at home. One day, her husband declared her to be an infidel and filed for divorce, taking their three children away from her. Though she missed them terribly, I think she felt that God had sent her more children than she could count to love and cherish in school, and we were privileged to have her with us.

Life continued through the summer term with various challenges ranging from the vagaries of the weather to political uncertainties regarding relationships with neighbouring countries. In late April, the warm wind blew up, *khamseen* in Arabic, and stayed with us throughout the day. There was much itching and discomfort as the sand blew in the children's eyes and ears, affecting their behaviour, and the temperatures and humidity were rising. Then we heard there had been attacks on Lebanese villages in the south of the country, followed a few days later by the unmistakable sounds of bombing and firing from the air, like a giant thunderstorm. And in the distance, we heard the air-raid warning siren. Apparently thirty-six Phantom jets flew over in pairs, aiming mainly at the Palestinian camps. One plane bombed three houses just behind us in the hills behind Kafarshima. I was visiting a family in the village with Hazel and three Lebanese teachers at the time, and how thankful we were that this had not happened an hour earlier when the children would have been leaving school on the buses.

The next morning, I discussed contingency plans with the teachers as to how we would manage the children if there were any danger in the classrooms which faced the airport. "We are some sixty-five miles from the border," I wrote to my parents reassuringly, "but just as I'd finished the story in Assembly – some ninety children altogether with their teachers – we heard the bombs and shooting again, so I said, 'It's time to sing,' and we sang the loudest song we knew – *I have hands that will clap, clap, clap* – and drowned the noise!" Further, I wrote home, "I now have had a tiny little taste of what affected the lives of thousands of your generation who lived through 1939-45."

Alongside all this was the reassurance that God was providing for us in terms of equipment and staff for the new classes we would need in the following school year. I was reading in 1 Kings 11:38 in my RSV Bible about the time when God spoke to Jeroboam, reassuring him of His presence on condition of obedience to God's commands, and the words just jumped out at me: "*...I will be with you and will build you a sure house...*" I felt convinced that this promise applied to our school; whatever the uncertainties, God was building, equipping and providing for us both now and in the future.

Meanwhile, term was moving to a conclusion. In the last week of May, we had no less than four parents' meetings – two in pre-school held during the morning and two after school to meet the parents of the kindergarten, Junior 1 and Junior 2. So many parents, who only the previous October had been suspicious and lacking in trust, came to see us, so grateful for happy children who were making progress in their education with us. It was a joy to write home, "I was just so thrilled for the sake of the five Lebanese teachers who work with me, because they were obviously encouraged too. More than one parent said to us, 'Tell me what you honestly feel about my son / daughter,' indicating to me that they were really beginning to trust the school and our activity-based teaching methods."

Next came the end of term open day and entertainment. Kindergarten were not performing as they did at Christmas, but Juniors 1 and 2 produced a musical play in Arabic with dancing, which entailed practices and general disruption of normal lessons! Then came the *khamseen* again, with windows and doors crashing in all directions. Not long after the open day, with only three weeks to go to the end of term, I wrote, "It's getting much hotter and stickier now, especially in the evenings when the damp rises over Beirut and the mosquitoes appear in their hundreds." And later, "I'm just getting so used to battling with biting flies, mosquitoes and other crawling insects, large and small. I even managed to squash a cockroach last night!"

Those last three weeks simply flew by! Flights home were booked, via Budapest to Heathrow and Manchester, and there were numerous goodbyes and end-of-term outings. I enjoyed an evening with Mona, my Lebanese teacher who helped with English teaching in the kindergarten. She took me through the souk in downtown Beirut for the purchase of gifts to take home. I was amazed at the way she bartered in Arabic to get the best possible price. I was a mere learner of the art.

We were sad to say farewell to Al and Dawn Fairbanks and their two little girls in whose house we had enjoyed our regular InterVarsity Fellowship Bible Studies. "We've really appreciated their open house and friendliness to us this year," I wrote to my parents. "Yesterday afternoon, I took Julie and Kirsty (aged eighteen months and three-and-a-half years) into the grounds of the American University, which stretch right down to the sea and back up again. It really is beautiful at this time of the year. This is the first time the general public have had the chance to walk through since the student strikes earlier in the year. The girls were so good … it's quite a change for me to be with English-speaking children!"

There were farewells, too, at the Alliance Church in Beirut, including a bring and share meal before the evening service. So many were leaving for the sum-

With Margaret at Jezzine.

mer months. Even the Lebanese would adjust their working hours to an earlier schedule – 7 am to 2 or 2.30 pm – and then drive up into the mountains and stay in rented accommodation for cooler temperatures. Also in Beirut was the home of the British Ambassador, Paul Wright. I found the invitation to celebrate the Queen's official birthday rather unsettling, but was glad to don my long skirt and attend with the other Brits on the staff. "It was all very friendly and easy with cocktails and buffet snacks," I wrote home. "It is a beautiful garden and strange to see so many British faces again! In the middle of the evening, we stood for the National Anthem and toasted the Queen, and this was immediately followed by the Lebanese Anthem and a toast to the President."

It was to the President's summer palace that we took the whole of Juniors 1 and 2 in one of the school buses, the day after school finished for the summer holidays. It was a beautiful drive with cooling temperatures as we drove the twisty road high in the Chouf mountains, south of the school. "Frangieh, the President, only spends fifteen days here, and he happened to be at Beit Eddine that very day – the whole place was full of life. While I was taking a photo of them all in front of a huge fountain, who should walk past but Frangieh himself with a bodyguard of four. Such excitement!" I wrote home. We sang Arabic songs on the bus to the accompaniment of a drum and two tambourines, and even stopped to celebrate a birthday with a lovely cake complete with candles on the way back down to school. A memorable end to the school year, and I was so full of praise.

There was one last trip into South Lebanon before flying home. This was to the town of Sidon to view the Crusader Castle and on up into the mountains to Jezzine. Since 1770, this town has been famed for its craft in making beautiful cutlery and other items such as letter-openers, the bone handles carved into the shape of birds' heads. The handles are made from cows' horns and then polished and decorated with inlaid mosaics of coloured bone and brass. The town itself is in the midst of pine forests, vineyards and orchards, with panoramic views of the surrounding localities scattered in the midst of a fertile plain and protected by the mountains of southern Lebanon. Margaret and I went with our friend Afaf from the InterVarsity Fellowship Bible study group, along with her widowed mother, Mrs Musallam. I marvelled at the beauty and fruitfulness of this country as we passed the fruit stalls on the Sidon Road: strawberries, cherries, apricots and citrus fruits in abundance.

My first eventful year in Lebanon was drawing to its close. "You'll have to let me read through all my letters to remind me of everything that has happened this year, and what a year!" I wrote home. "I just marvel at all the Lord has taught and is teaching me during this time abroad, and especially the need to walk really closely with Him day by day."

CHAPTER TWELVE

A Growing Challenge

It was the beginning of the autumn term, 1974, and I was glad to be back at Eastwood and settling in to the challenges of a new school year. It had been a busy summer back in the UK, sharing with friends and family about our first eventful year, and knowing God's call to continue in the Lower Junior department, offering a bilingual activity-based education that would enable every child in our care to flourish and grow mentally, physically and in their love of Jesus.

July had been particularly busy taking meetings. My Girl Crusader class in West Kirby was welcoming, especially as I showed slides of Lebanon and of the school and the children in my care. Quite a large group of all ages stayed behind after the evening service at All Saints, Marple, including my parents, and I was glad to show slides and tell them how much their practical gifts, the portable cassette tape recorder and the climbing frame, had been appreciated and enjoyed. Even more important was their prayer support, ably led by my former Sunday school teacher, Edith Bowyer, who was now the church secretary. She would not only type up my newsletters, duplicate and distribute them, but from time to time would send round small clips from my letters urging friends to pray. *"I will continue to rejoice, for I know that through your prayers and God's provision of the Spirit of Jesus Christ what has happened to me will turn out for my deliverance."*[1]

Particularly memorable was a talk I gave to my grandmother's Ladies' Class at her church in Ashton-under-Lyne. Granny Radcliffe, now in her mid eighties, had been a huge inspiration to me for many years. She had

---

[1] Philippians 1:18,19

Nawal with kindergarten,
including the two Marwans,
May 1974.

been a pupil teacher in Ashton before marriage to my grandfather and had always encouraged me in my desire to teach and to follow God's call on my life. Granny had presided for many years over this class, and I remembered going through the side door of the church to a large downstairs room on Wednesday afternoons in the school holidays and sitting at one of the long trestle tables covered in starched white cloths with little vases of flowers on each one. I would sit expectantly, feeling enormously privileged in the honoured place at Granny's left-hand side, waiting for the moment when she would ring her little bell. There would have been a talk upstairs in the church, and now the tea would follow: little sandwiches on each plate made from white bread, with the crusts cut off and filled with egg mayonnaise or meat paste. The corners would be gently curling at the edges as Granny made her speech. I especially liked the tiny fairy cakes, beautifully decorated.

Now, Granny was an honoured guest at the Ladies' Class, and I too felt honoured to be asked to speak about my first year's teaching in Lebanon. "There are so many words I could use to describe this year – frustrating yet joyful, frightening yet reassuring, demanding patience and wisdom beyond my capacity and teaching me so much that in myself I can do nothing. Jesus said, *'I am the vine; you are the branches. If you remain in me and I in you, you will bear much fruit; apart from me you can do nothing.'*[2]" And I recounted to the ladies how God had called me to teach in Lebanon just as He called Joshua to lead his people into the Promised Land after the death of Moses. With these dear ladies, I was able to speak a little about the country of Lebanon and its peoples, the joys and struggles of our first year, and my feeling of utter dependence upon the Lord and on the faithful prayer of Christian friends and family. Time after time, I had been faced with cultural adjustments that were entirely beyond my ken as well as opposition from some parents who, while in favour of our standard of education, disagreed with the daily Christian act of worship. I shared with

[2] John 15:5

124

the ladies about two little boys in my department of three- to eight-year-olds, both aged six and both named Marwan. The Lebanese father of the one had come to see me the day before I flew back to England, demanding to know why I taught his son that God sends the rain, without giving a scientific explanation. I asked them to pray that God would watch over this little lad as he grew up in such a home, especially as I knew his Canadian mother was sensitive to God's love expressed through Jesus. The other Marwan was living with a diagnosis of leukaemia and wore a simple black habit to school. It seems his grandmother had had a dream in which she was instructed by God that the boy must be put under a vow for the rest of his life. He was to wear the black habit until he grew out of it and, after that, a brown gown similar to a monk's habit. He too needed our prayers. I was touched by the response of Granny's Ladies' Class as they looked at the photos and we prayed together.

The journey back to Lebanon in September once again featured the adventures of the green suitcase and a last minute 'rescue' for its owner! "Not Sydney this time, merely Budapest," I wrote to my parents. The journey had started well, as I had decided to take up my sister's offer of borrowing her guitar to accompany the children both for Assembly and the numerous nursery rhymes and ditties we sang together. This was much easier for me than piano-playing and trying to watch the children at the same time! I had packed the guitar case with books and papers down the side and was greeted with, "What's this? A trumpet?" as I heaved it onto the baggage search at Heathrow, and we all had a good laugh.

On arrival in Budapest, I was told I needed a visa for Hungary in order to pick up my green case. Equally, I was adamant that as I was in transit to Beirut, this would not be necessary. On arrival in the transit lounge and meeting up with Margaret and Lebanese friends, the dispute continued, until eventually it was decided that neither I nor an English girl married to a Lebanese could travel on this flight for which we had tickets. Margaret kindly took the guitar case, and Elizabeth and I made frantic enquiries in a multitude of languages as to whether there was a quicker way to get to Beirut other than waiting days for the next flight – and I had no idea of the whereabouts of my green case.

We eventually decided to fly to Athens that evening on our Beirut tickets, doss down at Athens airport and then fly to Beirut from there. "I walked out to wave to Margaret as the plane had not yet taken off, walked back praising the Lord that we would get there only one day later, when suddenly my other stranded friend yelled across the transit lounge, 'We're on the flight; we can go!'" There was such drama as Elizabeth took hold of one handle of my heavy hand luggage and I the other and we dashed onto a coach laid on especially for us and raced across the tarmac towards the plane. There followed a wait for many long minutes as three Malév employees argued in Hungarian with the pilot about us. We had no idea what had happened to our passports or our cases. Margaret had used the guitar case to save me a seat and my passport was duly returned, so all was well.

What a joy it was to see Hazel and the Khourys waiting for us through the glass panel at Beirut airport, and then to embark upon the long procedure of form-filling regarding my case. The next day saw us down at the airport again to meet Kirstene from the BOAC jumbo jet direct from Heathrow. I waited as the luggage came off the Malév flight from Budapest... and there was the green case with the brown strap. It was such a relief, especially as once again it was loaded with clothes and gifts from England for friends in Lebanon.

School numbers had, as expected, grown exponentially. I found myself with about one hundred and sixty three- to seven-year-olds in the department, more than the whole school put together in the previous year. "It's wonderful the way so many of the things I spent ages negotiating for at the end of last term have been provided or are happening now," I wrote home. "Desks and furniture for the kindergartens and pre-schools are arriving, though I haven't seen the tables yet." Constrained as we were with a smallish room at the rear of the ground floor for the new Transition class for five- and six-year-olds, I had asked Mr Feghali to construct trapezium-shaped tables a little higher than those in the kindergarten, with Formica tops and matching chairs, along with new open locker cubicles and shelf units with castors for children's lunch boxes and maths equipment. The tables were normally positioned in pairs as hexagon shapes, with six children sitting round in a group, but they could also be arranged in other interesting ways. All the new exercise books I had ordered from Star Stationers in Beirut had arrived, along with a sizeable order of maths equipment from Philip and Tacey in England. All that remained was the consignment from E. J. Arnold that was due any day.

The week before the new term started was long and tiring. As well as organising the new classrooms, we were receiving parents and selling uniforms. "Seeing familiar parents again is a real joy," I wrote home, "and it's just like meeting old friends." It was wonderful to note their change in attitude and growth of trust in the school. "The new parents by and large are reasonably co-operative, but there is still that initial suspicion..." My prayer was that in spite of the growth in numbers, we would be able to maintain the individual touch, and that each child would be assessed and enabled to progress at their own rate of learning; most of all, that each child would come to know that they were loved and valued by Jesus.

Just as this time the previous year, the first week of term presented its own challenges and much for which to give thanks. The children whom we knew came with a great sense of confidence and enjoyment in showing off their English and, as I commented in a letter home, were "so civilised and controlled in their behaviour". The new children were feeling their way and testing their boundaries behaviour-wise, such that even the Arabic-speaking teachers were struggling to maintain order. Was the only authority the children would respect engendered through fear of being whipped or beaten? I was convinced that classroom control was funda-mental to sound learning and happy children, but not at the expense of fear and suppression. We aimed to work towards friendly, emotionally intact and busy classrooms, leading to productive learning and feelings of self-worth and security for every child.

I was blessed with teachers who were prepared to persevere in this matter and encourage each other. By the end of October, I wrote to my parents, "I can't describe to you what a joy it is to have all the teachers, Lebanese and expatriate, pulling together and really throwing themselves into their teaching." As for the children, "though they still flash all over the place like lightning, they are much more biddable and I'd even use the word 'civilised'!" I was hugely appreciative of the time and sheer physical and emotional energy these teachers expended as they persevered in love with small children who seemingly were used to nothing but having their own way.

We now had ten teachers in the department and six classes. To praying friends in England, I wrote, "Please pray that the Lord will continue to mould us together as one and guard our relationships with each other and our reactions to the children in every situation. Thank you for your partnership in prayer for us at the school. *'Do not be afraid or discouraged ... For the battle is not yours, but God's. ... You will not have to fight this battle. Take up your positions; stand firm and see the deliverance the LORD will give you*

... Do not be afraid; do not be discouraged. Go out to face them tomorrow, and the LORD *will be with you.'[3]"*

Amidst the challenges, there were indeed many answers to prayer, not least the way some of the children with special needs were settling. Ibrahim's older sister had moved up a class and was no longer with us in the department, but after an initial hiccup, he settled beautifully and became a well-loved member of his class. The little boy with leukaemia, Marwan, was back in school, only going to the hospital twice a week for X-ray treatment. The other Marwan now came to school with his three-year-old brother and took him very protectively to his pre-school teacher. Marwan was left-handed and a joy to teach. He would happily produce a page of English mirror-writing, because he would forget that English, unlike Arabic, reads from left to right! I wrote to my parents, "I've already had his mother come and see me to say how happy Marwan seems to be. So praise the Lord."

Just as I was beginning to despair about the non-arrival of the order from E. J. Arnold, there was a further answer to prayer. It was not until late October that we heard the boxes had actually arrived in Beirut. Our long-suffering agent needed the school permit number in order to see the consignment through customs at the airport. Only that very morning, Amine had been to collect the said permission from the Ministry of Education after two years of negotiation! But our patience was to be stretched further, and I was frequently heard saying to a teacher, "When the order comes..." In November, when the boxes had been stuck in customs for a fortnight and I had rung the agent almost daily, he suggested in jest that he and I should go to the airport at 10 pm one evening and smuggle it out ourselves! I felt like the persistent widow in Luke's Gospel who kept on and on pleading for justice. Finally, by the end of the month, we supposedly had customs clearance, but the boxes were not delivered until the following term. It was a great test of patience.

There was one more outstanding stationery need: simply for large sheets of coloured card. These had been ordered in quantity back in June, and I began to suspect the order had disappeared beyond recall. The teachers were keen to do artwork, mount pictures and make books with the children, and I hated to discourage them. So I gained permission to reorder the card, and Amine volunteered to pick it up the following afternoon. "So I rang," I explained in my letter to home, "it was 4.30 pm

[3]   2 Chronicles 20:15,17

and nearly going dark – impossible to place a paper order over the telephone – okay, I'll come in – took the *servis* car into town and arrived at 5.45 pm – traffic bad, now pitch dark. At 6.50 pm, after great discussions and a cup of Arabic coffee, special prices etc. etc., I left Star Stationers, so full of praise I wanted to sing all the way home!" I was learning to do business Lebanese-style!

Familiarity with taxis, *servis* cars and buses was a great help amidst the day-to-day challenges of school life, and there were some lighter moments. "I got in a *servis* car and couldn't remember whether it cost twenty-five or thirty-five piastres. So I hopefully handed the driver a twenty-five-piastre piece. 'Oh no,' he said, in Arabic, 'it's fifty piastres!'" I wrote home. "So I, in great indignation, somehow remembered the Arabic I needed and said, 'No, I wouldn't pay more than thirty-five piastres!'" The driver thought this was extremely amusing and happily accepted my twenty-five-piastre piece. I was also learning to barter!

I had no desire to drive in those days. There seldom seemed to be a spare stretch of road without congestion. "Last week a new law was passed to attempt to reinforce the parking restrictions on the main roads downtown," I wrote. "Small vehicle cranes are being used to tow away parked cars." I was passing one day when I witnessed a driver turning up just as his car was being towed away, "and then commences a terrific haggle with the traffic police… It's amazing to realise how wide the roads actually are without the usual double parking on both sides!"

I was also appreciating the feeling of being welcomed back into friendships made during my first year in Lebanon, both in connection with the school and the village, but also in InterVarsity Fellowship Student circles and at the American International Alliance Church. Along with Margaret and Kirstene, I rejoined the American University choir to sing a Christmas Operetta that I found much easier than Brahms' *Requiem*. The fellowship lunches after morning service at church were a great way to pick up friendships and get to know people, though I still struggled with savoury and sweet on one plate! One of the friends from the IVF Bible study, Afaf, celebrated her birthday on November 2nd, and a group of us enjoyed a night of Russian singing and dancing at the large UNESCO[4] hall in Beirut. The dancers were so athletic, with sorrowful songs as well as joyful, and wonderful costumes.

---

[4] United Nations Educational, Scientific and Cultural Organization

I had already enjoyed a weekend attending an IVF Conference at Kchag Conference Centre in the mountains with students and graduates, and so welcomed a further weekend with IVF friends amidst the pine trees, with splendid views over the Beirut skyline to the sea. The centre, by the end of November, was closed for conferences, and we had the barest of facilities, "i.e. water and electricity, but even the latter went off during a thunderstorm!" I related to my parents. "In the mountains, I managed to wreck my hairdryer by plugging a one-hundred-volt appliance into two hundred and twenty voltage!" Heavy storms and snow in the mountains always indicated cooler temperatures and very heavy rain at sea level in Beirut. Later I wrote, "I went into Beirut to shop yesterday morning, and the heavens opened as I waded down the streets!"

I was gradually building friendships with those outside of school, and my twenty-eighth birthday gave us an opportunity to invite friends to a bonfire party in the garden of the school. We had woken to a fresh, sunny day and the expectation of an all-too-short phone conversation with my parents and sister, along with lots of cards and 'newsy' letters. By the time some sixty or so friends had arrived, the garden was bathed in moonlight and there was a real campfire spirit. After the food, Kirstene led us with her guitar and country-style singing around the fire, and we ended with a short epilogue.

Just before my birthday, Hazel had asked for my thoughts regarding the possible renewal of my contract for another school year. I had asked my parents to pray for wisdom and peace of heart. "I tend to find this job so physically exhausting, and yet I have so much for which to give praise, especially as I look back over all the difficulties of last year." I asked them to pray "that He will give me His peace and inspiration to continue, despite all the daily pressures and demands from children and teachers". Hazel's birthday card included a verse of promise, *"Though I sit in darkness, the* LORD *will be my light,"*[5] followed by a prayer in verse.

> *Being in doubt, I say,*
> *Lord, make it plain –*
> *Which is the true, safe way?*
> *Which would be in vain?*
> *I am not wise to know,*
> *Nor sure of foot to go,*

[5] Micah 7:8b

My blind eyes cannot see
What is so clear to Thee –
LORD, make it clear to me!

There was a footnote in brackets, "I can't help hoping very much you'll be celebrating your next birthday here too, but I know His way is the only good one!"

Back in school, we were preparing for the forthcoming parents' meetings for children in kindergarten, Transition and Junior 1. This was our opportunity to show the parents round the classrooms and let them see for themselves the sheer volume of written maths and artwork the children had done in class. "Parents are working with us so much more now and really trusting the system," I wrote home. "Praise God, they know that fundamentally, though many mistakes are made, we do care for the little details of their children's welfare as well as whether they get good marks or not." In fact, I was still determined we would not award marks at all in the Lower Junior department. I was aiming to show the parents that teachers do so much more at this age than just teach factual knowledge and then compare one child's progress with another. They are, rather, guiding each child's learning by exposing them to appropriate multi-sensory experiences, by providing group interaction to promote healthy teamwork and language learning, and by constantly praising and affirming effort as well as progress. "Do keep praying for my teachers. ... They are working so hard."

The bilingual Assemblies were going well and provided a lovely opportunity not only to share God's love through Bible stories and simple songs and prayers, but also to bring the whole department together, bar the pre-school, on a daily basis. We were now over a hundred four- to seven-year-olds, along with their teachers and any visitors who happened to join us. Imagine the scene as the children were brought in from the garden in as orderly a fashion as we could muster at the end of playtime and settled in rows, some on chairs and the littlest children from kindergarten on mats at the front. "All very simple," I wrote home, "but do pray that Biblical truths will go home."

There was Noah who obeyed God and was kept safe from the storm along with the animals and all his family, and the joy of the rainbow – God's promise never to flood the earth again. There was David, finding God to be the helper who was always with him, even when in danger from the lion and from Goliath the giant. And there was Nehemiah, who was the King's helper, who knew and loved God and talked to God when he was sad. We often used puppets, pipe cleaner figures and moving pictures on the flannelgraph board, and always told the story phrase by phrase in English and in Arabic. Then we would sing together. I only knew about six chords on the guitar, but it was enough for the favourites, *Praise Him, praise Him, all you little children, God is love, God is love* and *I am H-A-P-P-Y*, both of which they would love to sing in both languages, along with simple songs like…

> *Talk to God, talk to God,*
> *He hears what we say,*
> *Talk to God, talk to God,*
> *Every, every day!*

…that illustrated the truths from God's Special Book, the Bible. One day I found myself saying to the children, "Can you think of something you would like to talk to God about? Maybe saying thank you for something you enjoyed or asking God to help you to be kind?" It was a special moment to witness two or three children coming to the front and saying simple prayers… and our hearts were moved.

At the beginning of December, we started telling the Christmas story in Assembly and preparing my five- and six-year-olds in Transition to perform a Nativity in song and mime. I very much wanted the entire class – all thirty of them – to be involved in some way, and prayed for inspiration. How about the whole class forming the circle of Bethlehem, holding hands which they would lift as the main characters wove their way in and out of the streets, and we would all sing, *Round and round the village; may we stay at your house?* We took every opportunity to practise, and gradually it came together.

At the end of the dress rehearsal in the main school hall on the first floor, one of the children said quite spontaneously, "I really enjoyed that, Miss Radcliffe," and I was so thankful. "So long as they enjoy it," I wrote home, "that's the most important thing, because then even the mistakes are acceptable!" Further, I wrote, "One of my naughtiest boys, whose mother told me she takes five tranquillisers a day because of Gilbert, is the innkeeper, and he has to lead Mary and Joseph right round Bethlehem (i.e. the circle of children from Transition) and into the middle of the circle where the stable is. He does this with great gusto, and when the shepherds come to see the baby, just in case they don't do it properly, he beckons them all into the stable and tells them where to stand." I added, "I'm not quite sure how Biblical this is!" Some of the parents were really helpful with costumes, and we were all stitching hems and making crowns as the excitement mounted. "I'm really having to pray to the Lord for that spirit of peace and serenity which only He can give." *"...in quietness and trust is your strength..."*[6]

We performed the Christmas entertainment twice to accommodate all the parents – one of the fathers was seen to be panning round the room with his cine camera plus large glaring light before we even started the programme. The kindergarten classes sang their favourite songs in English and in Arabic, all suitably dressed up. Junior 1 offered Christmas greetings in Arabic to

Christmas 1974.
Top: Christmas *haffleh*, Hilda translating.
Middle and bottom: Christmas story in Assembly, Mona translating.

the music of Haydn's *Toy Symphony* with their teacher, and then came the Nativity. I shall never forget how the children mimed their parts as we sang the timeless story of the birth of Jesus into our world, nor how the parents responded with an expectant hush as the tableau unfolded, followed by a round of applause as we drew to a close.

One of the friends from the IVF, Afaf, had invited me to go to Jordan with her and a couple of other friends for a few days over Christmas. My father had offered to pay my flight home for the Christmas break, but I had declined with one proviso: "You know that should any crisis arise at home

---

[6] Isaiah 30:15b

Mr and Mrs Whitman in Amman, December 1974.

in which I'm needed, I'll be there like a shot." I was warming towards my new friends and was keen to spend more time exploring the Middle East.

I was thrilled to be asked to share the driving. Having written to the Automobile Association (AA) for an International Driving Permit for use in Syria and Jordan, I was prepared, as my twelve-month visas for those two countries were still valid. I was keen, as I wrote home, "not to spend the whole time sightseeing but to have a real change away from the busyness of Beirut". And for the first time in my letters home, I mentioned a psalm that would become more and more meaningful in the coming year: "Psalm 91v1 is a wonderful comfort and reassurance. *'Whoever dwells in the shelter of the Most High will rest in the shadow of the Almighty.'"*

We were hoping to stay in Amman once again, only this time, instead of at the OM Girls' Guest House, we were able to stay in a little flat-roofed house with a garden. It was rented by a Navigators couple who were studying Arabic in Amman and leaving for Beirut over Christmas! "So they left their place for us – hot running water, central heating, cosy beds – how the Lord provides!" I wrote home. It was about four hours' driving time, with the usual long waits on the borders of Syria and Jordan. "I drove a little through Syria along the road which runs parallel to the Golan Heights, this time with less army activity."

On arrival in Jordan, after a thorough search, we were on the road to Amman and a lovely welcome from Mr and Mrs Whitman, the pastor and his wife of the Brethren church where we had worshipped at Easter. We were soon to meet the Kelseys, an American couple who ran the Language Centre for mission partners in the Middle East who are studying Arabic. "Christmas morning dawned bright and sunny, yet crisp and wintry, which seemed so healthy in comparison with the cold dampness of Beirut," I wrote home. We worshipped with the believers in Arabic, had lunch with the Whitmans and then started visiting friends in Amman. It seemed as if the whole of Amman was feasting! Muslims were celebrating the culmination of the *Hajj*, the pilgrimage to Mecca, and Christians the birth of Christ in Bethlehem. I continued in my letter home, "All the shop shutters are down and everyone is in holiday mood and visiting their relatives." We visited Afaf's relatives, the OM girls and other Jordanian believers, and, on each occasion, enjoyed delicious sweetmeats such as tiny pieces of baklava and strong bitter coffee in *fenjan*[7]. "I should think we must have driven up and down and round nearly every one of the seven hills of this city!" I commented in my letter home.

Entry into Petra by horseback.

Boxing Day saw us heading down the King's Highway to Petra. "There are now five of us in Afaf's Morris 1100, having collected another girl on one of our visits yesterday. Her name is Salaam, which means 'peace', and she is the daughter of one of the believers in the church," I wrote. Our first port of call was Madaba and the Greek Orthodox church of St George to view a mosaic map that was kept hidden under a large rug. It had been discovered in 1884 when the present church building was erected on the ruins of an earlier church from the sixth century. This mosaic would have originally covered the region from Galilee in the north to Egypt and the Nile Delta in the south. The walls and gates of Jerusalem are still clearly visible as well as the city of Jericho surrounded by palm trees. I loved the portrayal of fish swimming down the River Jordan, with one turning back against the flow to avoid an untimely end in the salt-rich and aptly named Dead Sea!

The King's Highway runs along the edge of the plateau above the deep Jordan rift valley and the Dead Sea. I wrote that we paused at Kerah "to view an old Crusader Castle which was besieged in the eleventh century by Saladin at the time of the Holy Wars, and is in a magnificent position overlooking the steamy Dead Sea". As we drove along this barren, twisty, mountainous road, I felt as though I were living in the Old Testament as I continued writing my letter. "There were farmers ploughing with wooden

[7] tiny cups with no handles

ploughs pulled by a couple of donkeys, small Bedouin encampments surviving with maybe a donkey used as a burden-bearer, a few goats, sheep and tents just like Abraham would have had."

By three o'clock, we had arrived in Petra and booked in at Petra Rest House for bed-and-breakfast. This time we decided to go the two-mile walk into the ancient city on horseback, supposedly docile creatures and provided for the purpose. Mounting a horse was a new experience for me, and mine was fine until we were on the way out again and another horse galloped past at quite a rate. My horse could not resist the chase and set off at a canter! "I felt as if I were flying through the air, and just clung on to its mane for dear life, shouting, 'Stop! Stop!'" I wrote in my letter. It had never occurred to me to pull on the reins; the jerk had caused my glasses to fall off and my young guide was running pathetically behind! "By some amazing miracle, I managed to stay on – just." I was so relieved when the horse came to a complete standstill as one of the men stood in front of it and my glasses were recovered. In spite of the adventure, I had loved seeing Petra by horseback. "The sun was setting as we left around 4.30 pm, and it cast a beautiful glow over the buildings literally carved out of the rock. Petra certainly lived up to its name, 'rose-red city half as old as time'."

We woke to frost on the car the next morning and continued on south towards Aqaba. "Superb scenery *en route*," I wrote to my parents, "especially as we descended from the plateau down into the barrenness and loneliness of the desert scrubland. It was how I imagine the moon's surface to be, and in parts the cragginess made it feel quite eerie. We passed by the occasional group of camels and Bedouin tents in the desert." A passport check on the outskirts of the town gave us a chance to take in our first view of the Gulf of Aqaba on the Red Sea and to peel off our winter woollies. Immediately opposite was the port of Eilat that had been developed in recent years since this area, the Sinai wilderness, had been taken over by Israel from Egypt. "I had to pinch myself," I continued, "to appreciate fully that just the other side of those craggy rocks was the vast area where the children of Israel wandered for forty years!" There followed in my letter home a sketchy little map of the northern part of the Red Sea, with the Gulf of Suez to the west and the Gulf of Aqaba to the east (see end of chapter).

We continued driving along the shoreline until we were in sight of the border with Saudi Arabia, leaving our passports with the officials and watching as Pam and Denise jumped into the warm water to swim and search for coral. Denise even had snorkel and flippers! "The rest of us were content with collecting pieces of coral and shells from the beach and made a cup of coffee on our camping Gaz stove! Our hearts were just too full of praise – the sun shining down and the soft lapping of the waves on this beautiful beach which almost belonged to us alone." This truly was a moment to treasure, as I had longed for rest and an escape from the busyness of Beirut living. The highlight of the day was yet to come, as we drove back into Aqaba and hired a glass-bottomed boat with an outboard motor from the Aqaba Hotel. We were amazed at the colour, the vibrancy, the beauty of the coral formations only a few feet below the surface. Only that morning, we had been shivering in the cold, such is the extremity of desert temperatures. And so to our return to Amman, taking the two-hundred-and-fifty-mile drive on the new Desert Highway, "a good fast road on which one can drive seventy miles per hour most of the way," I commented in my letter.

We anticipated that the journey back to Beirut the following day would be somewhat arduous, with two borders and the city of Damascus to negotiate, and it certainly was a marathon! We paused at a village in northern Jordan to visit the family of a couple of students who had studied in Beirut and were known to Pam through the IVF Bible study group. The one had sadly lost her father only two months previously and the whole family were still in mourning. The women of the house were wearing black, and we were offered only strong Arabic coffee. Dora was afraid to venture out except to her new teaching job. "It's very hard for believers," I wrote in my letter home. "She's afraid the neighbours will talk if she goes to church, and she has very little fellowship."

It fell to me to drive through Syria, and once again the whole atmosphere felt dark and oppressive. "We tried to find the ring road round Damascus, but somehow missed it and got caught in all the rush-hour traffic when the light was fading and everywhere was very drab." Having passed by a female military training base with young girls in khaki streaming out of the barracks, we were thrust into the thick of greater Damascus traffic. "The place is so polluted and you can hardly move for bicycles, donkeys, little three-wheeled two-stroke-engine carriages piled high with people and goods, and drab-looking carriages pulled by even-drabber-looking horses." And there were people milling everywhere down the main streets along with single deck buses belching out smoke like steam engines.

On finally reaching the border with Lebanon, we were met with the sight of a whole coachload of Turkish men returning from pilgrimage to Mecca. I described the scene in my letter. "While we were waiting, it was the time for evening prayer, so they all with one accord donned their little caps, unrolled their mats and started their prayer movements just outside the border post." Rain was falling in Lebanon as we drove the final leg through snow-covered mountains and then down through misty patches into Beirut.

There was still another week's holiday before the start of the new term, and I was quietly looking forward to it, full of praise for an unforgettable holiday. Little did I know what lay ahead of us as a school and how unpredictable the coming days would prove to be.

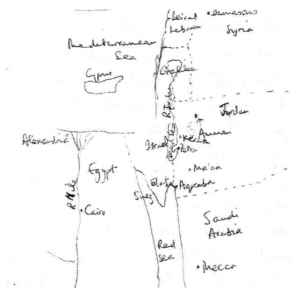

Hand-drawn map from letter.

CHAPTER THIRTEEN

Unsettling Times

Wednesday, March 5th, 1975 dawned bright and early, and I emerged from my bedroom around 7 am, only to find Hazel St John seated at the phone in the hallway, seemingly making endless phone calls. As she looked up, her words were, "No school today; the buses are not picking up the children from their homes because of road blocks surrounding the school and blocking the roads from Sidon and into Beirut." It was perfectly true. There were billows of thick, ugly black smoke from the burning tyres strung across the roads, belching upwards like miniature volcanoes wherever we looked from our fifth-floor flat in the school building. This retaliatory incident reflected the growing political instability of the country, and there was more to come. Only the previous Friday, we had sent the children home early on the buses because of a threat of demonstrations and roadblocks. We were learning to adapt to day-to-day events and give thanks to the Lord for His safekeeping.

School had not been easy since my return from Jordan. Right from the very beginning, life had been challenging in terms of my willingness to adjust to whatever came along each day. The first week was hectic, though I did manage two afternoons free from teaching to spend time with parents who were struggling to accept both our standards of behaviour and our teaching methods. There were new parents too, pressing us to squeeze their children into classes already full to bursting point and, "The wet, windy weather just makes life even more chaotic," I wrote home. "I do praise God that He is in control through the traumas. I was given a lovely promise from Isaiah chapter 1 and verse 19, which I was able to share with the teachers at lunchtime. *'If you are willing and obedient, you will eat the good things of the land…'*" I took this to be God's promise to us for the new term

139

View from fifth-floor balcony of burning tyres blocking the road, March 5th, 1975.

in spite of all the political uncertainties and my own indecision about whether to renew my contract for another year.

It proved to be a tiring term physically. How grateful we were for days when school was closed for religious holidays and thankful for loyal teachers who refused to go on strike for higher pay. An additional strain on the staff was the fact that we were running seriously short of stationery and educational equipment, as the order from E. J. Arnold had still not been released from customs at the airport.

My commitment to friendship with the Lebanese was being tested, too, over the simple desire to pray and do Bible study with a friend from the IVF Graduates Fellowship, "all highlighting the difficulties of adapting to this culture and its people," I wrote to my parents. "How wonderfully gracious the Lord is during these times. He has brought me yet another step along the road of complete dependence upon Himself." *"We were under great pressure, far beyond our ability to endure, so that we despaired of life itself … But this happened that we might not rely on ourselves, but on God, who raises the dead."*[1]

One morning, towards the end of January, in the midst of my daily reading from Isaiah 30, my uncertainty regarding the renewal of the contract was swept away. I shared with my parents, "The verses in the RSV that have really set the seal on all my wonderings about next year were speaking to me. *'…you shall weep no more. He will surely be gracious to you at the sound of your cry; when he hears it, he will answer you. And though the Lord give you the bread of adversity and the water of affliction, yet your Teacher will not hide himself any more, but your eyes shall see your Teacher. And your ears shall hear a word behind you saying, "This is the way, walk in it," when you turn to the right or when you turn to the left.'*[2] It was such a lovely reassurance that I was not on my own, even if the Middle East did explode like a time bomb as President Anwar Sadat of Egypt was reported to have said. "That's

---

[1] 2 Corinthians 1:8,9
[2] Isaiah 30:19-21 (RSV)

entirely in the Lord's hands," I wrote home, "and His place for me next year is Eastwood College, Kafarshima!"

Right now, practical matters were at the forefront of my mind. "One of my teachers has been sick all week," I wrote home, "and so I've had to fill in and have ended up teaching every single minute!" And still we had no good news from the airport because, having opened the boxes from E. J. Arnold, "the customs officials will not recognise it as educational equipment but merely toys, and

View of Beirut harbour from the Christian Medical Centre in Ashrafieh.

are expecting us to pay fifty per cent customs tax." The next day I went with Amine and the clearing agent and "we presented ourselves at the airport and I actually had the joy of clapping eyes on our precious, precious order!" The miracle was that it was completely intact. When I explained to the customs chief that we did actually use these so-called 'toys' for teaching, he actually agreed and we eventually struck a compromise, Lebanese-style. The stationery equipment could not possibly be classified as toys, and the tax bill would therefore be lowered. I was thankful that we had shipped by air and not by boat and that nothing had been pilfered. "And really, there has been such a super spirit amongst the teachers as they have 'made do' over and over again with little equipment," I wrote. "I just thank the Lord every day for their willingness and concern for the children."

It was not until a sunny Saturday in mid February that Amine knocked on the door of our fifth-floor flat to ask if I would like to go downstairs because they had just brought the boxes from the airport! "…*God is faithful; he will not let you be tempted beyond what you can bear.*"[3] With the help of Jill, one of the pre-school teachers who lived in nearby Hadeth, the boxes were unpacked and the items allocated to the different classes. "We've all had a new lease of life since the equipment has arrived!"

---

[3] 1 Corinthians 10:13

On the following Saturday, I happened to be alone in the flat when the phone rang, and it was Joan, my other pre-school teacher. She actually lived in the school building with her two children, aged nine and eleven years, and had driven to the Christian Medical Centre in Ashrafieh that morning to see the doctor about an ingrowing toenail that had been causing pain for a while. Dr Manoogian offered to deal with it immediately and "yes, she'd be able to drive back so long as she rested a short while after she came round from the anaesthetic," I reported in my letter home. Hence the phone call to ask me to let the children know that she would be home later than expected. I immediately volunteered to go to the hospital by *servis* and keep her company. "I arrived when the operation was just over and she hobbled to her car with a great bandage on her big toe, and yours truly had to drive home in the lunchtime Saturday traffic!"

I drove the whole weekend – into Beirut for church on Sunday morning and then for a trip along the coast road in the afternoon towards Sidon with Joan and the two children. We stopped at the village of Damour, where I discovered it was fatal to admire the beautiful blown glass vases in rich colours, Phoenician-style, displayed by the roadside. My mother treasured the large burgundy-coloured, narrow-necked glass jug I bought for her as I enjoyed my growing facility in bargaining. The weather was certainly warming up, even though the snow could be seen on Mount Hermon and the Lebanese mountains. Joan checked her insurance and I was thrilled. "I shan't drive often," I wrote home, "but it's lovely to know that I've got over my hang-up about driving in Lebanon. You just have to forge ahead and not look left or right, especially at roundabouts!"

It was a gift to be able to borrow Joan's navy blue Fiat 127 from time to time. To reassure my parents, I wrote, "We've really committed my use of it into the Lord's hands now and believe He will protect. It's a super little car, even though the front seat is stuck and I have to jam my handbag behind me in order to be far enough forward to drive!"

And so to the events of March 5th and my early experience of the civil disruption that was to take hold of Lebanon in the coming months and years. School reopened the day after the road blocks, and I prayed for wisdom regarding the drive into Beirut for the Bible study at Afaf's flat in the evening. All seemed to be quiet by 7 pm, "so I set off in Joan's little Fiat. Disturbance was definitely in the air, especially as I got nearer the city, but I just drove on regardless and parked the car near Afaf's building," I wrote to my parents. "We had a super study (first part of John 4), and around

8.30 pm, I had a phone call from Kafarshima. 'Don't try to come home, because the main roads through are already blocked.'" So I had no option but to take up Afaf's offer to stay the night. Lebanon was to be in mourning the next day for the untimely death of a former MP, and we woke to more road blocks. I was thankful that the school in Kafarshima was closed as we tried to shut out the filthy smoke billowing out from the paraffin and burning tyres all around us.

I retreated into Afaf's bedroom. My thoughts turned to those of the man in the book of Lamentations who felt utterly devastated and downcast, and I prayed, "Dear Lord, in this temporal, uncertain world, here I sit with burning tyres and filthy smoke surrounding the building. Young men and boys are just losing themselves in the emotional fervour of it all, and shooting is going on all around us. The whole of Lebanon is mourning a dead Muslim leader. O Lord, burden me afresh for these people... I simply praise You that I'm here with Afaf and her mother. Your ways are indeed higher than our ways and Your thoughts higher than our thoughts."[4] My prayer continued, "Thank You too, Lord, for Hebrews 4:12, *'For the word of God is living and active. Sharper than any double-edged sword, it penetrates even to dividing soul and spirit, joints and marrow; it judges the thoughts and attitudes of the heart,'* and that Your Word will accomplish its purpose and never return empty.[5] Thank You for probing deep down into my heart. Continue to make me willing for this, Lord, that I may ever live to praise Your name and know the victory You give in Christ." I was just pondering verses from Lamentations, *"He has barred my way with blocks of stone ... He pierced my heart with arrows from his quiver,"*[6] when there was even more shooting in the air and a march past of commandoes with black headgear, heralded by cars with megaphones declaring the glory of martyrdom. Lamentations spoke to me again, *"I say to myself, 'The LORD is my portion; therefore I will wait for him.'"*[7]

By late morning, most of the noisy shooting and burning around Afaf's building had subsided, so after lunch I tentatively made my way in Joan's car back to the school in Kafarshima. There was hardly a soul to be seen and most of the roadblocks had been disbanded. But the destruction was

---

4   Isaiah 55:9
5   Isaiah 55:11
6   Lamentations 3:9,13
7   Lamentations 3:24

Wild cyclamen in Kafarshima.

all too apparent: broken traffic lights, lampposts uprooted and burnt-out buses which had been used to block the main roads into Beirut.

The end of term drew nearer with all the busyness of writing reports and retelling the Easter story both in Assembly and across the curriculum. Thankfully, the political turmoil died down and there was no further disruption of the school routine. Looking back, I wrote to my parents, "The last few weeks have been tough, and I praise the Lord for His upholding. This is such a lovely time of the year with green grass and carpets of flowers, cyclamen, red anemones, wild poppies – beautiful!"

I was keen to present the Easter story in an age-appropriate and sensitive manner, and decided to use an idea I had gleaned years previously from a Scripture Union manual. We set up a painting easel in Assembly, and I pretended to be a child called Jane who was busy with green paint painting a green hill. She had seen a picture something like it in her house and she kept thinking about it. Then she painted three crosses on top of the hill. "That's a nice painting," said the teacher. "Do you know the story about that hill?" And Jane replied, "Well, I think it's something about Jesus, but I don't know what."

The next day we continued the story, with one of my Lebanese teachers translating phrase by phrase into Arabic. I recounted the story of the last supper. "I shall be going away from you," said Jesus, "but I shall come back again." Then there was the walk to the garden where Jesus prayed and His followers fell asleep, followed by the betrayal and arrest. "Had Jesus done anything wrong?" No. These people did not love Jesus, so they took Him away to a green hill where He was put on a cross to die – and I pointed to the painting. Two prisoners were being punished too, on either side of Jesus. God knew what was happening. Jesus' friends were very sad, but soon they would not be sad any more because something very wonderful was about to happen.

There followed the story of the cave tomb in a beautiful garden. Jesus was laid in the tomb and a huge stone was rolled across the entrance to protect the body. Gradually, God's salvation story was revealed as the two

Marys came early on Sunday morning. "Don't be afraid," said the angel. "Jesus is not here. He is alive. Go and tell His friends." There was the story of Peter and John running to the cave to see for themselves the empty tomb, and Cleopas and his friend walking to Emmaus. Morning by morning in Assembly, we recounted how sadness was turning into incredulity and then to joy, as Jesus revealed Himself to His friends in His risen body.

It was a joy to spend one afternoon with Transition making an Easter garden. The five- and six-year-olds worked in groups, one making the rock tomb from plaster of Paris, trying to be quick before it set hard! Another group used pipe cleaners to make little figures and dress them appropriately. There was Jesus, dressed in a white Kleenex tissue, along with the two Marys and Cleopas and his friend. Another group covered and painted little boxes and made steps up the side by zig-zagging a small strip of card. This was the village of Emmaus, which was positioned a pebble footpath away from the hill and the rock tomb. There was the garden itself, the flowers and the trees. Cress seeds were planted in a tin lid, tissue paper flowers were stuck onto twigs, and pipe cleaner stalks and trees sprouted from paper rolls, some with leaves, some more like palms. A few days later, the Easter garden was assembled in a large sand-covered box. It was so exciting to see the children all working together, chattering away in English with much enthusiasm and humming the song we sang in Assembly:

Jesus is alive,
Jesus is alive,
Praise Him, praise Him,
Jesus is alive.

There was only one more week before the end of term and the Easter break. "The sun is shining over the sea like a red ball of flame, and it is quite misty over Beirut," I wrote to my parents. I knew they were praying along with friends from church, and I wanted to encourage them. "Please keep praying and praising for the Lord's constant upholding physically and emotionally. He's bringing me into situation after situation in which I must rely on no man but simply on His grace and strength alone." "*My grace is sufficient for you, for my power is made perfect in weakness.*"[8] "*…he gives more grace. That is why Scripture says: 'God opposes the proud but shows favour*

8   2 Corinthians 12:9

to the humble.' ... *Humble yourselves before the Lord, and he will lift you up.*"[9] All these words were becoming more and more meaningful to me during these unsettling times.

[9] James 4:6,10

Chapter Fourteen

Out of Egypt I Called My Son

My letters home during the run-up to Easter were punctuated with details of how my proposed and much-awaited trip to Egypt was shaping up. The plan was to fly Egyptair to Cairo with Afaf and Pam, with whom I had travelled to Jordan over the Christmas holiday. Afaf had Egyptian friends who were meeting us at the airport and taking us to an apartment in downtown Cairo that we could use as a base for exploring the city. We also wanted to visit Nadia in Alexandria, who lectured at the Lebanese University in Beirut during term-time and joined us in the IVF Bible study group from time to time. As tickets were booked and visas stamped in our passports, I was able to write home, "It's truly wonderful the way it's all falling into place, and I can see we shall spend a good deal of time visiting!"

I was about to embark upon an Egyptian adventure like no other! The Egyptair flight to Cairo was delayed and there was a scuffle for the three of us to board the plane, during which time Afaf and I found ourselves in first-class seats being served a first-class meal, while Pam was relegated to a seat in the rear of the plane with far more inferior service. We were served a cold lamb chop, slices of mutton, fish and a slice of chicken breast with salad, followed by coffee and an apple, waitress-style with serviettes and knives and forks, all in one hour and forty minutes! On arrival at about 10 pm, we were met by Afaf's friend Samira, along with her husband and two of Afaf's cousins whom she had never met. It was exceedingly warm even at that hour, with the *khamseen* filling the atmosphere with a very fine dust. We were driven straight to the promised apartment and clambered up the stone steps and into bed.

Cairo Tower, Easter 1975.

It was not until the following morning that I realised where we were, in a poor part of a working capital city and far from tourist territory. The stairwell to the upper floors was rat-infested and our third-floor flat was small, with no running hot water, intermittent electricity and sparsely furnished, although certainly adequate as a base. The beds were hard, and we had endured a succession of noises during the night, including howling cats, barking dogs, prayer calls, chirping birds and early risers hawking their wares on the street down below. We were glad to *reconnoitre* a little in the area, and it was not long before we arrived at the nearby Coptic evangelical church for the ten o'clock service. To us, this was Palm Sunday, but not to the Egyptian believers who, that year, were to celebrate Easter during the first weekend of May. In fact, with them it was Mothering Sunday, and the pastor preached from Proverbs 31 about wise wives and mothers. He started his sermon at 11 am and by that time the church was practically full. It seemed that some of the congregation had been at work till then because Sunday is a working day in Egypt. I was thankful to Afaf for her whispered help with English translation from the Arabic thundering from the pulpit for some forty minutes. It was good to worship with believers and appreciate the warmth of their welcome.

As we came out of the church, we were hit once again by the *khamseen* blowing strongly from the desert, but Samira and her husband were keen to take us for a drive down the Nile to some barrages and a small park where we could picnic. Here we were surrounded by trees and were more sheltered from the hot, dusty wind. Even so, our first view of the Nile, dark brown, greasy and quite rough, was most unimpressive. The journey north revealed the extreme poverty of the farming peoples. The land appeared to be well irrigated by the many tributaries of the Nile Delta, but the crops were poor and the animals maybe only a donkey, a cow and some scraggy goats per family, along with two oxen yoked together pulling a plough. It all made for a rather pathetic sight.

Late afternoon, we returned to Cairo and were driven eastwards towards the airport and the suburb of Heliopolis. It was such a contrast from the Delta, cleaner and more residential. This was to be the first of our visits in order to make contact with Afaf's long-lost relatives. "They just poured in one after the other, cousins and their families, including all the in-laws!" I wrote to my parents. We finally sat down to a scrumptious meal at around 8 pm, followed by strong Arabic coffee in tiny cups such as we were always offered in Lebanon when the hosts were ready to let us go! One of the cousins drove us back to the apartment quite late, a friendly man in his early twenties studying at one of the Cairo universities. He was thrilled to meet Afaf and Pam, who were used to working with students, and to discover we were believers. It seemed that he and his teenage sister were the only believers in the whole family of nominal Christians. What a welcome and such concern shown by every single member of the family that we should not be at a loose end for one minute!

The next day dawned bright and clear, and after a better night's sleep and feeling refreshed, the three of us took a taxi to the Hilton Hotel in the centre of Cairo. The hotel was surrounded by lush vegetation and lotus flowers, and had a revolving door into the main reception area. From there, you could see right through to the smoothly flowing blue Nile and the island beyond, with the Cairo Tower rising above the trees. It was such a contrast to the gritty sandstorm of the day before. We managed to book an American Express tour of Old Cairo, "expecting to be with a whole coachload of people but were later pleasantly surprised to find it was just the three of us with a driver and a guide sitting in the front seat," I wrote to my parents. It was an intimate and fascinating tour.

We drove first to the Abdeen Palace of the family of the exiled King Farouk and now a history museum, featuring a large collection of military hardware. It was a truly magnificent Ottoman palace, home to the royal family who once ruled Egypt for over a hundred years. Then into old Cairo itself with its narrow dusty streets, overloaded donkeys and pathetic-looking horses pulling carts. Most memorable was being taken into the oldest Coptic church in Cairo, the church of St Sergius and St Bacchus, dark and smelling of incense. We crept gingerly down steep narrow steps into the crypt that had supposedly been built around the cave to which Joseph and Mary had fled with the child Jesus, thus avoiding Herod's slaughter of the innocents in Jerusalem. I pondered the prophecy of Hosea, "...*out of*

The Sphinx, Easter 1975.

Egypt I called my son,"[1] which is quoted in Matthew's account of God's protection of His Son, seemingly destined to a life on the move and who would ultimately fulfil the meaning of His name Jesus, to *"save his people from their sins"*[2].

From the church, we wandered through narrow streets with very few tourists in sight to an ancient Jewish synagogue. Once again, we encountered the history of God's people in the region, as the rabbi showed us scrolls of the Pentateuch, the first five books of Moses. Our final visit was to one of the many mosques of Cairo. I believe our guide told us there were twenty-nine in Old Cairo alone. On the way back to the Hilton, we sampled Egyptian perfume, highly concentrated and to be mixed with nine parts of alcohol! I succumbed to two tiny bottles as a gift for my mother, one from the essence of the lotus flower and the other jasmine. We returned to the apartment through the modern streets of Cairo, via the main railway station to book tickets for our journey to Alexandria later in the week, and called in to see Samira, who worked at the KLM airline office. She and her husband had offered to take us to the ancient pyramids and Sphinx that lie to the west of the city, about half an hour by road.

The following day was bright and sunny, "just right and so refreshing to experience dry heat after the stickiness of Beirut," I remarked to my parents. In tiny writing on a postcard, I wrote to my widowed grandmother, "The weather was glorious on Tuesday when we spent the whole day at the Giza pyramids and Sphinx, clambering right inside one of the pyramids." One of the seven wonders of the ancient world, dating back to 2500 BC, the pyramids reminded me of a history picture book I had read as a child. We did indeed make our way bent low through a narrow tunnel, lit by a few electric lightbulbs dangling precariously above our heads, until we found ourselves in the very centre. Here the Pharaoh would have been buried within a marble sarcophagus, awaiting the moment when it was believed his spirit would re-enter his body after death

1 Hosea 11:1
2 Matthew 1:21

and bring him life immortal. "The Great Pyramid was around four hundred and fifty feet high, built with huge slabs of stone brought down river from Luxor and Aswan where there are many more temples and pyramids," I informed my parents.

As we emerged from the tunnel, the light was blinding and the desert seemed like a moonscape. One or two tourists were braving camels, and Pam and Afaf were persuaded to take a ride. After my donkey experience in Petra, I was happy to decline and enjoyed taking photos instead! Samira and Shehir drove us a little further west into the desert, "from where we had wonderful

Giza Pyramids, 1975.
Top: Samira, Pam, Afaf and I.
Bottom: Pam and Afaf astride a
camel.

views to the east of Cairo and the luxuriant growth, palm trees of all varieties around the Nile, and west across to the desert through which camels and donkeys were threading their way." We picnicked at Sahara City and absorbed the peace of the place, before heading back into Cairo for more visiting. It was a privilege to be welcomed into homes again and receive such generous hospitality. One elderly aunt of eighty-four was hard of hearing and would not wear her hearing aid but, as I wrote home, "Afaf had greetings and gifts to present and it was a happy time."

Next morning, we were back at the Nile Hilton enjoying the Ladies' Powder Room before ascending the stone steps of the Cairo Museum for our booked tour. After two hours, my head was buzzing with ancient history, expertly recounted by our guide. "The Tutankhamun treasures are incredible," I wrote home. "He was only a boy king, who reigned from the age of nine until his death at eighteen from TB." I was fascinated by the secret embalming process prior to being mummified and placed in no less than eight coffins one inside the other, all heavily inlaid with gold and semi-precious stones, "and then buried with great ritual in a temple in Luxor along with all his belongings, food, models of items he would need

151

in the afterlife, his jewels, beds, chairs, clothes and many other objects he had used throughout his childhood". Nearby was a room in the museum reserved for Egyptian mummies, and there was Ramses II, the *"new king, to whom Joseph meant nothing [and who] came to power in Egypt."*[3] He, along with many other kings and queens found embalmed in the temples and pyramids alongside the Nile, were lying side by side in their glass cases. Parts of the Old Testament were springing to life as we grasped a little of the power and importance of the Pharaohs in ancient Egypt.

We left Cairo Museum and made our way across Tahrir Square to the Ibis Café at the Nile Hilton. This café had become a retreat for us, surrounded as it was by luxuriant, semi-tropical flowers and palm trees, oleander and hibiscus, even though we were in the centre of a bustling, overcrowded city. In the afternoon, I walked along the riverbank to All Saints Anglican Cathedral, while Pam and Afaf visited the university to meet with some of Pam's student contacts. I entered a light, airy building that has since been demolished to make way for a new road bridge across the Nile. Grey stone pillars drew the eye upwards and shafts of light cast shadows. "It was tremendously uplifting to be in the cathedral, especially as the choir were practising music for Easter to words from Isaiah 53, *'Surely He hath borne our griefs and carried our sorrows. He was wounded for our transgressions, He was bruised for our iniquities, the chastisement of our peace was upon Him,'* part of Handel's Messiah," I wrote to my parents.

As I listened, my eyes caught sight of a compelling piece about prayer engraved upon a pillar. I sat and scribbled it in my notebook.

Prayer

Prayer is being with God.
You come here to be with Him.

Perhaps He will take you up on the mountain to be with Him.
Perhaps He will take you into the light with Him,
or into the mist where you will not be able to see Him.
Perhaps you will be with Him in pain, or in happiness, or in tiredness.
He just says, "Come to Me," and you say "I will" or "I will not".

You know that if you say you will not come,
He does not leave off wanting you,

[3] Exodus 1:8

152

and you know what kind of wanting His is,
by the manger and the cross.

You know that if you come to Him,
He will ask you to help Him about His Kingdom,
and will give you that work for it which no-one else can do.

You know that He will bring you into the fellowship of His friends
and that you will be allowed to bring Him
into the fellowship of your friends.

And all the time you will fail Him so often
that some day you will have no self-confidence left;
only a growing confidence in Him instead.

Because He never fails you.[4]

These were words of hope and encouragement to me, and a timely reminder that the One who had called me to live and work in this part of His Kingdom would never cease to keep His promise, *"…I will never leave you nor forsake you."*[5]

That evening we had booked to take Afaf's friends, Samira and Shehir, to the *Son et Lumière* performance at the Giza pyramids. As we drove eastwards into the desert, my heart thrilled as we passed giant billboards and little open stalls selling all variety of delicious-smelling foods, *falafel*, *salata*, *shawarma* and the ubiquitous Coca Cola! There was a cool breeze blowing as we took our seats in the midst of the ancient burial tombs, and I shivered as yet more of Egypt's rich history overwhelmed my senses. Special lighting effects were projected onto the Sphinx and the pyramids and combined with recorded narration and musical effects, vividly recreating more than 3,000 years of history. It was an unforgettable experience and lives with me to this day.

The following afternoon was spent exploring and doing a little bargaining! "We went down the Nile in a sailing boat and afterwards in a horse-drawn cabby to the Khan el Khalili bazaar in the historic centre of Cairo," I wrote home. "I managed to get a few things, though bargaining was very necessary, and I was pleased to find fabric with hieroglyphs and pharaohs for myself and Margaret and Kirstene, as requested." Once again, the colourful sights, sounds and smells were overwhelming.

[4] author unknown
[5] Joshua 1:5

Craftsmen were at work in leather, alabaster and beaten copper wares, all beckoning us to come in and buy!

As rush hour traffic was mounting, we decided against buses or trams. The passengers were literally clinging on to moving vehicles, hanging out of the windows, even sitting on the top! Rather, we made our way back to the city centre by flagging down one of the Fiat 127 bright yellow taxis, which took us through all manner of streets and alleyways to the Sheraton Hotel, to meet with the wife and daughter of one of Afaf's cousins who both worked there. It was an easy walk back along the riverside to the Anglican cathedral to take part in the Maundy Thursday communion service, remembering the Last Supper, and then we decided to search out an Egyptian restaurant for our own evening meal. We were introduced to a popular Middle Eastern dish, *ful*, Arabic for broad beans cooked in a vinegar and oil sauce and served in a variety of ways, sometimes with vegetables, or with meat. "It seems to be the staple diet for the Egyptians as they have it for breakfast, lunch and tea," I wrote home. "We also had *shish kebab* roasted over a charcoal fire on sticks. It was delicious, especially with all the dips like *hummus*, *baba ghanoush*, *moutabil* and *labneh*, which I've grown accustomed to in Lebanon." I so warmed to the flavours and hospitality of the Middle East.

Friday morning saw us at Ramses Station for the three-hour train journey north to Alexandria. In the midst of the hustle and bustle, it was good to be met by Nadia, our Egyptian friend. "We were amazed to encounter a Muslim service on the station platform, with the preacher in full spate through a microphone and all the men sitting cross-legged on mats on the platform while passengers walked on and off trains and through their ranks!" Alexandria is Nadia's hometown, and it was a delight to be taken to the spacious apartment where she lived with her brother and family and her mother. We were to stay at Fairhaven, a conference centre attached to the Coptic Evangelical Church, now used as a residential school and training centre for children and young people with a range of learning disabilities. The accommodation was by no means five-star, "but at least there was hot water in the shower when the Butagaz cylinder was attached to the geyser!" I explained to my parents. "What a joy it was to stand under a hot shower and wash myself entirely from head to toe, the filth from the sandstorm the previous Sunday literally pouring out, especially from my hair."

That evening, Nadia took us by bus and foot along the seafront to King Farouk's summer palace, an impressive Ottoman and Florentine building with two towers of differing heights and long open arcades facing the sea on each floor. We were unable to enter the palace but marvelled at the architecture and lush Mediterranean gardens surrounding it.

We were out again the following day, roaming around Alexandria, visiting the museum, the Roman amphitheatre, Pompey's Pillar and the catacombs. "There were more Roman and Greek inscriptions here which contrasted with all the hieroglyphs we deciphered in the Cairo Museum," I wrote home. "It was at Alexandria that the Old Testament was translated into Greek, known as the Septuagint, in the third century BC." There was more Egyptian food that evening at a 'Ful ou Falafel' restaurant in town, and prices were noticeably lower than in Beirut. I attempted to describe the meal to my parents. "*Falafel* are like meatballs, only they are not made from meat – rather from ground beans mixed with herbs and parsley, fried in deep fat and eaten with *tahini*, a vinegary spicy sauce. I have grown to love these flavours from eating Lebanese food." Later in the evening, as we sat sipping sweet black Arabic coffee, Nadia delighted us with her piano-playing, études from Chopin and sonatas from Beethoven and Schumann, and her mother played a little too from old Arabic songs and melodies.

We returned to Fairhaven, and during the night I woke in a state of anxiety and distress. Questions were racing through my mind, especially regarding my relationships with Arab people. The air seemed to be too chilly for even my trusty hot water bottle to penetrate, and there was a dampness that as many as four blankets could not dispel. Eventually, through the darkness, I made my way to the bathroom along with my torch, my Bible and a blanket, and simply wept before the Lord. Was this what denying self would involve for me as I became so immersed in Arab culture and family life? The size and geography of the country of Egypt seemed so vast in contrast to Lebanon or even Jordan or Syria. I smiled through the tears as I remembered struggling to pronounce the word 'Egypt' as a six-year-old discovering the country on a map at school. Furthermore, I recalled one of the verses I had learnt as a teenager following the Billy Graham meetings in Manchester in 1961. *"If any man would come after Me, let him deny himself and take up his cross daily and follow me."*[6] I questioned my commitment as I sought to follow Jesus and serve Arab peoples. We had already faced a degree of civil disruption and

[6] Luke 9:23 (RSV)

danger in Lebanon earlier in the year. Little did I know then of the further uncertainties that were to come.

I wept again as the meaning of the next verse settled itself in my heart. *"For whoever wants to save their life will lose it, but whoever loses their life for me will save it."*[7] As though to reassure me, verses from the Psalms came to mind. *"Thou hast kept count of my tossings; put thou my tears in thy bottle! Are they not in thy book?"*[8] *"Those who sow with tears will reap with songs of joy. Those who go out weeping, carrying seed to sow, will return with songs of joy, carrying sheaves with them."*[9] Most powerful of all was the realisation that Paul's call to share Jesus with the Gentiles involved humiliation and bewilderment and tears. *"For I wrote to you out of great distress and anguish of heart and with many tears, not to grieve you but to let you know the depth of my love for you."*[10] I gradually made my way back to the bedroom, strangely relieved and at peace.

Sunday was chilly but bright and sunny, and "we had to keep reminding ourselves that it was Easter Sunday. The Eastern church would be celebrating later, according to the Julian Calendar," I wrote home. What a service of joy in worship, all in Arabic, and a great welcome! We had met some of the young people at Fairhaven. "The Egyptians are so easy and full of jokes, and these student believers were just bubbling over. They cannot meet on campus or hold any public Christian meetings in the university." After church, I was particularly interested to meet a teacher from a school in Alexandria and learn more of the Egyptian system of free state education post Nasser's reforms.

Our Egyptian adventure was nearly over, and we returned to Cairo for some final goodbyes to Afaf's relatives. "Imagine our astonishment," I wrote to my parents, "to find on arrival at the home of the first cousin that they had arranged a great family gathering in the home of yet another cousin and everyone had been informed of it except us!" I had mixed feelings because of my secret desire to ascend Cairo Tower on Gezira Island in the Nile, but nevertheless we were drawn into this family hospitality. I commented to my parents, "How close and protective families are out here; ties are incredibly strong and sometimes somewhat suffocating."

7   Luke 9:24
8   Psalm 56:8 (RSV)
9   Psalm 126:5,6
10 2 Corinthians 2:4

Our return flight to Beirut on Monday, March 31st was scheduled for eight o'clock, expected arrival 9.45 am, so alarms were set for 5 am. It was pitch dark and all the lights in the flat had fused! Candles sufficed, and we took a taxi to the airport for 6.30 am. My letter home recounts what happened next. "Afaf and Pam went to change their Egyptian money back into dollars, and we didn't finally come to book in for the 8 am flight till 7.15, only to find a crowd of men pushing and shoving at the check-in. When we reached the desk, we were just told the flight was closed and that was that!" In spite of our protests, all that was on offer were seats on the next Egyptair flight to Beirut, which left Cairo at 11.30 pm that evening, arriving 1.15 am on Tuesday, April 1st, the very day school was due to reopen for the summer term!

There was nothing for it but to accept another day in Cairo. "What a gift of a day it was from the Lord, with beautiful sunny warm weather!" I wrote home. "I shall never forget the three hundred and sixty degree panoramic view from the Cairo Tower as we sucked our ice-creams at the very top. You could see all over Cairo and the desert with nothing but sand and pyramids in the distance." At a height of six hundred feet and built by the then president, Gamal Abdel Nasser, in 1961, the Tower resembles a lotus flower, with latticework casing, and was then the tallest structure in Egypt and the whole of Africa. I had even tried to photograph it earlier in the week from the Nile Hilton when it was floodlit after sunset, though not very successfully! My secret desire had been fulfilled, and I was thankful. *"Take delight in the LORD, and he will give you the desires of your heart."*[11]

We eventually reached the airport again in plenty of time for check-in and all went smoothly, with no searching at customs. Likewise, we arrived on time in Beirut, and the taxi dropped me off in Kafarshima at 2.30 am! "How I got prepared for Tuesday's lessons after only three hours' sleep, I shall never quite know," I wrote home. "Praise the Lord for His overruling and His abundant love and protection right through the holiday, and I think most of all for what He taught us all of Himself in and through our relationships with each other as we look only to Him."

[11] Psalm 37:4

CHAPTER FIFTEEN

Peace that Passes Understanding

I was thankful to survive the first few days of the summer term, especially taking into account my enforced lack of preparation the day before term began, but I was concerned not to have received any news from home since early March. I reassured my parents, "I know it's not your fault, so please don't give up writing. Apparently, all mail is being sent up to Tripoli to be censored and franked because of letter bombs at the main post office in Beirut. Hence the delays." We too no longer trusted the outgoing mail from Beirut and would either post at the airport or, better still, ask friends to carry it by hand and post at their destination. Friends and family could no longer depend upon where our letters would be postmarked!

As well as letter-writing, I knew there was plenty to be done in the classrooms, sorting and cleaning for the new term. I wrote to my parents, "I had another mouse in my cupboard last term who kindly left it full of shredded papers etc.!" I still remember sliding open this particular cupboard door to retrieve some items for our Easter garden and paintings, only to hear some scurrying amongst the papers! I slid the door back again rather quickly, realising it would be better to leave well alone until the children had gone home and I could call Jusef the caretaker, who was a dab hand with a stick!

The weather was exceptionally warm and sunny for early April, with the *khamseen* blowing from the desert. "I feel as if I'm growing more Lebanese every minute," I wrote. "Praise the Lord for the love He's continuing to give me for these people. I find I have such a feeling of belonging in the country with the teachers and parents I meet every day and, of course, the children." On the first Sunday after our return from

Cairo, I had been invited for lunch after church to the home of Sandra, one of our English teachers in the senior school, who lived in a small ground-floor flat in downtown Beirut within walking distance of the church. Her son Gerard had recently been admitted to the kindergarten, and he and I were engaged in a battle of wills. I do believe this visit made a difference to our relationship in school, and prayed for opportunities for Gerard to experience success in his achievements and flourish within the school environment.

That afternoon, I had been invited to join Afaf and her mother for a drive north of Beirut to the Jeita Caves. These are spectacular limestone formations in underground caverns that I had first visited with friends from West Kirby who were calling into Beirut on a Mediterranean cruise, not long after we started the school. The upper cave had only been open to the public for a few years, and we were able to marvel at the dazzling rock formations as we stepped deeper and deeper in, via platforms and raised walkways. It was a feast for the senses and refreshingly cool, in contrast to the unseasonal warmth and humidity.

Back at school in our daily Assemblies, it was a joy to retell the stories of Jesus' many post-resurrection appearances to His disciples until the time came for Him to leave them in person. There were stories of how sadness turned to joy, breakfast was prepared for them on the shore, and how Jesus spoke with them lovingly of His imminent return to His heavenly Father. With Transition, we made a large collage picture of the 'breakfast on the shore' story, and the children were making good progress across the department. Then, quite suddenly, around 6.30 am on Monday, April 14th, we were informed there would be no school that day. There had been a clash in Beirut between opposing forces the previous day and shooting overnight. I was keen to reassure my parents, "While we are safe and well out of the danger zone here, it is obviously not wise to move from here or to bring children to school." I was concerned about what they would be hearing on the news back home, as we were listening to varying reports on the BBC World Service, which was generally reliable. After all, our village was only seven miles from Beirut, on the southern flanks of the city. Yet we were quiet and peaceful in Kafarshima, and none of us had heard any shooting in the night. As far as I could tell, closing school was merely a precaution. Nevertheless, I did try, unsuccessfully, to book a phone call home.

There followed a night of shooting and machine gun fire. "We do have a grandstand view from here across to the airport – which is still functioning but with masses of armed security – and over the Palestinian camps to the city." As my fifth-floor room was at the front, I took my duvet down to the fourth floor at the rear of the building and slept with Joan and her two children. "By morning, all was apparently quiet, with shops, schools and offices all shut and very little traffic on the roads," I wrote home. "There has been a lot of destruction and indiscriminate shooting." There was uncertainty in the air, and yet we had a great sense of God's peace and protection. "It's a gift from the Lord once again to catch up on letter-writing and other jobs and generally to restore ourselves physically as we face the rest of the term. Don't be tempted to worry, because we know with real assurance that we are in the Lord's hands," I continued in my letter home. " He is teaching me so much in these days of finding refuge in Him and in fellowship with other believers. We are realising more and more the importance of obedience to His instruction, '...*do not be anxious about tomorrow, for tomorrow will be anxious for itself. Let the day's own trouble be sufficient for the day.'*[1]"

I was still keen to speak with my parents if at all possible, and who knew when I would next be able to get a letter home? By mid morning, I had managed to book a call home for nine o'clock in the evening, eight o'clock UK time. We were midway through a time of prayer together when the call came through and I heard the familiar UK ring tone and my father's voice. "Hi Dad, Mum, Hazel, Robin." The line was clear as crystal, and I was able to speak to each of the family in turn! Such a blessing, especially as Dad was happy to ring both Margaret and Kirstene's families with words of reassurance. "Sorry not to give you any warning," I later wrote, "but I just felt it was important to let you know we're quite safe and just trusting the Lord for His continual protection."

The night-time shooting continued that evening. The following day, I was writing home once again. "Beirut as a city is at a standstill. All is uncannily quiet here, with the factories that surround us also at a standstill. Fortunately, though we daren't move from Kafarshima, we are still able to contact people by phone. How grateful we are for the relative peace here when skirmishes and road blocks are still occurring in many areas of the city." By Wednesday evening, a ceasefire had been announced by the Prime Minister. But would it hold? As the Lebanese husband of one of the

---

[1] Matthew 6:34 (RSV)

teachers said, "It's like an Aspro[2] to ease the pain and certainly no real solution." Nevertheless, that night was quieter, and I wrote home, "Quite a number of the roads are still blocked, but traffic seems to be moving again here." It was decided we should be cautious about reopening the school for another few days in order not to put the school buses in dangerous situations. "Many innocents have suffered losses in their families through indiscriminate shooting and explosions, and there has been quite a lot of damage to shops, factories and buildings. The main roads have been cleared, but there's a lot of broken glass in the worst-hit areas and it's not really safe to be out at night."

By the time school did reopen on Tuesday, April 22nd, we were sensing a strong desire for a return to normality. Some parents were still too nervous to let their children come back to school, but as one father said to me, "So long as you don't anger anyone who happens to be holding a gun, you're okay!" Letters from home were finally coming through and this was reassuring. "How the prayers of people back home have been answered," I wrote, "especially over all that happened on our Egypt trip and His wonderful provision, then two weeks of teaching in exceptionally hot, windy weather and now this week of troubles." Each day was a gift from God, whether we could open the school or not. I was thankful to have picked up strength physically and been able to catch up on schoolwork. "God seems to be teaching me more and more to pick enough manna for today and claim His strength for this day and no more," I wrote to my parents, "simply trusting the rest into His care." And to my grandmother, I wrote on the back of a postcard, "We are all just so thankful for safety during these troubled weeks and for a deep sense of God's peace in a situation which is still somewhat tense."

In early May, and with a few days' break for the celebration of the Greek Orthodox Easter, almost as if we knew of the impending travel restrictions as Lebanon stumbled towards civil disorder, I wrote home, "Margaret, Kirstene and I went with the IVF crowd on what turned out to be the most relaxing day's outing I've enjoyed for some time." The President's summer palace of Beit Eddine was a short drive south from Kafarshima up into the Chouf mountains. It was built in the early nineteenth century by the then Emir, the Ottoman-appointed governor of the region, and sits majestically on a hill surrounded by terraced gardens,

[2] Aspro is a brand name for aspirin, a mild analgesic used to relieve pain or inflammation.

Trip to Beit Eddine with LIVF friends (Nadia, Margaret and Kirstene on left), May 1975.

orchards and olive groves. It was in 1943 that Lebanon's first president after independence, Bechara el Khoury, declared it to be his summer residence. "We picnicked amongst the trees just below the palace, amidst a carpet of wild flowers – absolutely beautiful." During the day, I chatted with a number of people about renting accommodation for the next school year, as Margaret and Kirstene had both decided not to renew their contracts with the school. It would be 'all change' in our fifth-floor flat, and I was wondering whether the time had come for me to stretch my wings and move out of the school building. Coupled with this was the idea of having my own car. "I'm still praying very much re the car situation for next year," I wrote home, "and if it's right to continue living here with a new group of people and spend the extra money on a car, then I simply trust the Lord will show His will."

In addition to the trip to Beit Eddine, I was able to go with Sandra to the Piccadilly Theatre in Rue Hamra, the main street in Ras Beirut, not far from the Alliance Church. It was an unforgettable performance by possibly the most famous singer in Lebanon, indeed the whole Arab world. Her name was Fairuz. Piccadilly Theatre was a major venue for concerts, musicals and plays in Lebanon at the time. Modelled after the theatre of its name in London's West End, it attracted people from all walks of life in Lebanese society. Seated on plush red velvet seats and listening to Fairuz and her family performing was a real joy. The music was such a subtle fusion of Arabic folk melodies and romantic lyrics with live Western-style orchestral accompaniment, including some Arabic instruments such as the lute. The musical play we attended, *Mais El Reem*, included scenes from Lebanese villages in the mountains, with singing and dancing in traditional costumes. I was entranced and keen to experience as much of this country and its culture as I could. I wrote home, "Tomorrow I'm due to go out for the day with Afaf and her mother and uncle and numerous cousins. I think there are to be three carloads, so it should be a real Lebanese outing!"

We set off mid morning, driving north from Beirut along the coast road, passing Jounieh and Byblos and turning inland near Batroun towards Mseilha Castle, a little compact sixteenth-century fortress. It stands alone atop a detached rocky spur in the centre of the Dog River valley and is built like a ship to conform to the shape of the rock. Legend has it that the castle was near the site of

Trip with Afaf's family to Mseilha Castle, May 1975.

an ancient Roman settlement. We did notice traces of a Roman road passing through the valley as we walked through cultivated fields towards the castle. There was a picnic spot by the stream from which we could view it and an ancient arched bridge. It seemed such a privilege to be accepted by this close-knit family, who chatted away in Arabic and yet spoke excellent English to me. That evening, I continued in my letter home, "I hope to spend the last day of the Orthodox Easter holiday doing schoolwork and then back to school, I trust, for the remaining six weeks of term." But that was not to be.

School did open normally for two weeks, during which time the children enjoyed a school trip to Hadeth, a nearby village where the Hungarian State Circus had pitched their tents. The children were very excited at seeing lions, tigers and monkeys for the first time in their lives. They laughed with the clowns and held their breath as the acrobats and trapeze artists performed their stunts. It was followed by much interesting conversation, story-writing and artwork in school about clowns, elephants, circus rings and acrobats, with huge collage pictures decorating the walls of the classrooms.

Assemblies too were full of interesting stories of how Jesus' followers continued to know God's love and care even though they could no longer see Him in person. There followed the story of the mighty wind and the flames of fire as the Holy Spirit came to live in their hearts so that they would never be alone, just as Jesus had promised. God would always be their helper and we could always pray:

Thank you, God, for love and care,
Round about us everywhere.

163

One of our favourite songs spoke of these truths too:

God is a Father,
He is always there;
Whatever happens,
He still will care.

On the last day of term we sang together:

Jesus loves me, this I know,
For the Bible tells me so.
Little ones to Him belong,
They are weak but He is strong.
Yes, Jesus loves me,
Yes, Jesus loves me,
Yes, Jesus loves me,
The Bible tells me so.[3]

I too was clinging on to these simple promises as the government and the country now launched into one crisis after another. I wrote to my parents, "I can't praise God enough for the way He lays it on people's hearts to pray. Prayer is a powerful weapon against Satan's fiery darts, which can be so subtle and persistent, and truly He is answering in the most remarkable ways!" I was still in prayer about the possibility of having my own car in the autumn after my planned summer break in the UK. Imagine my delight when Afaf offered to lend me hers when I needed to run a friend home from the IVF Bible study one evening! I had driven Afaf's Morris 1100 when we were on holiday in Syria and Jordan, but never in Lebanon. This was the answer to my prayer for now, because the purchase of a car, even second-hand, was beyond my means. As I wrote home, "The Lord has given me a wonderful peace about it all." There was also the question of accommodation for the following school year that was still unclear. "I am now, however, the proud possessor of a single bed and a collapsible round table," I wrote home. "The bed and mattress have cost me about eight pounds and the table five pounds, and I've also got an iron for just over one pound!"

The last summer outing with our IVF friends was to Baalbeck, two hours' drive from Beirut. The town is home to a huge temple complex, including the Roman ruins of the temples of Bacchus and Jupiter. Known

[3] Anna B. Warner (1827-1915)

in Greco-Roman times as Heliopolis, sun city, the town borders the fertile plain of the Beka'a Valley and boasts smaller ruins of the Round Temple of Venus, town walls and important Roman mosaics from private homes. "I was completely overwhelmed by Baalbeck," I wrote home. "The actual size of the remaining pillars of the three Roman temples which once stood there, set against the background of the anti-Lebanon mountains (Mount Hermon range) is absolutely staggering. None of the postcards or slides I have seen can do it justice." It was a long and happy day as we picnicked and marvelled until dusk, when the *Son et Lumière* began to light up the night sky. I shall never forget the vivid description of Roman Emperors driving through Baalbeck to offer sacrifices to the great god Jupiter. "One could almost see the Roman chariots and merrymakers as they marched through in triumph." No wonder Paul wrote to the church of God in Corinth in the first century AD, *"...thanks be to God, who in Christ always leads us in triumph, and through us spreads the fragrance of the knowledge of him everywhere."*[4]

Sunday mornings at church in Beirut continued, followed by lunch out with friends. During the week, we were able to hold parents' meetings for the kindergarten children. One-to-one Bible studies continued too, until Wednesday, May 21st when there was another flare-up between opposing left- and right-wing political factions in East Beirut. It was only four weeks since the previous gun battles had died down. We had tried to keep the school open for as long as we could, but parents who lived near the besieged Beirut suburbs were understandably cautious and kept their children at home. The next day, Thursday, was declared a General Strike – and therefore no school, as the bus drivers would not be allowed to work. This was followed by a ceasefire that was ignored, as the gunfire continued. I realised it was totally unsafe to travel into Beirut to lead the IVF Bible study that evening because of the risk of being caught in the midst of sniping and indiscriminate shooting from cars. By Friday morning, a second ceasefire had been broken and the fighting continued. "We could hear it more at night, artillery and mortar fire blasting off and, of course, the inevitable shooting."

I had been asked by Hazel to speak at her coffee morning for English-speaking mothers, which was held every alternate Friday in the sitting room of our fifth-floor flat. All had been arranged for another teacher to take my class that morning, but as school was closed, the coffee morning

4 2 Corinthians 2:14

was postponed. I was actually quite thankful, as the noise and disruption was beginning to take its toll. I wrote to my parents, "I'm really sure the Lord had His purpose behind all this. He just knew that I was in no fit state emotionally or spiritually to be taking meetings. In fact, I just didn't know how I was going to face either Thursday evening or Friday morning, and by His grace He overruled."

I had already been struggling with extreme tiredness due to broken nights. "It's been as much as I can do to stagger down to school in the mornings. I've simply been clinging to the Lord, who has proved so wonderfully how He provides just the right people at the right time, as well as comfort and relief from His Word." Colossians 1:11-14 became increasingly precious: *"…being strengthened with all power according to his glorious might so that you may have great endurance and patience, and joyfully giving thanks to the Father, who has qualified you to share in the inheritance of his holy people in the kingdom of light. For he has rescued us from the dominion of darkness and brought us into the kingdom of the Son he loves, in whom we have redemption, the forgiveness of sins."*

On Saturday morning, a third ceasefire was announced and a military government formed with a Brigadier General as Prime Minister, solely as an interim measure before returning to civilian government in order to bring fighting to a halt. At around 10 pm on the previous evening, as the new government was declared on Lebanese radio, "there was an enormous amount of gunfire and shots all around us like pop-gun shooting, and we all with one accord moved into the corridor!" How we laughed when we realised the shooting was all part of the celebrations for the new Prime Minister! It was a quiet night after that and all seemed calm on the roads, though we detected cautiousness about the new military government and wondered whether the ceasefire would hold. I wrote to my parents, "We are learning more and more out here in these present circumstances to live no more than one day at a time. It's pretty nigh impossible to plan ahead for anything and it makes one realise how precious each day is."

The national cautiousness was well founded. The evening of the third ceasefire was alive with street fighting in Beirut, and it was impossible to drive into the city for church on the Sunday morning. "We were able to have our own service here with the Khoury family, who came down to our flat from upstairs." Listening to the BBC World Service news from London confirmed the worst night of fighting yet. "The frightening thing that keeps people in their homes," I wrote to my parents, "is the snipers and armed men driving through the streets and likely to shoot quite indiscriminately." As the news bulletin drew to a close, there was a brisk phone call from the British Consul to say that all British people should regard themselves on a twenty-four-hour curfew until we had further news of developments. The military government had run its course and the new three-day-old Prime Minister had been forced to resign. "We've just heard that the whole military government has

Granny Radcliffe.

resigned and gun battles have started again," I continued in my letter home. "Please, please pray for this country, that the Lord would keep the witness of His church strong." More and more we were realising the truth of Hebrews 13:14 (RSV), *"For here we have no lasting city, but we seek the city which is to come."* It was good to remind each other of Jesus, the One who was preparing a place for His followers in that glorious city to come. *"...our citizenship is in heaven. And we eagerly await a Saviour from there, the Lord Jesus Christ."*[5]

Even though we were unable to reopen the school for the rest of the month, I was able to write home, "We are so, so fortunate out here in Kafarshima to be able to walk about the village and go and visit people, whereas in Beirut there are still barricades, numerous security check points and sporadic shooting." Some days the news was more encouraging, as I wrote home on Tuesday, May 27th: "News this morning is better and it seems a civil war has been averted." The next day, I added, "There was a little shooting during the night and a few explosions, but it really does seem to be dying down. Please ask the church to continue in prayer for His people here and especially that Lebanon might remain an open door for the gospel and that peace may return."

Hazel's friend, who was flying to England that week, was able to take our letters for posting to family and friends. I wrote to Granny Radcliffe in tiny writing on the back of a postcard I had bought in Baalbeck. It depicted

5   Philippians 3:20

Lebanese folklore dancers in their traditional costumes with a backdrop of the magnificent Roman temples there. "We visited Baalbeck for the first time a few weeks ago. Thank you for your prayers. These last few days have not been easy, though we have certainly not been in the midst of the shooting ourselves. How wonderful it is to know the peace that passes understanding, especially in these unsettled days. People are moving around more now. More and more, I'm finding God's Word is so full of promises, especially Matthew 6:34: *'Do not worry about tomorrow, for tomorrow will worry about itself. Each day has enough trouble of its own.'*"

To my great joy, I was actually able to speak with my eighty-five-year-old widowed grandmother very soon after writing the postcard. I had been trying to ring my parents for over a week, forgetting that it was Spring Bank Holiday week in England and they would quite likely be on holiday in our caravan in Abersoch, North Wales. On Sunday, June 1st at 7.45 am UK time, I tried again to no avail, so on the spur of the moment I asked the operator if she would be willing to try another line, Ashton 1238, Granny's number. "To my surprise," I wrote to my parents, "we were through in seconds! I suppose Granny has the phone by her bed. I told her we are obviously not going out except for around the immediate neighbourhood and that we are enjoying hot weather. I was so happy to hear her voice – and your news too." I continued, "We are loathe to travel around too much and will certainly not bring the school buses while there is danger of shooting from cars and kidnapping between rival political groups."

We were hoping to reopen on Monday, June 2nd for the local children in Kafarshima and surrounding villages, with a skeleton staff for those families who lived near enough to the school to bring their children in safety. There was no doubt that this was a test of faith to prove, as I wrote home that "the wisest thing is to trust the Lord for the next twenty-four hours and commit the future, which still has so many unanswered questions, into God's hands and rest in Him". In my prayer diary, I wrote, "Lord, help me to view each new day as if it were my last and live it for You. Holy Spirit of God, please lead me today, one step at a time." On Monday morning, we cautiously reopened the school. I wrote home, "Although we only had a handful of children, it's lovely to feel we are doing something positive for the children round here whose parents feel it's safe enough to bring them. We live twenty-four hours at a time." Further, I wrote, "Keep praying that the Lord would restrain the intentions of wicked men who are seeking to stir up trouble and highlight contro-versy, keeping people in this state of fear and tension."

The remaining weeks of June leading up to the end of term were extremely volatile in terms of who would actually arrive in school on any particular day. It was becoming increasingly tiring for both staff and children as the days grew hotter and stickier. Though the stories and rumours were unsettling and the nights sometimes disturbed by shooting in the distance and the occasional bang nearby, we kept remarkably safe within the school building and the immediate environment. As I wrote home, "So far, in Kafarshima we have been wonderfully protected, and we just praise the Lord for this." I also reassured my parents that we were heeding the warnings from the British Consul. "Kidnapping and torturing incidents are horrifying and make one feel physically sick. For this reason, we are being very careful about travelling around and definitely not after dark."

There was one incident that occurred at that time that I decided not to recount to my parents. I was in the back seat of a *servis* car as we drove through nearby Hadeth on the main road into Beirut. The driver overtook a large Mercedes car, parked outside the hospital with its boot wide open. I took a cursory glance inside the boot and noticed a mutilated corpse covered in blood. We had passed in a flash, and I shuddered in disbelief. Why should the Lord allow me to witness such a horrific sight? It hit me hard: *this sectarian warfare is real, and it is happening right on my doorstep.* On reflection, I felt I could now empathise more readily as I listened to people's stories of similar atrocities. Yes, the times were becoming increasingly dangerous. I was blessed in knowing the peace of the Lord's overruling and protection in response to the prayers of friends and loved ones.

I had started reading from Colossians in my daily 'quiet times', and shared in my letter home, "Tremendous promises from His Word to lay claim upon – being filled with the knowledge of His will, spiritual wisdom and understanding, and, most precious of all at this time, *'being strengthened with all power according to His glorious might so that you may have great endurance and patience.'[6]*" I continued, "Praise Him for this oh-so-necessary daily strengthening from His Word."

On the Friday before the end of term, I was able to fulfil the promise I had made to Hazel to speak at her ladies' English coffee morning held in

[6] Colossians 1:11

the lounge of our fifth-floor flat. This had been postponed four times, and I would have been sorry to miss the opportunity to share with this group of English-speaking ladies. Each one had married into a Lebanese family and was living in Lebanon, bringing up her children in this culture. The group included Joy, Jill and Joan who taught in the pre-school, as well as Suzette from South Africa with whom I enjoyed one-to-one Bible study, and the Canadian mother of Marwan in my Transition class. All lived locally and were keen to study the Bible and share the ups and downs of raising a family within a cross-cultural marriage. I respected them all, especially as I myself still had much to learn cross-culturally. It was a real privilege to share thoughts from the Bible about working with children as parents and teachers and invite discussion as we went along.

I read from 2 Kings chapter 4 and then spoke of Elisha's visit to Shunem, where he stayed regularly with a well-to-do Shunammite woman and her husband. In gratitude, Elisha prophesied that they would have a son, and so it came to pass. The boy grew until one day tragedy struck. He suffered a very bad headache in the heat of the day in his father's field and later died in his mother's arms. She laid him on the bed where Elisha rested when staying with them. With the mothers, we spoke of how they would feel if something like this happened in their families, especially at this current time of unrest in the country. Might the Shunammite woman have become bitter towards God, who had given her this child and now seemingly taken him away? How did she react? Even though she was from a different culture, she had great faith that Elisha, the man of God, would be able to help. Twice she told both her husband and Elisha's servant that she knew all was well in spite of the pain of her loss; such faith that, through Elisha, God could do something for her child! We spoke of times of anxiety over our children and considered this woman's faith. Whatever problems we faced with our children, and I saw many in the classroom, God can always do something and, furthermore, bring peace of heart. As the woman said, *"Everything is all right."*[7]

Elisha responded and took action immediately as he returned to the house and sized up the situation. There was no interrogation, simply acceptance and a desire to prevail upon God in prayer. Elisha did not understand why this had happened any more than the boy's mother, but he clearly believed that the boy could be restored to life and that God could

7   2 Kings 4:26b

do it. I told the mothers that I believed this to be true at a spiritual level every time I stood before the children and prayed with them in Assembly.

Elisha was willing to completely identify himself with this precious child. What an example for us! If we desire to do this with children in our care, we need to find that simple childlike faith that Jesus urged us to exercise. *"Truly I tell you, unless you change and become like little children, you will never enter the kingdom of heaven."*[8] What exactly is it about a child's attitude that caused Jesus to commend it and, furthermore, make it a condition for entering the Kingdom of God? Jesus goes on to say that *"whoever takes the lowly position of this child is the greatest in the kingdom of heaven"*[9]. It is the child's attitude of simple trust that delights the heart of God.

Elisha acknowledged before God his utter helplessness in the face of this tragic situation. Scripture simply tells us he *"prayed to the LORD"*[10]. It was no ordinary prayer. He lay over the child, mouth to mouth, eyes to eyes, hands to hands. He completely identified himself with the child. To me, this was the secret of teaching effectively, and I discussed with the mothers how this identification applies to our relationship with the children in our care. 'Mouth to mouth' signifies language, learning to speak the language of a child and, more importantly, to listen to what they say to us. Were we prepared not to speak down to a child but to speak simply and clearly and give explanations? Could we let the children know that we do value their thoughts but are not going to be manipulated by them? 'Eyes to eyes' indicates learning to see the world through the eyes of a child. So much of a child's initial learning comes from what they see. How can we find ways of guiding what a child sees while not over-shielding them from life? What about the television? Getting to bed in good time? 'Hands to hands' points to how we learn to think and feel as a child does. My experience in teaching thus far had shown me that a child has an acute conscience and is very aware of right and wrong, of fair play and injustice. How can I listen and help him to process his thoughts and feelings? How can I model fairness and generosity? What would Jesus do?

Finally, we discussed how totally Elisha identified with the boy in his prayer that God would bring the Shunammite's son back to life. What a huge responsibility we have to our children, trusting that God would work

---

[8] Matthew 18:3
[9] Matthew 18:4
[10] 2 Kings 4:33

End of year staff party in Khourys'
sixth-floor flat.
Top: Mona in foreground.
Bottom: Jill in foreground.

in each heart by His Spirit and that each one would become a follower of Jesus.

I was thrilled at the answer to prayer concerning a car for the following term. It was most unexpected as Joan, who had lent me her two-year-old Fiat 127 with only 28,300 kilometres on the clock, decided to return to Sierra Leone where her husband was working and, after a brief discussion about payment, simply handed me the keys! Joan also suggested I should occupy her flat on the fourth floor of the school building on my return in September. Even though I had prayed and searched for accommodation outside the building, this proved to be the safest place for me in the even more uncertain days to come.

My flights home for the summer months had been booked by our friendly travel agent some weeks previously. He had achieved the best price by booking a three-month excursion ticket with Royal Jordanian Airlines, to include a two-night stopover in Amman, Jordan, staying with the friends whom we had visited the previous Christmas. I had given the flight times to my parents in an earlier letter and it ended with "London-Manchester BE4076 2nd July 17.50 arr 18.35. Please keep the date free for the Grand Reunion!"

The end of term came all too quickly, with renewed fighting, mainly at night. Rockets and artillery fire were heard in the southern suburbs of Beirut between Kafarshima and the city centre. I had barely a week to pack and prepare for the flight home. The day after we finished school, the Khoury family invited the whole staff team, including those who were leaving, for a farewell gathering in their apartment on the sixth floor of the school building. There was a huge table laden with scrumptious Lebanese nibbles – savoury pastries such as *sanbusak*, *lahma bi ajeen*, *fatayer* and *filo* pastries. There were stuffed *kibbeh* torpedo-shaped meatballs as well as sweet pastries such as *baklava, konafa, ma'amoul* with both date and nut fillings, and *ghorayebah*. It was a memorable feast, tinged with sadness as a number of the staff team were leaving and the days ahead in Lebanon were so uncertain politically. Amine made a speech, thanking the teachers for all their hard work as we drew to the end of the second year of Eastwood College. Hazel added her thanks and also congratulated Amine on achieving his BA degree from the American University of Beirut. She entertained us all by reading her limerick after the style of Edward Lear.

To Amine

There once was a boy named Amine,
his equal has seldom been seen.
He sat in the class
and saw as in a glass
the school that he hoped to begin.

His father, surprised, yet agreed,
that with people to help and to lead
he'd give him the place
as a permanent base.
"Nashkur Allah!" he always replied.

With invaluable help from Miss Jones
and visits, committees and phones
he collected a team
to give form to his dream,
the people to add to the stones.

The first was his friend, truly clever
with money, accounts, in all weather.
So Samuel Nasrallah
with Hazel to follow
joined in with his Eastwood endeavour.

Then others, they helped with this feat
Edmond and Tony who worked in the heat.
They dug up the earth,
brought playgrounds to birth
while banana trees beat a retreat.

'Twas Madame supported him too,
with uniforms, orange and blue,
with food and advice
she's invariably nice
to the staff and to guests, not a few.

Now see them arrive in a van or by air,
from Lebanon too, each part to prepare.
There's Kirstene, yes Poole,
who sure is no fool,
and Wendy who leads below stair.

You also should meet Margaret Readdy,
so resourceful and witty and steady.
They'll be leaving us soon
to our sorrow and gloom,
she and Kirstene, complete with guitar.

And Sarah, Armande and Andrée,
they've helped each in a different way.
They've cheered up us all
big, medium and small,
as to Eastwood they add something gay.

So now to a man, a BA,
we bring our best wishes today.
We hope you give praise
as at Eastwood you gaze,
"Nashkur Allah, Hamdillah" for aye.

22nd June 1975

In spite of the renewed fighting, I was able to drive Joan and her two children to the airport for their early flight to Freetown and then take over the car! I visited friends in Beirut, including Afaf and Nadia, whom we had visited in Alexandria at Easter. That evening, I stayed the night with Afaf, only to find myself stranded in her building for the whole weekend as it was unsafe to drive back to Kafarshima. On Monday, June 30th, I was due to fly to Amman, but it proved impossible to reach the airport and I was only half packed! Thankfully, the next day, a new cabinet was formed and a ceasefire announced, so I drove back to the school during a lull in the fighting and finished my packing. Flights duly rearranged, I flew Beirut-Amman-London-Manchester on Wednesday, July 2nd. It was a marathon of a journey, over twelve hours, and so good to see my father at the terminal in Manchester. I was reminded of our final Assembly at school and the story of Moses and the burning bush. When God told Moses to go back to Egypt, He gave him a promise: *"My Presence will go with you, and I will give you rest."*[11]

This is His peace that passes understanding, loving faith at rest. *"And the peace of God, which transcends all understanding, will guard your hearts and your minds in Christ Jesus."*[12]

[11] Exodus 33:14
[12] Philippians 4:7

CHAPTER SIXTEEN

Shooting Permitting

It was early on Tuesday, September 16th, and I was sitting on my suitcase urging it to close so that I could fasten the buckles and bump it down the stairs. My father was waiting outside to take me to Manchester Airport for the 7.45 am shuttle flight to London Heathrow. From there, I was scheduled to leave on the Royal Jordanian Airlines flight to Amman and then to Beirut, due to arrive at 8.20 pm Lebanese time. I had said goodbye to the rest of the family the evening before. Dad and I made a pact at the airport before I left him for Departures. It was simply "no news is good news", and I promised to write as often as I could, sending letters with kind friends flying out of the country.

I was always excited to be flying back to Lebanon, and this day was no different in spite of the political uncertainties. I loved the views from the cabin window as we descended over Beirut to Amman. All seemed deceptively quiet that day as we flew down the Lebanese coastline, over the wide bay of Jounieh and the apartment blocks of the city, inland over Syria and down over the seven hills of Amman, towards the airport. After a brief wait in the transit lounge, it was a fifty-minute low-level flight back to Beirut.

I had been back in England for just under three months, and the weeks had flown by! After the initial first few days of absorbing the absence of shooting and the smell of roses, the lighter evenings and the fresher air, I was keen to visit friends and family to thank them for their loving support and their prayers. I had arrived home on July 2nd, having left Beirut airport some ten hours or so after the latest ceasefire had been announced. It had been without doubt the most violent of the three political crises so far in 1975, starting in April, recurring in May and again in June just as the school year was drawing to its close.

Only two evenings before arriving home in England, when the shooting and machine gunfire was at its height, I had received a phone call from Joy, the English wife of a Lebanese pastor and mother of one of the children in Transition. We were so thankful for underground telephone cables at that time. She was asking me to ring her parents in Newark on my return to England and assure them of her safety and that of the family. I remember her words so clearly. "Be realistic," she said, "and don't hide anything from

Taken for the *Stockport Advertiser*, 14th August, 1975.

them. Tell them we have a God who is completely trustworthy and who keeps His promises." She went on to tell me of what had happened the night before. For some days, she, her husband Sami and the two children, aged five and nine, had been sleeping on their mattresses in the centre of the six-storey block of flats in which they lived, in a particularly hard-hit area of Beirut. Bullets and rockets were literally ricocheting off the buildings by the minute. That particular evening, before falling into a fitful sleep, they had been reading from Psalm 91 together as a family. *"Whoever dwells in the shelter of the Most High will rest in the shadow of the Almighty. I will say of the LORD, 'He is my refuge and my fortress, my God, in whom I trust.'"* Continuing the psalm, there were so many promises to cling on to. *"...he will save you ... He will cover you ... his faithfulness will be your shield and rampart. You will not fear the terror of the night, nor the arrow that flies by day ... 'Because he loves me,' says the LORD, I will rescue him; I will protect him..."* And so they committed themselves to the Lord for another night of shooting.

In the early hours of the morning, Joy woke up with a very definite conviction that their building was about to be hit badly by some sort of

177

machine gunfire. She decided to wake her husband and two children and warn them that something was about to happen, but to remember God's promises in Psalm 91, particularly with respect to God's faithfulness being a shield of protection round about them. Just as she was speaking, there was a terrific explosion as the balcony on the fifth floor immediately below them was literally blasted off and crashed to the ground. Simultaneously, the sound of breaking glass was heard as electric light bulbs, placed in the shape of a large illuminated cross on the wall of the neighbouring building, fell to the ground, shattered by rocket fire. Later when Sami spoke to me on the phone, his words were simply, "We were saved by the Cross."

During the summer months in England, I was able to share with family and various groups of praying friends that the situation in Lebanon was still tense as the balance of power shifted from one political group to another. As Joy had said, I was as realistic as I could be, very aware that we too had been shielded and protected throughout those difficult months. I shared how during times of shooting and kidnappings, all schools had been closed along with shops and offices. Whenever it had been safe to travel, life had gone on steadily between the ceasefires, but with a self-imposed curfew after dark. I was convinced that our school was part of the ongoing work of Christ in Lebanon and could truly thank God for that country where there is freedom, unique in the Middle East, for the preaching of the gospel. I was equally convinced that teaching there was God's continuing call on my life, in spite of the ups and downs of the summer term.

I based myself at home in Marple and travelled from there a great deal. Not long after my return from Lebanon, I found a little job as a dinner lady at a primary school in Old Glossop, a short drive away from our home. I lasted just six days! Dinner ladies are special people and I have a huge admiration for them, especially when the weather is too wet for the children to go out to play! I did, however, succeed in helping my mother's sister Pat gain confidence in driving her Fiat 127, a similar model to the car I had acquired in Lebanon from Joan.

1975 was a glorious summer, and as well as visiting family in the Manchester area, I was able to reconnect with friends in the Wirral and worship at St Mary's Upton. In early August, I drove my brother Robin and Granny Radcliffe to Cheltenham, and we stayed with my father's sister, Una. Later in the month, I drove down the M6 again to visit friends in Cheltenham from college days and worshipped at St. Barnabas. Precious were these times and good to thank so many, including friends at All Saints Marple, who had given so much encouragement and support, not only to me but to my parents, especially when life became so uncertain. My box of slides and the projector were always to hand along with photos of the school and the children. Printed in the church magazine for September 1975 were my heartfelt thanks: "Should I not have the opportunity to see all of you personally who have prayerfully supported the school in Lebanon during these last two years I have been working there, please accept my thanks now for your partnership in prayer. Hopefully, I shall be returning to Beirut on September 16th for a further year's teaching. Please continue to pray for us there, that the Word of God and the claims of Jesus Christ may go out powerfully in truth and excellence whatever the conditions." As Paul wrote, *"In all my prayers for all of you, I always pray with joy because of your partnership in the gospel from the first day until now."*[1]

On Sunday, September 7th, shooting broke out in Tripoli, north Lebanon. Dad and I watched it on the TV news that evening. What to do? I clearly recall my father's words: "God called you to this work. You knew it was right to renew your contract, so we must let you go in faith that He will keep and protect you at all times, whatever the circumstances." It was just over a week before I was due to fly back to Beirut for the new school year. Everywhere I travelled that week, I solicited prayer for the Lebanese at a time of growing street violence among different political factions. I asked for prayer, too, for myself, as I embarked upon this third year at the school working with the teachers, the children and their families whom I had grown to love so much.

Tuesday, September 16th was a very long day, and I prayed my suitcase would be transferred successfully from one flight to another. All went according to plan. I was glad to be met in the pitch dark by my Lebanese friend Afaf, who took me to her flat in Beirut for an overnight stay. In my first letter home, I wrote, "The first highlight of the year was undoubtedly your phone call on Tuesday evening. We had barely been back at Afaf's for maybe thirty minutes or so and I could hardly credit it – thank you so much. It meant more to me than I can tell you." My father had a promise he wanted to share and he read it out to me down a crystal-clear phone line: *"The LORD will keep you from all harm – he will watch over your life; the LORD will watch over your coming and going both now and for*

[1] Philippians 1:4,5

Vines growing on rooftop in
Kafarshima, September 1974.

evermore."[2] I later wrote, "How wonderful it was to hear you all on Tuesday evening. Events have been many and various since then, but through it all those promises from Psalm 121 have been fulfilled again and again."

I was glad to be back in Lebanon. Next morning, Afaf left for work in a friend's car and kindly lent me hers to drive to Kafarshima and the school with my suitcase in the boot. The plan was to drive the car back the following day and return to school by *servis* or taxi. All seemed normal as I readjusted to driving on the right and made my way out of West Beirut through the southern suburbs and out onto the Sidon Road to Kafarshima, a journey of about seven miles. There were a couple of weeks to settle in, help the new teachers to adjust and prepare the classrooms before we were due to open school on Wednesday, October 1st. As I drove, I was looking forward to creating my own little home in the flat at the southern end of the fourth floor of the school building that had been vacated by Joan and her family. It comprised a kitchen-cum-sitting-room, fully glazed with an extensive view west towards the airport and glorious sunsets over the Mediterranean Sea. There was one bedroom with a fitted wardrobe facing east, which was flooded with sunshine in the mornings and had a small balcony overlooking the narrow path leading up into the village. The bathroom was just off the main corridor that led from the lift to the flat. Joan had left net curtains for the large windows at the front and pretty floral curtains in the sitting room and bedroom as well as some furniture and kitchen equipment. I was pleased to be able to add my own bed, coffee table and iron!

I anticipated a welcome as I made my way up the drive that led to Eastwood College and I was not disappointed. On honking the horn, the caretaker Jusef arrived and pulled back the huge metal gate to reveal the family's barking dog and some of his children. Samer, Rosa and Lina were in school with me, and it was good to see them all again. How thankful I was for the provision of my own flat in the security of the school building. My slightly battered suitcase was hauled out of the boot and carried to the

---

[2] Psalm 121:7,8

180

lift, and after hugs and kisses all round, I escaped to the sixth floor for lunch with the Khoury family. They had been away for part of the summer, but were pleased to be back and gave me an equally warm welcome. Hazel, the headmistress, had already returned to her flat on the fifth floor. She had spent part of the summer in Morocco, where her brother and family and her sister Patricia lived, caring for their elderly mother. We met during that afternoon for a cup of tea, and Hazel shared more about how her mother had gradually weakened and died from the frailty of old age. How thankful the family was that Hazel had decided to visit Tangier at that time.

I had a particular memory of Mrs St John that I shared with Hazel. As we were leaving Tangier at the end of our visit to the mission compound a few years previously, the elderly lady had asked to see us to say goodbye. She prayed for me from her bed and then handed me a small piece of folded paper. On the one side, it read, "Goodbye message." "Read this on the plane," she said. It was very brief: "Numbers 6:24-26. With my love." I looked up the verses in my Authorised Version (AV) when I arrived home. *"The Lord bless thee and keep thee: The Lord make his face shine upon thee, and be gracious unto thee: The Lord lift up His countenance upon thee, and give thee peace."* I had no doubt that the blessing was not only for then but also for now, as we were about to face yet more disruption, danger and uncertainty.

That evening, I started cleaning and unpacking in the flat, and met the two new teachers who had arrived that day from London. I slept well in my own bed, but it became obvious, as shooting was heard nearby the following morning, that the situation was deteriorating and roads becoming unsafe. It would not be possible to drive Afaf's car back to West Beirut that day, but Jill's husband Halim did arrive via back roads from nearby Hadeth, with the battery for my Fiat 127 fully charged along with half a tank's worth of petrol in tin cans! During the summer, he had given the car a thorough service and "spent a deal of time rubbing down the rusty parts of the bodywork and repainting," I was pleased to recount to my parents. Furthermore, "because I had forgotten to leave him the key for the petrol cap and as the fuel gauge doesn't work unless you bash it hard, he, thinking there was no petrol in it at all, had wrenched out the old cap and fitted a new one which is far superior!" I was so grateful. He also brought all my plants that Jill had cared for during the summer, and I placed them around the flat. "All roads into town are now declared unsafe," I wrote home, "and there was a ceasefire in the late afternoon which was broken within ten minutes. It was announced on the 4 pm news bulletin from London on the World Service that the Foreign Office had advised Britishers not to visit Lebanon without good reason." Here I was, having arrived back in Lebanon and just in time.

There was a great deal of shooting and some explosions in Kafarshima during Thursday night, and the girls upstairs slept on the floor in the corridor. I was thankful for my wax earplugs, which I often wore when sleeping overnight with friends in Beirut to dull the noise of the traffic. From 6 am on Friday morning, an eerie quiet prevailed in the village. I ventured out to shop locally, and later in the day drove with Hazel on the back road to Hadeth to bid farewell to the Adaimi family, whose son had been with us in the school. I had enjoyed regular Bible study with Suzette using *Navigator Study Notes* throughout the year. "She and her Lebanese husband, along with their son Mac, are going back to South Africa to settle there for good," I wrote home. "Who knows how many must have fled, not only to the mountains but out of the country altogether, because of the unsettled conditions," I continued in my letter. We were so glad to be able to see them at that time, because what followed was a dangerous night.

We had been studying Philippians chapter 1 together with the Khourys, a few verses each evening, and then praying together. That evening, Madame Khoury said to me, "This night, you sleep on your mattress in the corridor on the fourth floor." I understood this would be safer after the previous night's shooting in the village. She also reminded me to close the shutters and leave all windows open at the side and rear of the building. Around 10 pm, I could hear explosions in the distance. It was hard to settle, so I did odd jobs around the flat, showered and washed my hair. I eventually settled down to sleep just after midnight, by this time far too drowsy to drag my mattress into the corridor, despite Madame's warning. I fell into a fitful sleep. It was still pitch dark around 4 am when I became aware, despite earplugs, of the reality that the school building was in the midst of firing lines and a furious battle. The noise was deafening and there were bullets flying around and above the building. Mine was a corner bedroom with two outside walls and a balcony with two windows on each wall, so I knew I could not stay there. I stood in the corridor for a second or two, glanced at the end window and then staggered into the hallway by the lift shaft where, for no apparent reason, I found a chair! The mattress stayed in the bedroom because I knew I would not sleep and I felt the urgency of moving to the centre of the building.

The noise was ear-shattering, so I settled down in a corner on the chair, away from outside walls. I simply prayed through all I could remember from Psalm 91. *"...his faithfulness will be your shield and rampart. You will not fear the terror of the night, nor the arrow that flies by day, nor the pestilence that*

First bullet hole in my sitting room window, fourth floor, September 1975.

stalks in the darkness ... A thousand may fall at your side, ten thousand at your right hand, but it will not come near you. ... no harm will befall you."[3] I was thinking of the others too on the fifth floor and the Khourys on the sixth and seventh floors.

As dawn broke and the racket outside eventually subsided, I came back into my kitchen, stooping down to avoid attention, made a coffee and went back to bed. I woke at around 9 am, and walking down the corridor to the bathroom, I was amazed to see shattered glass and splinters of wood on the floor. On looking up, I saw a small hole towards the top of the door to that room and, on opening it, realised that two bullets had pierced through the front windows. One bullet had hit the opposite wall and sunk into it and the other had whizzed right across the room, through the closed door, across the corridor and into the plaster of the opposite wall. My legs turned to jelly; this was exactly the spot where I would have been sleeping had I taken my mattress into the corridor. I was overwhelmed with awe at the extent of the Lord's protection that night. *"For he will command his angels concerning you to guard you in all your ways."*[4] I also found a small bullet hole in the sitting room, but no damage apart from broken glass.

On recounting these events to my parents, I referred to the verse where Paul reassures all those who were praying for him, *"...I know that through your prayers and God's provision of the Spirit of Jesus Christ what has happened to me will turn out for my deliverance."*[5] I thanked them for "their faith to believe that the Lord would go before and protect whatever the circum-

[3] Psalm 91:4-7,10
[4] Psalm 91:11
[5] Philippians 1:19

stances". I truly believed that this protection set the seal on the Lord's call to me as I identified with the Lebanese at this uncertain and dangerous time in their history. We had many bullets in the building that night, so it was no real surprise to me when Hazel came down the following morning to be told we would all have to evacuate the building.

There followed two glorious weeks of recuperation from the shock and trauma of those few days under attack. We were by no means idle, and full of hope that the situation would quieten down and in due course we would be able to return to Kafarshima and reopen the school for the autumn term. We stayed initially in a guest house in Shemlan, a quiet village stretching along the ridge of the Chouf mountains that lay behind and above Kafarshima. The villa belonged to the Toroyan family who had children in school, and it had glorious views over the headland of Beirut (Ras Beirut), the airport and the Mediterranean Sea. "Shemlan is a favourite spot of mine," I wrote home, "and it's well away from snipers and noise. This time is a blessing in disguise, I think, because we are able to get to know each other and give the new girls a little 'holiday' which helps lessen the culture shock, and especially so as they arrived into such unfortunate circumstances."

When Margaret and I had first arrived in Lebanon, Hazel had taken us to Jisr el-Qadi, a village not far from Shemlan. We visited a potter working on his wheel who reminded me of the potter in the Old Testament prophecy of Jeremiah. "...I went down to the potter's house, and I saw him working at the wheel. But the pot he was shaping from the clay was marred in his hands; so the potter formed it into another pot, shaping it as seemed best to him."[6] Inspired by the visit, Margaret had written a poem that reminded me that we were still being shaped by the Potter's hand to fulfil the purpose for which He had called us, even in these uncertain days.

The Potter

A lump of mud and water;
undefined, useless, ugly,
common clay.
It stands void of meaning
on the workbench of life;
powerless, immobile.

---

[6] Jeremiah 18:3,4

184

The Potter comes,
gently lifts the clammy mass
onto His wheel.
Slowly, surely, His fingers move,
break down and knead
the unpromising material.
At first resisting,
gradually the clay becomes more pliable,
finally yields to his touch,
The Potter can begin.

Almost imperceptibly a shape takes form
quietly, slowly, inch by inch the vessel grows.
It is unique for
there is no mass production in this workshop.
Sometimes pressure is exerted
to eradicate a flaw.
He moulds so patiently,
nothing is allowed to mar
the vessel He has planned.

His practised eye selects
the instrument best suited to His task.
Then skilfully He scores
the smooth damp sides,
not to destroy
but to perfect
the exquisite design He had envisaged
before the world began.
Only the Master Craftsman could
create this thing of beauty
from a clod of common clay.

It is complete at last.
Finally the wheel spins
slowly to a halt.
The Potter rests,
satisfied.[7]

---

[7] Margaret Readdy, March 1974 (used with permission)

These two weeks in Shemlan were an ideal opportunity to experience the natural beauty of Lebanon and introduce the new teachers to some of our families. The days were fresher and the nights cooler than lower down the mountains. It was good to drive around making visits to reassure parents and their children that we were preparing to reopen school just as soon as the ceasefire held and it was safe to send transport. We were also able to drop down the twisty roads from Shemlan to visit Lebanese staff who lived in the other mountain villages like Bchemoun, home to Mona, one of my most loyal teachers. I loved visiting this household.

Mona lived with her brother and sister-in-law and their two children in the family home. A flat-roofed house, it was set back from the road and positioned at a lower level so the tops of the vines could be seen, providing shade from the beating sun. Visitors were ushered into the cool of the shuttered sitting room and urged to sit on one of the immaculate upholstered seats around the edge of the room to await a cool drink of lemonade or 7UP. As I got to know this family better, and in the cooler months, I would be invited into the parlour, a much cosier room with a central wood-burning stove with pipe above reaching through the ceiling. The washing would sometimes be draped around the stove and the children would be playing shyly in its warmth. It was a real privilege to be accepted by this Lebanese family and be able to practise my Arabic informally.

After our first quiet night in Shemlan with the ceasefire holding, I was able to drive down to Beirut in my Fiat and bring Afaf to Kafarshima to retrieve her car from the school parking area. "It was really hot as I drove along deserted roads with my half-tank of petrol," I wrote home. "I wasn't stopped till I reached the street where her building is, and then only by young lads with rifles wanting money for 'the cause'. I was stopped twice, and each time I just said I was sorry and couldn't speak Arabic and mercifully they let me go." Afaf returned with me to the school and was then able to follow me on the twisty drive back up to Shemlan. The next day, she invited me to visit her uncle and family in nearby Souk el-Gharb where they had a summer residence. It was a beautiful house surrounded by vines dripping with bunches of grapes of all varieties, flowering hibiscus and scented jasmine. I loved invitations to Lebanese homes and being immersed in Arabic culture and language. It was hard to believe from this distance that the country was so volatile politically and that reopening the school would be so hard to achieve.

There were others we knew from Beirut and Hadeth who had fled to Shemlan, including missionary friends of Hazel from Lebanon Evangelical Mission. On the first Sunday, we were able to join them in the mission house for morning worship and fellowship together. The following Sunday, likewise, as I wrote home, "We worshipped with the other missionaries in Shemlan in the morning, had lunch with the Khourys in the rather posh Hotel Hajjar in Souk el-Gharb just along the ridge, and then went to the Anglican church in Shemlan for evening prayer." I loved this little church. It was cool and refreshing. A sense of God's peace descended upon us as we listened to the familiar words from the *Prayer Book* and Rev. David Penman from the Lebanon IVF preached from God's Word: *"All authority in heaven and on earth has been given to me ... And surely I am with you always, to the very end of the age."*[8]

The following day, I took Hazel in the Fiat on my first real mountain drive. We were following David Penman on a long detour through the Lebanese mountains back down into Ras Beirut in order to arrive via safer roads into the north of the city. I described the journey in my letter home: "It was up twisty mountain roads and down into deep valleys all the way for two hours or more. What a stupendous drive, especially so as there was a really bad thunderstorm on the way back, but the Fiat bore up wonderfully as we battled along the narrow roads in second gear with hailstones beating on the windscreen!"

That night was quiet, so the next day Hazel and I ventured down to Kafarshima and the school. "I decided to stay the night and clean up the flat. At about 10.30 pm, I was sitting peacefully having a coffee, when suddenly there was a tremendous explosion just across the road and the sound of shattering glass." Such a shock! I crept out onto the balcony to see what had happened, "and there followed a second explosion!" I wrote home. I hurried to the lift shaft in the centre of the building, but there were no more. "It transpired that an employee at the furniture factory opposite the school was settling his private grudge against his boss."

Wednesday, October 1st was the day school should have reopened, but clearly this was not possible. There followed another night of mortars, rockets and reported kidnappings. Next day, I wrote home, "I was able to visit Mona in Bchemoun, who had a great sorrow because a very dear friend and her daughter were on the Malév plane from Budapest which crashed into the sea just six miles north of the airport on Monday evening."

8   Matthew 28:18,20

It was a privilege to don dark clothes and sit with this family in their shock and grief, drinking bitter coffee and upholding them in my prayers.

The following weekend, I drove along the coast road into Beirut and stayed overnight with Afaf and her mother. I later wrote home, "It was quite an experience to drive through Ras Beirut to church this morning. There are still water shortages, lack of street lighting and piles of rubbish being burnt in the streets." I was glad to arrive safely at the Alliance Church and be encouraged from Ecclesiastes 12:8: *"'Meaningless! Meaningless!' says the Teacher. 'Everything is meaningless!'"* It certainly seemed that way during these dangerous days. It was so good to be reassured that though life is brief and transitory, *"here is the conclusion of the matter: Fear God and keep his commandments, for this is the whole duty of all mankind. For God will bring every deed into judgment, including every hidden thing, whether it is good or evil."*[9] We were urged to "keep constantly praying for reconciliation and peace, and for those who have suffered so much in this latest outbreak, which has certainly been the worst," I continued in my letter home. That evening, I drove back to Shemlan for one more night and was able to receive holy communion at the Anglican church with David Penman preaching once again. This was to be my last time of worship in this little church.

Finally, it was deemed safe enough in Kafarshima for us all to return to the building. The caretaker Jusef and his family had worked hard to clear the debris and they gave us a great welcome. Sadly, the short period of calm "proved only to be a lull in the fighting," I wrote home. "It was, however, long enough to bring about a relaxation of tension and the confidence that maybe we could start school in the not too distant future, but who knows when?" Every ceasefire, albeit temporary, raised our hopes, only to crash again when there was renewed fighting, often after nightfall.

In the midst of a down patch, following a day of visiting Lebanese teachers who lived locally and listening to endless political discussion in Arabic, I had an unexpected phone call from my parents. "You've no idea what an encouragement it was to me to hear you both speaking as you did last night," I wrote later. "Have you read Proverbs 25:25[10] lately? It was just as natural as breathing to speak with you once again. Truly a thousand miles is but a fraction of an inch when the Lord is between us and we are

[9] Ecclesiastes 12:13,14
[10] *"Like cold water to a weary soul is good news from a distant land."*

united in prayer." I asked them to pray for the believers "that their faith will be really deepened and that they will see these times as urgent ones for witnessing to His saving grace and comfort in time of need, and not simply wallow in their own doubts and fears about the insecurity of the whole situation." In the school, I asked them to pray for Hazel and her responsibility for the staff and for Amine, facing the strain from the financial point of view. "We are completely at a standstill, banks closed, no-one able to come to pay fees and no-one with any cash to do so," I continued. "Please share with those who are praying at church and thank them on my behalf." I was so grateful to have a degree of independence and the opportunity to reflect in my fourth-floor flat. "Yet I am seeing quite a lot of the others upstairs, and we are praying together each evening." *"...I will continue to rejoice, for I know that through your prayers and God's provision of the Spirit of Jesus Christ what has happened to me will turn out for my deliverance."*[11]

The following week was busy. Hazel and I collected teachers from Bchemoun, Damour, Ras Beirut and Hadeth for a very encouraging staff meeting. "As you know, these days we have to trust God for every opportunity to travel, to meet, to shop," I wrote home. "Having had to cancel one staff meeting due to renewed fighting and kidnapping, we were finally able to hold it midweek. There was a wonderful spirit among us, and we made the rather momentous decision that we would start school on Monday, October 20th and trust that having announced it in the newspaper, at least people from the immediate vicinity would attempt to bring their children."

The decision inspired us to prepare for school to reopen, and I was proud of how my teachers worked in their classrooms, making them bright and attractive to welcome the children. I decided to open windows that had been shut all summer and wrote home for sympathy from my mother's nursing instinct. "I dropped a window on my face, which has resulted in a bad head and a slight black eye!" There was no serious damage but "my specs flew right across the room and one of the arms broke off! What a mercy that the lenses stayed intact." At last we were ready, after countless timetable and furniture changes, to reopen the school.

I spent the weekend with Afaf and her mother, planning to return with two of the teachers early on Monday morning. Sunday was unusually calm

11 Philippians 1:18b,19

and quiet in Beirut. There were very few of us in the congregation at the Alliance Church that morning, and I was glad to greet one or two as I took my place in the pew. The American pastor and his wife had already left for the States following their Embassy's advice, and I vaguely wondered who would take the service and preach from God's Word. I noted from the newssheet it would be Rev. Gordon Gale, an American missionary living for some years in Beirut. The family rented a rambling second-floor apartment within walking distance of the church and had clearly decided to stay for the time being. His subject that morning was prayer. "Is this the greatest need of this hour? Our situation now did not come upon us without God's knowledge, and so He has something to say to us. But we must be in the place of prayer." He proceeded to unpack the truths of Jesus' teaching in Luke 11:1-13 which had been read to us earlier in the service.

I was quickly drawn into Gordon's exposition and found it easy to take notes. When Jesus was asked to teach His followers to pray, He not only gave them a pattern of words that came to be known as the Lord's Prayer, but He also stressed persistence in prayer. *"So I say to you: Ask and it will be given to you; seek and you will find; knock and the door will be opened to you. For everyone who asks receives; he who seeks finds; and to him who knocks, the door will be opened."*[12] It is the prayer of the heart, the mind and the will that emphasises a deep inner determination that opens the door for God the Father to meet our need. "Prayer is more than asking," he said. "It's going through until there is a deep conviction that we've been heard."

Gordon referred to prayer meetings he had attended when working in India. The subject for prayer would be given and many would pray short prayers until a silence descended and a place of assurance was reached that God had heard and would answer. Furthermore, God Himself is so committed to prayerful communication with those He has created that His Holy Spirit *"helps us in our weakness. We do not know what we ought to pray, but the Spirit himself intercedes for us through wordless groans."*[13] When that place of assurance is reached, we simply dwell in the peace and offer praise and thanksgiving for all God is. *"Amen! Praise and glory and wisdom and thanks and honour and power and strength be to our God for ever and ever. Amen!"*[14]

[12] Luke 11:9,10
[13] Romans 8:26
[14] Revelation 7:12

How can prayer accomplish so much? Gordon likened the command of Jesus to pray with perseverance to the teaching of James. *"But when you ask, you must believe and not doubt, because the one who doubts is like a wave of the sea, blown and tossed by the wind. That person should not expect to receive anything from the Lord. Such a person is double-minded and unstable in all they do."*[15] The doubter does not receive because he lacks faith, but the one who perseveres accomplishes much through the power of God. *"If any of you lacks wisdom, you should ask God, who gives generously to all without finding fault, and it will be given to you."*[16]

Gordon went on to describe the role the believing person plays in channelling the power of God into human need. Set within the present context of so much political upheaval and discontent, lawlessness and danger in Lebanon, this teaching came with power indeed. "God's power," he said, "is available to accomplish great things for good in His world. Prayer is the vehicle, the channel that routes the power of God into the situation of need." And Gordon stretched out his right arm to signify God's power and his left arm, the need. "We, as it were, grip hold of God and channel His power as we bring the need to Him." To those who say, "Why pray at all, for the sun shines on the good as well as the evil?" it is as if the Lord says to us, "I want to bless you," and He puts the desire into our hearts and then says, "Will you please ask for it?" Gordon continued, "God is desiring to give Himself, and He is seeking vessels through whom He can communicate His desires. He wants people who will identify with Him and be the means of releasing His power." *"The prayer of a righteous man is powerful and effective."*[17] God's economy is such that He needs men, women and children to pray, because His Kingdom consists of humans made in His image. In conclusion, Gordon called on us to "have the faith in God for this hour. He is answering the prayers of many years for Lebanon."

I certainly wanted to identify with the Lebanese people to whom I had been called, and was committed to obeying God's instruction, *"Be strong and courageous. Do not be afraid; do not be discouraged, for the LORD your God will be with you wherever you go."*[18] I believed God was saying to me, "You are facing a situation in which it is seemingly impossible to do what you came here to do. It is what you are that matters, and that depends upon what you receive through your prayer, channelling My power to those

[15] James 1:6-8
[16] James 1:5
[17] James 5:16b
[18] Joshua 1:9

who are needy and fearful at this present time." I was conscious, too, of the power of the prayers of those at home, and was encouraged. The next day I wrote home, "It's not easy to keep writing to you, but I know I must. Humanly speaking, the situation here seems to be getting more and more hopeless, but the Lord is working His purpose out. His people are learning more and more to be in the place of prayer as they experience His protecting and comforting power." I continued, "We have to praise Him, too, for every opportunity to get about, share with others and encourage each other."

CHAPTER SEVENTEEN

Walking in the Midst of Trouble

Sunday, October 19th had been a calm, quiet day in Beirut, and that evening I wrote to my parents, "The Lord's day was packed full of worship and teaching at church and then came the worst night yet in the city centre. The Lebanese security forces fought back the whole night, from around 11 pm till dawn at 6.30 am. Afaf's building was not actually shelled, but we could hear the explosions and machine gunfire which sounded very close." I was pleased to add, "The Lord's peace and assurance of protection were certainly something very wonderful." I was eagerly anticipating finally being able to reopen the school as we had planned and prepared, but, as I wrote home, "It was impossible to move from Beirut till the middle of Monday afternoon, when the armed men would be sleeping for sure." Kafarshima had been quiet, and school did reopen with thirty-five children in total, sixteen of whom were in my department. "We await with anticipation to see who will come tomorrow and how we shall end up organising the morning."

Though disappointed not to be there for the first day of school, I was delighted to take up Hazel's suggestion to bring Bahia, my very reliable kindergarten teacher, back to Kafarshima to stay with us in our fifth-floor flat. Her building in West Beirut had been badly damaged in the previous night's shelling. As I wrote home, "This means that Bahia can teach the few children who came today from her class. Maybe more from the area will come tomorrow if parents reckon it's safe, that is now we are open, but many, many families have either left the country altogether or taken their winter clothes up to the mountains and are staying there." In spite of disappointments, I knew that prayer was being answered in incredible ways; I wrote, "I'm learning more and more not to take a single step

193

without reference to Him and then simply to pray that the Father's Name should be glorified in whatever situation I find myself."

On Tuesday morning, October 21st, my first day back at school, the numbers reached thirty-five in my department, a good number but far fewer than had registered the previous term. It was a real joy to be teaching again in spite of such unusual circumstances. That evening, I wrote to my parents, "What stories of suffering – fathers having lost their businesses; shops, offices, factories and homes completely burnt out. Yet it's good to be open for the immediate area, so long as we are careful where we send the buses." Sadly, our optimism was short-lived and I wrote again, "Early Wednesday morning, around 3 am, we were shot out of bed once again with more gunfire and explosions in Kafarshima itself. I was pretty sure when I went down to the classrooms in the morning that we would have a very skeleton school." It was not even safe to send the buses round the village, because shooting on the roads could still be heard. It was quieter in Kafarshima on the Wednesday night, but on Thursday the local situation became more critical as shooting continued for the whole day. I slept during the afternoon out of sheer exhaustion, but was aware of the constant bombardment over and around the building, echoing through the village behind us.

That evening, a twenty-four-hour curfew was imposed throughout Beirut and the suburbs. The local news spoke of severe measures being promised by the government. The atmosphere was tense, but nevertheless we gathered to pray till around 9 pm and even then the main battles were starting up again, until, for no apparent reason, from 9.30 pm right through till daybreak a strange quietness descended. We were thankful for a better night's sleep. I wrote home, "The following day, we were still unable to move even in Kafarshima, and during Friday night, though fairly quiet here, shooting and burning of factories began all over again in the heart of the city." It seemed a gloomy picture and a further blow to our hopes to be able to keep the school open, if only for the local children.

Contingency plans were clearly in order. As well as requesting prayer for the Lebanese in their bewilderment and confusion, for unity amongst believers and for the rulers and the government, I wanted to reassure my parents of the precautionary measures that the British Embassy was taking in the event of total breakdown of law and order. Hazel St John, our headmistress, had been appointed by the Embassy as warden for Kafarshima and the surrounding district. That weekend, an emergency meeting was held at the Embassy, and on her return Hazel gathered those of us with British passports to explain the measures the Ambassador had discussed with them. As I listened, I was reassured and I felt my parents and praying friends would be too. I sensed within myself a growing conviction that as long as there were children able to attend school from the local area, it was God's plan and purpose for me to stay in the place where He had called me to work. I wrote honestly to my parents, "The Ambassador does not advise a panic departure before such time as the Embassy itself may be driven to close." British subjects who had no overriding reason to stay were urged to leave and, as we already knew that the British Community School had closed, this ruling was not unexpected. I continued in my letter, "The Ambassador also advises us to be prepared to be flown out if there were a sudden deterioration and to have a bag packed with essentials." In my heart I was hopeful this would not have to be the case for me.

There followed another noisy night in Kafarshima with sporadic shooting, so on Sunday, October 26th we decided to worship together with the Khoury family on the fifth floor. "We praised God for each other and all He is teaching us as we pray together." As I wrote to praying friends at All Saints, Marple, "Your prayers are being answered in remarkable ways. Studying together from Philippians, we have realised how tremendous it was that Paul could write such a letter of rejoicing even while imprisoned, witnessing to the guards." *"Yes, and I will continue to rejoice, for I know that through your prayers and God's provision of the Spirit of Jesus Christ what has happened to me will turn out for my deliverance."*[1] I continued in my letter, "May this be an encouragement to you." It certainly was to me, and though I had a heavy heart because of all the suffering involved, I knew a deep inner peace which made it possible to go on day by day preparing for school and welcoming whoever was able to come. In my letter I wrote, "Praise God for His timing of events and His protection, and pray with us that we shall all be guided by His Spirit to make the best use of the time He gives us, whether to move about or stay put, and just to be in the right place at the right time." *"...you, LORD, are a shield around me ... I lie down and sleep; I wake again because the LORD sustains me. I will not fear though tens of thousand assail me on every side. ... From the LORD comes deliverance. May your blessing be on your people."*[2]

[1] Philippians 1:18b-19
[2] Psalm 3:3,5,6,8

So life continued for the next couple of weeks. We never knew each day just how many children or teachers would be able to come. Neither did we know how often it would be possible to send letters home with friends flying to England or further afield. Planning for learning opportunities and providing stability and a welcome for the children who did arrive in school, even if we saw them infrequently, demanded a great measure of inventiveness and creativity on the part of the teachers. Small numbers afforded great opportunities to integrate singing and artwork with one-to-one teaching of the basic skills of reading, writing and maths in both Arabic and English. Each morning we were able to have time together for Bible story and prayers, starting with the story of creation and the world God made, emphasising God's love for the world and His desire to befriend and help us to be kind to others. We much enjoyed making a large frieze of the creation story with the sea, mountains and dry land, followed by flowers, grass and trees, and not forgetting animals and pipe-cleaner people!

"I am writing now in between teaching small groups of children (I think we have about twenty today brought by their parents from Kafarshima), and it's quite exciting to feel we can stay open on a voluntary basis. We can't send the school bus even round the village because of petrol shortages once again, and also it won't be really safe for a week or so even if this ceasefire holds. I think it's the tenth in the space of six weeks." No sooner had this letter been sent on its flight to Heathrow than my father blessed me with a surprise phone call. My mother was at the church choir practice, and Dad thought he would dial the school number and see if he could catch the line directly without having to book a call with the operator. I had washed my hair that evening and was sorting through some old family photos just before going to bed, trusting that I would be able to make it home for Christmas. "What a special joy it was to hear your voice and the reassurance of your love and prayers. I know such a peace that it is His will for me to be here," I wrote home later. I had been reading from John's Gospel and the words spoke to me vividly. *"You did not choose me, but I chose you and appointed you so that you might go and bear fruit – fruit that will last..."*[3] It was as if God were saying to me, "You did not choose to come back to Lebanon for a third year, so why are you here and why have I given you peace in the midst of so much tension? Here's the answer:

[3] John 15:16

it is because I, God, chose you and I appointed you to do the work with these children that I called you to do."

We did hear of expatriate families, British and American, some with small children, who had decided to take early home leave. At one point, I found myself feeling quite upset about it, asking myself whatever I should do if the Embassy were expelled and all the Brits with them. I wrote home, "Isn't it incredible how the evil one attacks? I recalled Job with the hedge around him[4] and God's promises of protection throughout the Psalms, *'You will not fear the terror of the night, nor the arrow that flies by day … I will rescue him … He will call on me, and I will answer him; I will be with him in trouble…'*[5] Praise Him for all He is teaching us these days and how gracious He is in giving such peace from the promises of His Word." There was to be more grace made available as the situation intensified. I knew I could trust the One who had chosen and appointed me to teach in this school as long as we could keep the doors open and it was safe for the children to come.

Life was never dull and seemed to be gradually returning to some sort of normality. The night of my phone conversation with my father was quite dramatic, as I later wrote home: "We had a real thunderstorm that evening, but I couldn't really tell the difference between planes taking off (there are hardly any at all nowadays as most have been diverted to Damascus or Amman), shooting in the distance and claps of thunder!" For the whole of those two weeks of our 'imprisonment' in Kafarshima, we only heard shooting in the distance from Hadeth and the city centre during the night. During the daytime, snipers were out and about, shooting as they pleased, especially first thing in the morning and just before dark, to warn people of the night curfew. At that time, there was no heavy bombardment of the school building as had happened in September, and cars were beginning to move more freely during daylight hours. I wrote home, "I had been invited to lunch with a missionary family who live in Hadeth. The minute I arrived, we sat down to eat and the shooting became almost deafening – from cars, from rooftops… Some ceasefire!"

Petrol was becoming increasingly hard to find, and at the weekend I left for Beirut with the red light flashing on the fuel gauge. Just after I arrived at Afaf's flat to greet her on her birthday, yet more shooting

[4] Job 1:10: *"Have you not put a hedge around him and his household and everything he has?"*
[5] Psalm 91:5,14,15

erupted in the tourist area between the big hotels that had been taken over by rival factions. Praise God, I was safe inside her flat. Early on the Monday morning, I returned to Kafarshima in time for school with the petrol gauge still flashing red. I was aware that life was tense in the city and felt so grateful for where I lived in the school building with its lovely open view across to the Mediterranean Sea to the south, the city to the north and the village rising up behind us. The following day after school, Tuesday, November 4th, I took three of the teachers in the car to visit Jill Mattar in the neighbouring village of Hadeth. "I was overjoyed to find a petrol station on the way back with no queue and plenty of petrol!" I wrote home. "There were five or six men waiting around, and they filled the tank to capacity with petrol spilling all over the place! Then came the oil top-up, water check and windscreen clean. I think half the village came out to watch, and then the owner knocked twenty-five piastres off the normal price per litre! I just couldn't believe it – praise God for His provision in every detail!"

Political talks continued, and I wrote home, "We praise God for a breathing space when people can leave their homes to replenish their food stocks, especially those who've been trapped for days in city apartments." For the rest of that week, there was a marked improvement in the security situation, and the roads were safe enough to venture out for visits and shopping. I was thankful to receive letters from home with family news. One letter included a lovely offer from my parents to pay for me to fly home for a break for Christmas. I was hopeful that this would be possible, even though far fewer flights were coming in and out of Beirut airport. I continued writing home, especially when there was the incentive of a willing 'postman' flying out of the country, and was glad to be able to write with more positive news. "It was great to have a week of peace when one could move around more freely and stock up with food. We continued to have the school open unofficially during weekday mornings. It was so good to be reminded in church yesterday of how the church universal has been lifting this country to the Lord, and we are certainly experiencing His protection during these dangerous days."

As I was writing home one evening, there was a slight disturbance in my flat on the fourth floor. "I've just noticed a mouse creeping out from under the fridge. It's not the first time, and I know where they come in – up the drainpipes and in through a slight gap between window frame and wall, which I must block up." So I searched around for my tin of rat powder, sprinkled it on a chunk of bread and pushed it under the fridge. "It makes me feel quite cruel," I continued, "especially as I can hear it scratching around under the fridge."

By Monday, November 10th, the latest ceasefire was holding well, and it was deemed safe enough to send the school buses to collect children from surround-

Khoury family evacuate by tank, November 1975.

ing villages. I wrote home with the good news. "By Tuesday, we had eighty children in school and really felt we were beginning to get organised, and parents were gaining confidence and wanting to put their children in school again and pay fees." How we rejoiced – but our euphoria was short-lived. I continued in my letter home, "At 7.30 pm, we were just sitting down around the table on the fifth floor to do Bible study together, when gunfire and shelling erupted once again and continued throughout the night."

By noon the following day, the guns finally fell silent and the village was deathly quiet. There was not a car on the road, and the newly reopened factories around us were at a standstill. We were once again caught in the crossfire between rival factions, and many bullets hit our building. The Khoury family suffered the most damage, as they lived on the top two floors. We had to smile on the fifth floor, as a bullet pierced straight through some book shelves, removing the D from 'Danger' in one book title, thus reducing it to -anger, *Saints at Work* by Jean Rees! Another bullet whizzed over the light fitting in the dining room, a chandelier, and landed in the wall immediately above the sideboard containing china and glassware. Danger of yet more damage had thankfully been averted! I suffered three bullets in my sitting room on the fourth floor, and there was plenty of shattered glass to clear up. The Khoury family had relatives in Aley in the Chouf Mountains above Kafarshima, and most of them decided to evacuate the building the next day in an armoured tank provided by the security forces. I wrote to my parents, "It was really quite exciting to see them all huddled inside the tank to avoid the bullets!"

It was quiet until 6.30 pm, and those of us still in the building prayed together in one of the kindergarten classrooms on the ground floor and then buried ourselves in our sleeping bags in preparation for another night of bombardment. An hour or so later, I popped upstairs with extreme caution, only to find yet another bullet had scattered glass all over my sitting room once again. I confessed to my parents, "To be quite honest, I was nearly at breaking point and the noise was deafening. However, the Lord was very gracious and we were all there to support each other." We slept amazingly well that night, huddled together on the floor in the kindergarten library, but the following morning the shooting resumed and I spent most of the day on the ground floor, repairing children's books and sorting out my cupboards. Hazel left during the afternoon with the two English girls and Alice, a Lebanese from Sidon who was staying with us and helping in the school. I wrote home, "How brave she was to leave when there was not a single car on the road and any minute the shooting might start up again." I continued, "I was absolutely petrified to even get behind the steering wheel of my Fiat, and it took me all the courage I could muster to step out on the balcony to bring in my washing, which had been there since Tuesday afternoon!"

Not long after Hazel left, the sky darkened, followed by heavy rain and thunder, the first of the season. Word came from the village that some sort of truce had been agreed between the two warring factions. As we prayed together in the evening, Bahia, my Lebanese colleague in the kindergarten, and I gave thanks for the prospect of a quieter night, but it was not to be. I wrote home, "At 2 am, the ceasefire was broken violently and we both had to move pretty quickly from our beds and down onto the ground floor once again. It was without doubt the worst night so far, with many explosions and continuous heavy gunfire till the early morning." This time I decided to settle in the corridor right in the centre of the building and away from outside windows, to dull the noise and for extra protection.

So it was that snuggled in my sleeping bag, almost entirely zipped round, with mice scuttling about, the Lord sent a special dispensation of His Holy Spirit to reassure me of His promise from Joshua: "...I will never leave you nor forsake you. ... Be strong and courageous. Do not be afraid; do not be discouraged, for the LORD your God will be with you wherever you go."[6] I felt a deep sense of warmth despite the draughts in the corridor; such grace as I was swept along in the joy of praising the One who had called me to this place, the One who was utterly in control, not just of my life but of all that

---

[6] Joshua 1:5,9

seemed so senseless and destructive.[7] I felt totally embraced by this glorious Being filling me with His Spirit, and found myself laughing! Could this be the joy that Jesus had prayed for His followers just before His crucifixion? *"...that they may have the full measure of my joy within them. ... My prayer is not that you take them out of the world but that you protect them from the evil one. ... Sanctify them by the truth; your word is truth."*[8] Could this be the joy of which Nehemiah spoke following months of opposition to the rebuilding of the city walls and Ezra's reading of the Law? *"Do not grieve, for the joy of the LORD is your strength."*[9]

At around 7 am on the Friday morning, there descended an uncanny stillness. I crept upstairs and into my kitchen on the fourth floor and quickly made a cup of coffee. All was quiet, so I stayed upstairs to eat breakfast. No sooner had I moved from the kitchen to the sitting room and sat down with my breakfast tray, than the shooting started again. I heard the glass shatter and smelt the burning. A bullet had pierced through the window above my cooker where I had been standing and embedded itself into the plaster of the wall immediately behind where I was now sitting. The shock was immense. I could but praise God for yet another instance of His marvellous protection and timing.

The shooting continued sporadically throughout the morning. Bahia was able to leave, but I simply could not summon up the courage to drive out onto the creepily quiet road. Every morning that week, I had been reading wonderful promises from the Psalms of David, and clung onto God's Word as I continued working in the ground-floor classrooms. *"...I trust in you, LORD; I say, 'You are my God.' My times are in your hands; deliver me from the hands of my enemies ... How abundant are the good things ... that you bestow in the sight of all, on those who take refuge in you. In the shelter of your presence you hide them from all human intrigues; you keep them safe in your dwelling from accusing tongues. Praise be to the LORD, for he showed me the wonders of his love when I was in a city under siege."*[10]

By the end of that day, I felt satisfied that all was tidy in the classrooms and enjoyed spending time downstairs with the caretaker and his family who lived on the ground floor and guarded the entrance to the school. I later wrote home, "At about 10.30 pm, all seemed quiet and it was lovely to be able to sleep the whole night in my bed on the fourth floor!" God's

[7] See Introduction.
[8] John 17:13,15,17
[9] Nehemiah 8:10
[10] Psalm 31:14,15,19-21

Word was becoming more and more my 'Book of Instructions' for when and how to move. *"You are my hiding-place; you will protect me from trouble and surround me with songs of deliverance. I will instruct you and teach you in the way you should go; I will counsel you with my loving eye on you."*[11] My dear friend Afaf had already offered a safe haven for me with her mother in their home in West Beirut, and we were in touch regularly by phone, even praying for each other down the line. The promises from God kept coming. *"The angel of the LORD encamps around those who fear him, and he delivers them."*[12] *"The salvation of the righteous comes from the LORD; he is their stronghold in time of trouble. The LORD helps them and delivers them; he delivers them from the wicked and saves them, because they take refuge in him."*[13]

By Saturday afternoon, I knew the time was right to make a move. I finished the work downstairs and packed my suitcase. That morning, as I checked out my 'Book of Instructions', the Lord gave me a command and a wonderful promise: *"Depart, depart, go out from there! … you will not leave in haste or go in flight; for the LORD will go before you, the God of Israel will be your rear guard."*[14] In my letter home, I shared that "I had a picture of my little Fiat driving out from the school and from Kafarshima completely surrounded and protected by the Lord on all sides." By 3.30 pm, when I had expected a lull in the fighting, the shooting had still not stopped and I was more frightened than ever, but I knew people were praying and that I had to go. I made one final phone call to Afaf to say I was on my way, ran down the stairs, waved goodbye to the caretaker, his wife and the children, and set off down the school drive. There was an eerie silence punctuated by occasional gunfire shots as I turned left onto the deserted road. It suddenly occurred to me to reach over and wind down all the windows in order to avoid yet more broken glass should a sniper's bullet hit my car, but all was well. I was totally protected by my heavenly Father according to His promise.

On arrival at Afaf's home, I was amazed to find that life had been continuing as normal whilst I had been besieged in Kafarshima and that the ceasefire in Beirut was still holding. I was pleased to write home, "I had a shocking headache that evening, and it was a joy to be able to sleep the clock around away from that incessant gunfire. How I praise Him so much

[11] Psalm 32:7,8
[12] Psalm 34:7
[13] Psalm 37:39,40
[14] Isaiah 52:11,12

for His deep down peace, which comes from praising Him and acknowledging His control over the events as I was in the midst of them."

By now, it was clear to me that being able to reopen the school before Christmas was very doubtful indeed, though it was important to keep my work permit up-to-date in spite of the uncertainties. Flying home for Christmas on a month's excursion ticket was advised, but it was impossible to make a definite booking and only expensive scheduled BA and MEA flights were leaving from Beirut airport at the time. I was blessed indeed to be able to stay temporarily with Afaf and her mother. In fact, Mrs Musallam told me I was her refugee! I was hopeful I would be able to use the time to study Arabic more and keep in touch with friends on the phone.

The reassurances from God's Word continued. *"Though I walk in the midst of trouble, you preserve my life. You stretch out your hand against the anger of my foes; with your right hand you save me."*[15] The day after I left Kafarshima, I had good cause to trust in these words. It was a joy to attend church in the morning and spend time sharing experiences of the Lord's protection in these dangerous times. Afaf and some of our IVF friends had planned to drive up into the mountains to visit some missionaries who were staying in the village of Ain Zhalta in South Lebanon. I had at first declined the invitation to travel with them as I was utterly exhausted, but at the very last minute I felt it was right to go, having spent so much time indoors the previous week. I agreed to leave church early and meet Afaf at 12.10 pm at the latest, but sadly the sharing time delayed me and I did not reach the appointed meeting place until 12.30, only to find they had gone! I knew which route they would take and chased them up the mountain in my trusty Fiat! After about a half-hour drive, I caught them up, parked my car in Aley and jumped in with them. Afaf had brought along her mother to give her an outing but there was room for me too!

Ain Zhalta is a mountain village with glorious views over the cedars of southern Lebanon, and the air was bracing. We enjoyed a refreshing time of fellowship with the missionary friends and set off home in good time to reach Beirut by nightfall. Having picked up my car where I had left it, I suggested the road down to the coast through Aramoun would be the safest, as we had heard reports of kidnappings on alternative routes. Aramoun is set in the midst of forest and is known for its ancient mulberry trees. Red-roofed stone houses are stacked above each other up forested mountainside that seems to rise vertically above the twisty road. As we

---

[15] Psalm 138:7

continued in convoy down the road, night was falling and it grew misty and overcast.

I led the way with two friends in my Fiat, and Afaf was following with her mother and two English girls. The village was behind us, and we were not far from the coast road that led south to Sidon and north back into Beirut via Khalde and the airport. The road was by no means deserted, but suddenly two armed gunmen jumped out from the side of the road and stopped the car in front of me. My heart fell as I too was motioned to stop. As the car in front was waved on, I assumed the same would happen to me and reached for my passport on the dashboard. Imagine my consternation when the one gunman shouted to his friend, "She's English," in Arabic and told me to get out of the car, at the same time as holding on to my passport. By this time, the other two were crouched in the back of the car, and the gunman was trying to manoeuvre me to sit with them so that he could drive the car off with his friend in the front and us in the back! As it dawned on me that it was no use arguing and I would have to hand over the keys and trust the Lord to protect us, I heard Afaf's voice distracting the gunman and demanding to know what he wanted. She spoke in a strong Palestinian accent, which clearly arrested his attention, and within seconds she had pushed the two English girls from her car into mine and let the gunmen – by this time there were three of them – into hers and told me to drive on back to Beirut.

It was really quite dark by this time, as the dusk passes quickly at this latitude, but there were plenty of other cars around shining their headlights on us! In my stunned state, I drove on, wondering whether we would ever see Afaf and her mother again. On reaching the main road, I paused for Afaf to overtake, and as she honked her horn one of the gunmen actually poked his long rifle out of the rear window and waved it up and down! I knew the Lord would protect them and prayed they would not have to drive all the way down the coast to the Palestinian camp on the outskirts of Sidon. We had indeed walked in the midst of trouble and – praise God! – our lives had been preserved. It took me a little while to take everyone home and then drive back to the Musallams' flat to await their return. It was such a relief to see lights on and Afaf's car parked outside the building. It transpired that these gunmen were teenage Palestinians who knew that the Lebanese Forces were surrounding the area and wanted to get away quickly. When they realised Afaf and her mother were of Palestinian origin, they trusted them both and were soon chatting quite amicably. Mrs Musallam was even able to witness to them of God's love and was determined to keep them in her prayers. I think it took her a little longer to forgive me for taking them down the Aramoun road!

Very soon after this experience, I was in touch with Sami, the Arabic pastor of our church and husband of Joy, who had taught the pre-school at Eastwood in our first year. He mentioned the risk of kidnapping, especially for men, as there were still so many armed men on the streets. He had recently had a potentially dangerous experience when travelling from one side of the city to the other. He was driving his Volkswagen van and realised the two cars ahead of him were being motioned to stop by armed gunmen. Sami made as if to stop but in front of the two cars instead of behind them. As the gunmen were approaching the van, he put his foot on the accelerator and sped off at quite a rate, expecting to hear a bullet at any minute. I asked Sami how he had had the presence of mind to act in this way. "I knew," he said, "that if I stopped, as soon as they saw the Christian registration on my Identity Card, I would be kidnapped, but if I made a dash for it, I had a fifty-fifty chance of escaping." He went on to tell me that when he arrived home, he had no words with which to thank God until he read Psalm 138. "Even God gave me the words to say in gratitude for my preservation," he said. *"I will praise you, LORD, with all my heart ... for your unfailing love and your faithfulness. ... When I called, you answered me; you greatly emboldened me. ... Though I walk in the midst of trouble, you preserve my life. ... The LORD will vindicate me; your love, LORD, endures for ever – do not abandon the works of your hands."*[16] It was the very same promise of God's protection from danger that God had fulfilled for me on the Aramoun road!

There followed a further three weeks for me as a refugee at the Musallams' flat before I was to hear from Sami again. I was able to make local visits within the city to friends from school and the IVF, and share an increasing awareness of God's presence and safekeeping. One afternoon, a friend and I were visiting Bahia when, without warning, the traffic became more and more congested. We realised we were caught in somewhat noisy cross gunfire. After inching forward little by little, accompanied by much honking of horns to add to the general cacophony, we eventually came through! *"You have not given me into the hands of the enemy but have set my feet in a spacious place."*[17] Another visit during that time was to an IVF friend

[16] Psalm 138:1-3,7,8
[17] Psalm 31:8

who lived not far from Afaf. Lina cared for her housebound widowed mother as well as holding down a busy secretarial job in the city. We often shared God's Word and prayed together, and it was a blessing to me. Our favourite verse at this time was from Psalm 16: *"I keep my eyes always on the LORD. With him at my right hand, I shall not be shaken."*[18]

From my haven in Beirut, I longed to receive news from Kafarshima. For ten days, nighttime shooting was heard in the distance, and every morning I failed to catch the phone line to the school. The fighting was intense and there was no electricity, water or telephone. Eventually, we managed to catch the line – and how good it was to speak to people in the village again! On Thursday, November 27th, I picked Hazel up from the missionary flat where she was staying in Beirut, and we drove to Kafarshima to see what was happening. Furthermore, I really felt the need for a change of clothes! We simply trusted the Lord for His protection.

As soon as we reached Chweifat, the village to the south of Kafarshima, we could hear shooting and turned off onto a narrow back road as the coast road was deserted. On arrival in Kafarshima, just behind the school, there were positioned about half a dozen armed men from the militia who supposedly guarded the village. I stopped the car and Hazel spoke with them in Arabic. One of the men came to me and in beautiful English said, "Leave your car here and we will guard it." I was so relieved after my previous encounter with armed men on the Aramoun road that I just replied, "It's lovely of you to speak to me in English," and he grinned from ear to ear. We were then escorted down the narrow path to the back of the school under the shooting, and it was such a joy to be greeted by Jusef the caretaker and his wife Asia and the children. I wrote to my parents, "If this family hadn't been willing to stay, I can't think what would have happened to the school, especially as the warring factions appear to be attacking the building itself. Jusef has actually made friends with both sides, and because of this, no armed men have entered the school." There was such excitement as Hazel and I were plied with buckets full of oranges, grapefruit and tangerines, newly ripening in the garden. Hazel made many phone calls, and I was able to teach Jusef's children a little. I also prepared some materials for the Sunday school we hoped to start for the English-speaking children in Shemlan, where we had stayed earlier in the term.

With some apprehension, I mounted the stairs to my flat on the fourth floor. I was met by yet more broken glass, scattered like sugar all over the

[18] Psalm 16:8

kitchen and sitting room, but mercifully no other damage. The tally of bullet holes in the window had reached six, and my plants looked just like I felt, drooping and desperate for a drink. The bombardment was continuous, so I cautiously crept on all fours, aware that the slightest movement could evoke further shooting. There had been no electricity for over a week, so the fridge needed a good clean, especially as I had left some minced meat in the freezer compartment. I figured the bread in the bread bin was good enough for a biology lesson, well covered as it was in colourful mould. Having collected a change of clothes and waved goodbye to Jusef and family, I returned thankfully with Hazel to the car. As we approached, one of the gunmen spoke: "Miss Radcliffe?" I nearly dropped all my belongings in shock. He was the father of two of the children in the kindergarten. I later related the encounter to my parents. "I went through the 'how are you, how's your wife and your children' exchange of greetings as cheerfully as if I chatted with armed men with shooting all around every day of the week! He quite agreed with me that we could not live in the school and was amazed we had not already left for England. So I reassured him we wanted the fighting to stop and thus be able to have the children of the village in school again as soon as possible."

The whole experience was devastating, in spite of these personal touches. Hazel and I were relieved to return from this scene of desolation to the relative safety of the streets of Beirut. Deep down I was desperately upset. The trip to Kafarshima was a stark reminder of the futility of all this warfare and strife, the thousands killed and wounded, the kidnappings, the cruelty and wanton destruction of houses, shops and factories. All I could do was lament with David, *"Hear my prayer, LORD; listen to my cry for mercy. When I am in distress, I call to you, because you answer me."*[19] *"...my soul finds rest in God; my salvation comes from him. Truly he is my rock and my salvation; he is my fortress, I shall never be shaken."*[20] I was reminded, too, of God's call to me to this land of Lebanon and its people. *"Be strong and courageous. Do not be afraid; do not be discouraged, for the LORD your God will be with you wherever you go."*[21] To my parents I wrote, "God's promises and His nearness are so real these days," and thanked them for their faithful prayers. And to my grandmother, "God is wonderfully showing His power and strength during these difficult days, and He is teaching so many

[19] Psalm 86:6,7
[20] Psalm 62:1,2
[21] Joshua 1:9

of us the real secret of joy and peace, patiently waiting upon Him and acknowledging that He is in control even during times of heavy gunfire and complete lawlessness. The promises of His Word are becoming more and more precious."

The following Sunday was my twenty-ninth birthday, and it proved to be quite a non-stop day. After morning service at church, I offered to take two nursing friends home to Ashrafieh in East Beirut, a journey I had made many times before. All was well until I started to drive back to the Musallams' flat for Sunday lunch. The roads were eerily quiet and I somehow lost my bearings. I shall never know how I eventually found my way, having driven round and round the area, crying out to the Lord for His help. How thankful I was finally to find my way out! Following a quick lunch, I made my way south and up the twisty mountain road to Shemlan for the Sunday school we had started for the English-speaking children there. All went well until we suffered a power cut due to torrential rain and finished our storytelling by paraffin lamps! That evening, the Lord spoke to me. *"He reached down from on high and took hold of me; he drew me out of deep waters. … the LORD was my support. He brought me out into a spacious place; he rescued me because he delighted in me."*[22]

By the first week of December, reopening school was beginning to look hopeful. The security situation was improving throughout the country, and a number of Beirut schools were planning to open for the first time since the beginning of term. I wrote to my parents, "We're expecting to have at least two weeks' school before Christmas if we open again next week. If that's possible, then I should be able to leave on Friday, December 19th and be home for a fortnight. But on the other hand, if the situation deteriorates, you might find me home before this letter gets posted!" And so it proved to be – in a most miraculous way.

Meanwhile, the Khoury family returned to Kafarshima, and the Lebanese staff were alerted and seemed keen to come. Phone calls were made and a great deal of cleaning and repair work was set in motion. Hazel and I drove back to the school midweek to clean up and prepare, "especially with the task of hiding bullet holes in the windows of the classrooms!" as I wrote home. I now had a tally of seven bullet holes in my sitting room, yet more glass like sugar scattered everywhere and quite a collection of bullets. "Nothing is seriously damaged," I continued in my letter. "Most of the bullets went into the plaster, one in the door and one in

---

[22] Psalm 18:16,18,19

the edge of a large wooden fitted cupboard." How thankful I was that Jusef the caretaker came upstairs to clean the floors, but in his enthusiastic manner he managed to knock over a side table, breaking a pretty vase that had been a birthday gift from a dear friend in Birkenhead. This breakage, however, seemed a minor mishap compared to the destruction all around us. I was looking forward to being able to move back into my flat over the weekend.

But that was not to be. By the end of that week, the security situation was deteriorating once again, with the seeming inability of the government to rein in the warring factions and bring about a stable ceasefire. Nights were regularly disturbed by sudden outbursts of firing and heavy explosions. On Saturday, December 6th, the wave of kidnappings and killings surged – eighty reported killed that night and a twenty-four-hour curfew imposed. It would be impossible to return to Kafarshima and reopen the school. I huddled myself with my disappointment under the kitchen table in the Musallams' flat and buried my heavy heart in God's Word. *"Therefore we do not lose heart. Though outwardly we are wasting away, yet inwardly we are being renewed day by day. For our light and momentary troubles are achieving for us an eternal glory that far outweighs them all. So we fix our eyes not on what is seen, but on what is unseen, since what is seen is temporary, but what is unseen is eternal."*[23]

My disappointment reached a peak on Monday, December 8th, when all signs of life were snuffed out and we could not move other than up and down the stairs inside the building. Afaf knew how I was feeling and shared my sadness, as she too was unable to leave her flat and go to work. We prayed together a lot during those days in between our games of Scrabble and regular phone calls to check on friends. I wrote home, "Praise God that He is the God of the impossible and praise Him for His Word so full of promises of safety. Isaiah 57 spoke to me this morning, when I felt so touchy and weary about the whole seemingly endless, hopeless situation: *'You wearied yourself by such going about, but you would not say, "It is hopeless." You found renewal of your strength, and so you did not faint.'*[24] It exactly described how I felt. *'…whoever takes refuge in me will inherit the land and possess my holy mountain.'*[25]" It was as if God's Word was immediately relevant to my sense of desolation. *"'I live in a high and holy place, but also*

[23] 2 Corinthians 4:16-18
[24] Isaiah 57:10
[25] Isaiah 57:13b

*with the one who is contrite and lowly in spirit, to revive the spirit of the lowly ...
I will guide them and restore comfort to Israel's mourners, creating praise on their
lips. Peace, peace, to those far and near,' says the LORD. 'And I will heal them.'"*[26]
Furthermore, I recalled the opening verses of Romans 5, *"...we have peace
with God through our Lord Jesus Christ ... we boast in the hope of the glory of
God ... we also glory in our sufferings ... hope does not put us to shame, because
God's love has been poured out into our hearts through the Holy Spirit..."*[27] God's
love came flooding in and I praised Him.

The fighting across the city had definitely stepped up a gear, to include
the sea front hotels as well as the suburbs. And then, for me, the miracle
happened. The phone rang at the Musallams' flat on the evening of
Tuesday, December 9th. It was Sami, the Arabic pastor of the Alliance
Church. His message was clear: "It is too dangerous for you to stay here
any longer. My wife Joy and the children are in England and you should
be too. It is time for you to fly home."

"But how can I leave?" I stuttered. "I have my passport but no ticket,
and most of my belongings are in Kafarshima."

"I can guarantee an excursion ticket for you for one month," Sami
replied. "You are a member of our church and we will pay for the ticket."

"But Sami, we can't move from here..." My remonstrations were to no
avail, and I knew – in fact, it took my breath away – that this was God's
provision for me, His way of escape. Only that morning, I had been reading
from Isaiah 52, *"This is what the LORD says: 'You were sold for nothing, and
without money you will be redeemed.'"*[28]

"Wait for a lull in the fighting tomorrow afternoon and go to John
Khoury with your passport, and he will write a ticket for you for the 12.30
pm MEA Boeing 747 flight to London Heathrow on Thursday, December
11th," Sami continued. John was a travel agent who was working from
home close to the Musallams' flat. Little did we know at that time that this
would be one of the last flights to leave Beirut airport before the fighting
forced the airport to close.

So it was that I acquired the ticket and instructions for travelling to the
airport. I was to make my way to the Beirut International Hotel for 9 am
and board the MEA airport bus. Afaf came with me and it was hard to part
company. I was deeply appreciative of the way she and her mother had

[26] Isaiah 57:15,18,19
[27] Romans 5:1-5
[28] Isaiah 52:3

opened their home to me for those difficult weeks. The journey to the airport was without incident apart from endless sniper fire, and I was aware of unmarked escort vehicles overtaking the bus, falling back and then overtaking again, all the way through Beirut and down the airport road. For now, I was being taken from the devastation and destruction of the country I loved to the relative safety of England.

There was one more challenge to overcome on that momentous day. How was I to reach my family in Marple, Cheshire with very little cash to my name? Somewhat refreshed from the five-hour flight in a jumbo jet, on arrival at London Heathrow I made straight for the BEA counter, clutching my luggage and my precious sterling. Would I be able to afford an internal shuttle flight to Manchester's Ringway airport? The next available flight was due to leave Heathrow at 7.15 pm, and I was informed that the fare was £14.25. I had in my possession one crisp brown ten-pound note featuring Florence Nightingale, given to me by Granny during the summer, along with four green one -pound notes, one of which was a gift from Hazel for my birthday, and thirty-five pence in coins. This left just ten pence to make a phone call to my parents! The ticket duly acquired, I headed for a public phone and dialled my home number. My mother answered and then, at the sound of my voice, promptly fainted on the end of the line! With my ten pence running out, I called out for my father, who mercifully came to the phone and, in his usual calm tone, said, "Where are you?" How thankful I was that he had arrived home from work only minutes before I rang. "I'll be there," he said as I shouted the expected arrival time in Manchester above the ambient noise of the airport concourse. With that, the line went *ping, ping, ping* and my ten-pence-worth was finished.

"*...my God will meet all your needs according to the riches of his glory in Christ Jesus.*"[29]

---

[29] Philippians 4:19

CHAPTER EIGHTEEN

Blue Peter and Bible College

On the Sunday following my flight home, I sat quietly in the pew at All Saints, Marple with my parents. It was an all too familiar place, and yet my heart was elsewhere and I was deeply troubled. So many questions were racing through my mind. Why should I be able to escape the hostilities and the turmoil that had engulfed Lebanon? What would happen to the school, the children, the teachers and the country I had grown to love? There had been the mounting disappointments during those nine months of growing unrest and now the loss of all that had become so dear to me: the work with the children and so many good friends and teaching colleagues. It all lay heavily on my heart, and I was hardly aware of what was going on around me. There was a Christmas tree beautifully decorated at the front of church, people's smiling faces, and well-meaning friends asking how I was and speaking of their Christmas plans.

The service proceeded with its familiar liturgy, and God spoke to my bewildered spirit through the reading: *"...as servants of God we commend ourselves in every way: in great endurance; in troubles, hardships and distresses ... in hard work, sleepless nights and hunger; in purity, understanding, patience and kindness; in the Holy Spirit and in sincere love; in truthful speech and in the power of God..."*[1] The list of Paul's hardships continued: *"...dying, and yet we live on; beaten, and yet not killed; sorrowful, yet always rejoicing..."*[2] These final words brought a lump to my throat and, through my tears, a flash of insight and such a sense of release as I resonated with Paul's commendation of his own ministry to the Corinthians. To me, they spoke of

[1] 2 Corinthians 6:4-7
[2] 2 Corinthians 6:9-10 (emphasis added)

212

my own link with the Lebanese believers I had only a few days previously left behind. Now I could actually rejoice from my heart and truly acknowledge that God was still in control of that terrible situation, rife with evil and lawlessness. I knew that He would protect His own. I could weep and grieve and yet rejoice in God's utter sovereignty and compassion for this suffering nation.

I was in possession of a month-long excursion ticket, Beirut-Heathrow-Beirut, and hoping to return to the school in early January 1976 before the ticket expired. News bulletins were not at all promising, and it was clear from Hazel's letters to me that this was a false hope. Fighting continued in Kafarshima around the school building, and many of the children had gone overseas or into the mountains for the remainder of the school year. I simply had to continue trusting in God's Word. *"Many are the plans in a person's heart, but it is the LORD's purpose that prevails."*[3]

Still living at home with my parents, it was just two days after the ticket expired that I offered to drive my twelve-year-old brother Robin back to Kingsmead School in Hoylake for his final two terms. I had taught in the pre-prep department of the school previously and still had friends there, including the headmaster and his wife. "I hear from Hazel St John," said Mr Watts, the head, "that you're unable to return to Eastwood until the situation settles. Would you consider working with us for the time being as a supply teacher? If the Lebanese situation improves dramatically, you must feel free to leave with our blessing." I was taken aback with amazement at God's leading, and accepted without hesitation. Mr Watts continued, "We would pay you according to the current teachers' pay scale and provide accommodation for as long as you are with us."

The accommodation took the form of a small one-bedroom flat at the top of a large Victorian house just along the road from the school, and was ideal. I invested in a warm duvet with pretty covers and did my best to insulate the rattling sash windows with strips of newspaper! There was no doubt I was feeling the cold, but it was a joy to have my own place at this time of recovery from the trauma of months of uncertainty and danger. As winter gave way to spring and spring to one of the hottest summers on record, this garret flat truly became a place of comfort and healing, to which I often escaped between teaching sessions in the school. The supply work was as interesting as it was varied. For the spring term, I coached junior children, some struggling with maths and some with French, in

[3] Proverbs 19:21

small groups and one-to-one. I also had the privilege of working with an inspiring special needs teacher, who introduced me to best practice in multisensory learning for children with complex specific learning difficulties / dyslexia. The summer term approached, with still no chance of a settled peace in Lebanon, and I was asked to teach full time in the pre-prep department. The class teacher of the five- and six-year-old class was starting maternity leave, and to my great delight I taught again in the very same classroom where I had started my teaching career seven years previously. *"LORD, you alone are my portion and my cup; you make my lot secure. The boundary lines have fallen for me in pleasant places; surely I have a delightful inheritance."*[4]

In February 1976, there had been a brief respite from the fighting in Lebanon, and Hazel had written in upbeat mode, thankful that I had been offered teaching at Kingsmead. She mentioned that Kafarshima was quiet and essential repairs to the building were going ahead. Eastwood would be reopening on March 1st. She subsequently wrote that over a hundred children came and paid fees, so staff salaries could be paid, but she was not hopeful about prospects for the future. Her realism proved correct. Ten days later, the brief respite from fighting was over and with it any hope of reopening for the rest of the school year. Amine, who owned the school, came to England for a spell of theological study at Romsey House Theological College in Cambridge, and this gave me the opportunity to invite him to Marple during the Easter break to meet my parents. It was a memorable visit, during which Amine recounted the story in some detail of how as a young teenager he had had a vision for starting what he imagined to be the ideal school in Kafarshima.[5] On his return to Cambridge, Amine sent an Easter card to my parents and wrote, "With many, many thanks for all your kindness and hospitality, which I greatly appreciated and enjoyed. Praise the Lord for arranging this opportunity of meeting that I counted as a privilege and a pleasure. Yours in Christ, Amine Khoury."

It had been my hope to be able to return to Eastwood for the start of the new school year in September 1976, but as the summer progressed this looked less and less likely. In June, I had been asked to speak at the after-school Christian Union club at a senior comprehensive school in Wallasey, another previous teaching 'pad', and it was a joy to meet up with staff and

[4] Psalm 16:5,6
[5] See chapter 8 for the full account.

pupils whom I knew. As I walked along the staff corridor, a familiar voice called me into her office. It was Miss Cook, the headmistress. "Hello Wendy," she said. "I heard you were coming. Would you like your old job back in September?" I knew one of the RE teachers was retiring, hence the vacancy! Once again, I was stunned into silence as the enormity of God's provision sunk in. Only that month, June, I had received a letter from Hazel in Beirut with the chilling news, "There is no security whatever at present. There is no sense or guarantee that any solution is as yet in view, sad as it is, and neither side seems the least likely to give in." Hazel concluded, "I feel more than ever, Wendy, though with very great regret, that if you are offered a good post for September, you should accept." And so I gladly accepted Miss Cook's offer.

It proved to be a demanding year teaching secondary RE once again, including external examination work. I wrote to friends in December that year, "For this school year, the Lord has taken me back into RE teaching at a comprehensive school for thirteen- to eighteen-year-old girls in Wallasey. I do continue to solicit your prayers for the work in this new battlefield. The missiles are more subtle, of course, though biros do occasionally zoom across the classroom!" I was blessed with accommodation in Meols, near Hoylake, the first floor of a warm, semi-detached house next door to friends from Kingsmead School who were caring neighbours. I often came home from school somewhat frazzled, to find a hot meal in the porch and a message of encouragement from Pat next door. The house itself had been vacated for the year by its owner, who was visiting her family in South Africa. *"Many, LORD my God, are the wonders you have done, the things you planned for us. None can compare with you; were I to speak and tell of your deeds, they would be too many to declare. ... I desire to do your will, my God..."*[6]

One of the highlights of the autumn term in Wallasey was the *Blue Peter* appeal for Lebanon. The thirteen-year-old girls in my form were still happily watching after-school TV and soon informed me of the fact that BBC's *Blue Peter* had launched their Lifeline-Lebanon appeal, collecting used stamps and postcards for medical supplies to be sent to aid relief in war-torn Lebanon. They suggested that we should start collecting! In the classroom, we could hardly keep up with the response, and soon not just my form but the whole school was busily collecting from friends and family. It was a great opportunity to think of others in need and share my own love for this beleaguered land and its peoples, especially the children.

[6]   Psalm 40:5,8

I had two examination classes and a Biblical syllabus, non-exam classes for a range of abilities, along with weekly sixth-form discussion periods. Here I could share a little about the situation in Lebanon from friends who wrote interesting letters, testifying to God's keeping power.

Lina wrote from Beirut, "Nowhere is safe now. The bombs reach everywhere, anytime. One doesn't know when he goes out of his house if he is going to come back safely or not. But we are in God's hands and care. He is keeping us safe." She quoted from Nahum, *"He cares for those who trust in him..."*[7] Hazel wrote of the tragedy that struck our senior Arabic teacher, Georgette, and her family who lost home, shop and all their possessions on one terrible night of arson and pillage. Their village of Damour, ten miles south of Kafarshima, was looted and burnt, and many of their neighbours were tortured and killed. Hazel wrote, "By a miracle of God's goodness, they escaped." By Christmas 1976, the family of five were able to live on the fifth floor of the school with Hazel, who was pleased to have their company. Following prayers, Georgette whispered to Hazel one evening, "Isn't it wonderful how God can turn what seemed all loss into real gain?"

Many of the letters from friends and colleagues contained wonderful testimony to God's protection in times of real danger. I clearly recall hearing from Jill Mattar, one of my pre-school teachers and mother of Nerissa and Helene, both of whom attended the school. Her husband Halim was a hairdresser in Hadeth, the neighbouring village, and worked from their first-floor apartment in a spare room that had been turned into a salon. There was a separate door from the corridor into the salon, that afforded privacy for the family. Halim would normally be found in the salon each weekday, but there came a day of particularly heavy fighting in the streets around their building, with shells ricocheting off the walls. Nobody was venturing out, and Halim was resting in his bedroom after a noisy night.

Suddenly, a mortar shell hit the empty salon and another hit the girls' bedroom round the other side of the building. Nerissa was sitting right by the window in front of the dressing table. She spotted something coming in the mirror, ducked and then walked out of the room, shocked but relatively unscathed. Shattered glass, shrapnel and debris had passed over the top of her and completely covered the room. It then seemed like hours to Jill before Helene emerged a few seconds later, likewise in a state of

7   Nahum 1:7

216

shock. She had been sitting on her bed further away from the outside wall. When Jill peered into the room, she reported a Helene-shaped area free of debris on the bedspread and the little girl was unharmed. *"The angel of the LORD encamps around those who fear him, and he delivers them."*[8]

It was between the salon and the kitchen, away from outside windows, that the Mattar family would hide for safety during the worst nights of bombing. I recall Nerissa sending me a picture of their cat with her kittens, distracting them all with their playfulness, until everyone curled up to sleep from sheer exhaustion.

Friends living in Beirut and working with students in the universities were struggling with the sheer unpredictability and lawlessness, and wrote confirm-

Top: Jill's house with bullet holes. Bottom: Bricked-up mortar shell damage at Nerissa and Helene's home in Hadeth.

ing the uncertainties that faced them on a daily basis. Richard Thomas, one of the IVF staff workers, reported, "The extent of killing, looting, torturing, kidnapping, arson and senseless destruction of property has been incredible. The city centre of Beirut is littered with debris and refuse; some of the suburbs have also been badly hit." Antoine, who led the Graduates' Fellowship Bible study group, wrote of the announcement for military rule, "It may be the end of agony or the beginning of greater strife and suffering, but I know that our God is the Lord of history and the nations as well as individuals. This fact gives me great peace and comfort." As the situation worsened, he later recorded, "At times we felt that we were really abandoned, had it not been for His grace that kept us going and hoping in the midst of despair and suffering. I can personally testify to the love of our Lord, who has protected me from imminent danger and rescued me

---

[8] Psalm 34:7

from death several times. I could see His hand in the numerous acts of love and mercy in the midst of hysterical killing and hatred." Richard later wrote, "We praise the Lord for these uncertainties that test our faith. We pray that the Lord, through His Holy Spirit, will revive this land to give beauty for ashes here; not just the beauty of landscape, but of souls redeemed and used for His glory." This prayer resonated in my own heart too, as I longed for peace in this suffering land.

By November 1976, there was some encouragement as far as the school was concerned. Amine, the owner, presently studying in Cambridge, received a phone call from Kafarshima to say that all was quiet in the district, the roads were open and parents were coming each day to ask when Eastwood would reopen. Hazel was preparing to return and several of the Lebanese teachers likewise. Amine wrote, "Although the political problems are still unresolved, the actual fighting that has claimed more than sixty thousand lives has stopped. It also seems that life is going back to 'normal'. As a result, all schools are expected to open by the new year if they have not already done so." He continued, "In human terms, it looks almost impossible, but still, isn't our God the God of the impossible? Is it not also that in such impossible situations, God proves to be more real in our experience, more loving, more caring? What a comfort to know that when we truly walk with Him and serve Him, it is in His unfailing and infinite mercy and strength that we do so." The date for reopening was set for January 10th, 1977, but I knew without a doubt that the Lord had given me the teaching post in Wallasey at least for the academic year until July of that year.

Knowing that Eastwood had reopened galvanised me in the early months of 1977 to search God's will for the timing of my return. I was thrilled to hear from Hazel that Jill had taken over the running of the kindergarten and pre-school and was using my flannelgraphs for telling Bible stories in Assemblies. She had assistance from Mona, Lamia and a Lebanese teacher living in the village who had offered to help, Hélène Mansour. Hazel wrote, "I do feel it's very wonderful, Wendy, how the Lord is helping us through these days, and even in the midst of everything (especially anxiety over the staff), there is a sense of peace in the certainty that the Lord is still in control and that He has a purpose for our lives which is being accomplished, however much all we expected has been swept away." She continued, "I do pray you will experience this too, in these days which may well be so difficult for you." Would it be right for me to resign at the end of May and return to Eastwood in September, or should I continue with my current RE post in Wallasey until political conditions in Lebanon were more stable? Family and friends were praying for clear guidance, and the answer proved to be neither of these options!

I decided to approach the UK secretary of the mission to which Hazel belonged, David Bentley-Taylor, and seek his advice, especially if I were to consider a longer term involvement in teaching in Lebanon. David conferred with mission leaders and subsequently recommended a year at Bible college before attempting a return to the Middle East. He felt that to take a year committing myself to a deeper study of God's Word would be valuable preparation for the future. My initial reaction was one of bewilderment. I so longed to be working once again with the people, the children I'd grown to love, until one Sunday in February I was sitting in the pew at St Mary's Upton and the preacher spoke from 2 Timothy 3:16,17: *"All Scripture is God-breathed and is useful for teaching, rebuking, correcting and training in righteousness, so that the servant of God may be thoroughly equipped for every good work."* Surely this was my desire: to be resourced and equipped from God's Word in order to serve Him better in the future.

I applied to four Bible colleges and gradually the options were eliminated, until April 16th when I drove to South West London for an interview at Redcliffe Missionary Training College, Chiswick. As I made my way up the drive through an allotment garden, I spotted a beautiful magnolia just coming into bloom by the rear entrance. This somehow spoke of God's gift to me of a time of rest and an opportunity to experience more of His Word and the beauty of creation. *"What he opens no one can shut, and what he shuts no one can open. ... I have placed before you an open door that no one can shut. I know that you have little strength, yet you have kept my word and have not denied my name."*[9] At the end of the interview and tour around the college, I was informed very graciously by the principal, Miss Nora Vickers, that they would be glad to see me in September 1977 to study for one year! Though I knew it would not always be easy, this was a gift, and I started to look forward to studying again with just a little trepidation. The fees were affordable and God would provide term by term. This would be time to step aside from a busy teaching schedule and become a learner in a small community of thirty students from thirteen different nationalities.

[9] Revelation 3:7,8

During the spring and summer of 1977, I took every opportunity to speak to church groups, including my grandmother's Ladies' Class at the Methodist church in Ashton-under-Lyne. Using slides of Lebanon and the school, I solicited prayer for the country and the school, especially as Eastwood was now functioning with similar numbers attending to when we first opened in October 1973, approximately one hundred and thirty to one hundred and forty children of all ages. Amine wrote in his Christmas letter, "I ask you to pray for Lebanon and specifically for the freedom and witness of the believing Church. Pray, too, for the work of Eastwood and for the ministry of Hazel St John and myself and the rest of the staff who will be joining us." He concluded, *"So do not fear, for I am with you; do not be dismayed, for I am your God. I will strengthen and help you … I will uphold you with my righteous right hand."*[10] I also asked for prayer that the Lord would show me exactly when it was His time for me to return and join the staff team once again.

My time at Wallasey drew to a close with some tearful farewells. I remember having a bunch of flowers thrust into my hands with the words, "Thank you for all you've learnt us this year, miss!" There had been some great opportunities to work and witness with those teenage girls, and I had made good friendships with the staff. My RE examination class did well, and I was now looking forward to my year at Redcliffe College.

During the summer of 1977, I was pleased to be able to take part in a conference of international students, organised by the International Fellowship of Evangelical Students (IFES) to which the Lebanon IVF was affiliated. I joined the advance party with Katie Higham, PA to the General Secretary, whom I had met at their London office in Harrow. The Leadership Training Conference was to be held at Oak Hill College, Southgate, London, where during term time young men trained for Anglican ministry. Following a struggle to park, Katie and I were welcomed and shown around the accommodation. After some discussion, we were invited for lunch in the refectory of this all-male bastion of learning. As we entered the room, Katie turned and said, "Now I know where all the Christian young men are!" I pondered this thought with some amusement until later that evening, in my rather sparsely furnished student's bedroom, God spoke through His Word. I was reading from 1 Corinthians where Paul replies to the concerns of the Corinthian believers about marriage and singleness. Following some teaching on the marriage

---

[10] Isaiah 41:10

commitment, he writes, *"I wish that all of you were as I am. But each of you has your own gift from God; one has this gift, another has that."* He continues, *"Now to the unmarried and the widows I say: It is good for them to stay unmarried, as I do."*[11] I felt an enormous sense of relief as I read on. *"I would like you to be free from concern. ... An unmarried woman or virgin is concerned about the Lord's affairs: her aim is to be devoted to the Lord in both body and spirit."*[12] Suddenly, my status in life was clarified. Singleness was God's gift to me for the time being and as I anticipated a return to troubled Lebanon in due course.

It was an inspiring conference and such a privilege to meet international students from countries where personal freedoms were limited. I recall being moved by conversations with three South African students from differing sides of the apartheid divide, one white girl and two black men, sharing their faith and their struggles. There were delegates from Warsaw and Budapest who shared the trauma of living as believers under communist regimes. John Stott's teaching about Christian leadership in hostile environments and times of oppression was pertinent to my situation too. I was about to embark upon a time of receiving from the Word and delving deeper into God's purposes for me and my involvement in Lebanon during its time of trial and tribulation.

I was still in touch with Afaf, my friend who had, with her mother, provided a refuge for me in the early stages of the Civil War in Lebanon. She was now working in the London office of her firm in Beirut. That summer, we spent a glorious few days in Scotland, touring in her sister's VW Campervan. With the castle behind us, we walked the Royal Mile in Edinburgh and eventually arrived at Arthur's Seat in Holyrood Park. I had been asking the Lord for His promise to me for this next chapter of my life and reading from Exodus of Moses' desire for reassurance after his return from receiving the Law on Mount Sinai. *"...the LORD replied, 'My Presence will go with you, and I will give you rest.'"*[13] Furthermore, *"...the LORD said, 'There is a place near me where you may stand on a rock. When my glory passes by, I will put you in a cleft in the rock and cover you with my hand...'"*[14] This fresh revelation of God's holiness and protection came to life as we climbed our way to the peak of Arthur's Seat. I spotted a small rock jutting out from the grassy hillside with a cleft just big enough for me to crouch inside.

[11] 1 Corinthians 7:7,8
[12] 1 Corinthians 7:32,34
[13] Exodus 33:14
[14] Exodus 33:21,22

Many times, I returned to this promise and it brought comfort and hope. Likewise, in the New Testament, Paul wrote, *"For you died, and your life is now hidden with Christ in God. When Christ, who is your life, appears, then you also will appear with him in glory."*[15]

College routine was a discipline set within the bonds of community life. Alarms went at 6.15 am on weekdays and 6.30 am on Sundays. By 6.30 on weekdays, each student had made her way to a different part of the building – bedrooms, bathrooms, stairwells, landings, common rooms – for an hour of quiet devotional time. In the winter, I was often to be found hugging the nearest radiator. By 7.45 am, the whole college, staff and students gathered for fifteen minutes of 'family prayers'. This was followed by breakfast at 8 am in the communal dining room, six at a table. I could never make much conversation at breakfast, having been up so early! 6.15 am in the dark was not my best time of day, and I suffered from early morning catarrh as we were so near the river. Furthermore, I had been allocated breakfast duty that involved laying up tables, thankfully the night before, and washing up before and after the meal. At 8.30 am, the bell went for housework to begin! There was a duty rota for this too, and for twenty minutes the students would be seen wielding dusters and sweepers of all varieties throughout the college building. By 9 am, we were all assembled behind our desks in the lecture-room-cum-library, ready for the first two lectures of the day. As there were a number of students who spoke English as a second language, I, along with other native English speakers, was asked to take notes with carbon copies, which involved pressing very firmly on my notepad and writing as clearly as I could! As with the timing of breakfast, when coffee break arrived at 11 am, it was exceedingly welcome! A third lecture followed, with lunch at 12.30 pm, and by this time I was more conversational. We were then free from formal commitments until high tea at 5.30 pm.

During the spring term, I was allocated two-and-a-half weeks' kitchen duty, working with one other student and the college cook / caterer, preparing and serving all the meals. All the lectures were taped on huge reel-to-reel recorders, and one was expected to catch up by listening in the evenings. I confess I never did, as I was always too exhausted! I had looked forward to kitchen duty and was keen to learn about catering for large numbers. Shirley Saunders, the caterer, had high standards and a menu rota that made economical use of all ingredients. We worked around a

15 Colossians 3:3,4

large wooden table, cutting and chopping, peeling and preparing. Once a fortnight, there was a clear-out of the two large fridges and a huge pan was set up on the stove. This was curry day. Out came leftover vegetables, meat, chicken, scrambled egg, rice, sandwiches, pastries, followed by all things sweet – jelly, trifle, cake, stewed prunes, rice pudding – in fact, the entire contents of both fridges. I was staggered. Several large spoonfuls of curry powder were eventually added to the mix and it was well stirred. Curry was not a favourite of mine, and I had long been suspicious of its contents. Now I knew! There was an alternative for non-curry eaters and, needless to say, that was always my choice.

In spite of the rigours of kitchen duty – I resorted to support stockings as we seemed to be on our feet the entire day – the college routine proved to be healing and restorative. I wrote home, "There's a great spirit amongst the students and I love the international flavour. It's a real joy to be here." The morning lectures were taught mainly by visiting lecturers who excelled in Biblical exegesis and missionary application. I especially recall Rev. Ben White's teaching on 1 and 2 Corinthians and Dr Marion Ashton's on John's Gospel and Biblical Psychology. Lectures were also timetabled on Doctrine and Church History. My only concern was about the old-fashioned nature of some of the tutoring, especially that relating to child study and Christian work amongst children. Afternoons were spent on outreach from college into the surrounding area.

Miss Vickers had graciously made it clear to me that she believed the Lord had brought me to a smaller college like Redcliffe to alleviate pressure following a torrid few years, and therefore my practical assignments were to be kept to a minimum. Nevertheless, I was asked to take a weekly service at a local old people's home and go door-to-door visiting with another student at Brentford Towers. I later did some youth work at St Luke's, Shepherd's Bush on Uxbridge Road, and on Sundays took a lovely Sunday school class with four- to seven-year-olds at Holy Trinity, Richmond. Redcliffe boasted a small choir, ably led by Catherine Young, the vice principal, which I was pleased to join. We often practised during the afternoon for singing engagements on Sunday evenings in various churches nearby. I bought myself a long black velvet skirt in Richmond and loved helping to lead worship in this way. All these activities provided valuable learning opportunities to pray, prepare and work together with other students.

At the weekly 'mission outlook' spot, I was asked to speak about Lebanon. I soon discovered that the college had taken a prayerful interest in God's work in the Middle East and particularly in the last few years of political upheaval, war and civil strife. I shared about the measure of peace in Beirut at the end of 1977 and requested prayer for the staff of the Christian schools, one of whom was a former Redcliffe student. I spoke of the continuing freedom to teach the Scriptures and shared how the war had resulted in migration from the south of the country as the homeless flocked to Beirut as refugees. Many believers were now involved in aid and relief work. More living stones, new believers, were being added to God's building, and His Word was being shared in unprecedented ways. The Bible Society headquarters and shop in central Beirut had been attacked and looted, and Scriptures were finding their way into the hands of those seeking meaning to life amidst the strain of lawlessness. *"…in him you too are being built together to become a dwelling in which God lives by his Spirit."*[16] I asked prayer for 'my' school in Kafarshima, to which I hoped to return in September 1978, and that Lebanese believers would be able to endure the continued uncertainty. *"Now to him who is able to do immeasurably more than all we ask or imagine, according to his power that is at work within us…"*[17]

Saturdays were free days, and I delighted in exploring the surrounding parks and gardens. I often cycled over the bridge to Kew Gardens and would walk with visiting friends and family in Richmond Park, enjoying the deer and the squirrels. Spring and summer brought blossoms and flowers galore. I was able to drive the eight-seater college van, and often packed it with other Redcliffe students on Sunday evenings and drove to All Souls, Langham Place for evening service. During the summer term, Afaf had joined the college in preparation for future work with Lebanon InterVarsity Fellowship (LIVF) in Beirut. Rev. John Stott, recently returned from there, had preached at one of the evening services and was standing in the porch bidding people goodnight. As we approached, he searched under his robe and produced a letter from Rev. Colin Chapman, the Regional Secretary of the International Fellowship of Evangelical Students (IFES) in Islamic Lands, based in Beirut. Addressed to Afaf, this was an invitation to be his secretary / staff-worker from September onwards. She had been praying for exactly this and could now prepare herself for a return to Lebanon and her mother in West Beirut.

[16] Ephesians 2:22
[17] Ephesians 3:20

I too was keen to move forward with preparations for returning to the school in Kafarshima. It seemed prudent to pursue my application to Middle East Christian Outreach (MECO), and I duly appeared before the Mission British Council on May 17th. I had previously visited the council chairman, Dr Harold Langley, in his Yorkshire home for an informal chat. My hope was to be accepted as a short-termer (three years), seconded to Eastwood College, working with Hazel St John as before. As far as the mission was concerned, the options were clear. If I were prepared to teach in one of the mission schools, that would be acceptable, but if not, due to current political and security uncertainties in Lebanon, it would not be possible for the mission to second me to a different school. I understood their concerns but knew deep down that Eastwood was where I belonged.

One evening early in March, I had been summoned to the students' phone booth at Redcliffe. The call was from Edmond, Amine's younger brother, who was staying in London. He spoke of the sad and sudden death of Hélène Mansour, the primary teacher who had taken my place in charge of the Lower Junior department since the school had reopened early in 1977. Edmond urged me to return as soon as possible. Hazel too had written "of the big sorrow we had in the death of Hélène by a stray sniper shot as she drove from Hadeth into Beirut one afternoon. It was a great shock and very sad for her family." Hazel continued, "The children in school really loved her and I miss her so much." This news left me in no doubt as to where I should be teaching on my return. David Bentley-Taylor from MECO was very understanding and urged me to apply to be a mission associate on my return, in order to share in prayer support and fellowship with other missionaries.

During my time at Redcliffe, God's promise had returned to me time and again for the present and the future. His call was clear: *"My Presence will go with you…"*[18] *"Have no fear of sudden disaster or of the ruin that overtakes the wicked, for the LORD will be at your side and will keep your foot from being snared."*[19]

---

[18] Exodus 33:14
[19] Proverbs 3:25,26

CHAPTER NINETEEN

Return to Lebanon

Hélène Mansour's death had left a big hole in the staff team at Eastwood. I was keen to return and prepare for the new term, but was under no false illusions about the future. As my year at Redcliffe College drew to a close, I wrote to praying friends with gratitude for their loving support and a plea: "Please keep on praying, for the way ahead back to Lebanon is not easy. The country has no stable government and is politically very insecure." I continued, "The national church is there, and it is still possible to obtain visas to work in Lebanon." On a personal level, I was touched by expressions of support from Eastwood. Jill wrote, "It was wonderful to hear that there is a definite chance of your coming back this year. The ground floor needs you very badly, and I hope you will find that this is the Lord's will for you." She did also warn me that locks on cupboard doors had been forced open at some stage, resulting in a free-for-all of books and stationery! "I hope you won't find it too depressing a sight after all your hard work." She continued, "Mona asked me to send her love to you and tell you how much you are missed." And Hazel echoed the sentiment: "I am tremendously grateful that God is leading you back to us here – everyone is looking forward to your return." I was encouraged to step ahead in faith.

Hazel had written in May 1978 that Eastwood was hoping to open for the new school year on Monday, October 2nd, and requested that I attempt to be back in Lebanon around September 20th. Amine would pay for the ticket, both outward and return, on a two-year basis as previously. It fell to Hazel to purchase it before she came to England to visit friends and family in the summer. There was a pressing need for fresh supplies of kindergarten materials, and I was requested to purchase these in England

and arrange for shipment to Lebanon. As Hazel had also written, "Amine has not wanted to spend more than for bare necessities, since he still has a debt to pay for the post-war repairs of the school building." To bring me up to date, she continued, "The situation politically has not been easy, but we are carrying on with just the odd day or so when we have to stay closed. One feels grateful for the freedom we have to teach the children about Jesus in days when there is so much fear and insecurity in so many homes."

Just before my return to Eastwood there was a further encouragement. I was bridesmaid to my younger sister Hazel, who was married to Neil on July 29th, 1978 at All Saints Church, Marple. What a joyful occasion it was! Memorable was a mention in Neil's speech at the Reception of the fact that I was due to return to Lebanon in September. "We pray God will continue to guide and strengthen you, Wendy, for what lies ahead on your return." My heart was strangely warmed by this expression of support from my new brother-in-law.

I finally landed once again on Lebanese soil at 7 am on the morning of Friday, September 29th, 1978. My flight had been delayed for two weeks because there had been renewed fighting in East Beirut and its suburbs, which included Kafarshima. "Praise God," I wrote home, "for an indescribable peace right through the whole lengthy business of getting here." The flight from Manchester to London was on time, but from then on there were delays. The 5 pm Malév flight to Budapest took off an hour or so late, which shortened the wait in Budapest. I stayed in the transit lounge along with some Hungarian men and a few Lebanese families. At 1.45 am, when the flight to Beirut was called, I was snoozing fitfully with my head on my handbag as a 'pillow'. Thankfully, arrival in Beirut was on time. "It was a wonderful experience to see the sun rising above the clouds. Oh, how I love flying!" I wrote in my first letter home.

Afaf had flown back to Beirut in August to be with her mother and had started the enormous task of cleaning the Lebanese InterVarsity (LIVF) office, turning it into a place of welcome and hospitality for the student Bible studies and other social gatherings. Both she and Hazel were at the airport to meet me and waved through the glass screen as I made my way through the hustle and bustle of customs with no difficulty at all. It truly was like coming home, though not to Kafarshima at this stage. My first port of call was to the mission school for the Blind in West Beirut and a flat on the third floor of the building where I was to stay *pro tem*. Hazel had a bed ready for me and I slept till the early afternoon! There was much to

227

chat about over a cup of tea, and I walked round to see Afaf and her mother for a meal in the evening. I was just about to leave before dusk, when there was a flare-up below their flat – the first sign of hand-to-hand street fighting – so I ended up camping down at Afaf's. She even found my toothbrush and the other toiletries that I had left there three years previously!

The following day's fighting was much worse in East Beirut where Sami lived, my pastor from the Alliance Church. He managed to travel safely to Afaf's building in West Beirut in the morning to collect a letter I had brought from Joy his wife (still in England with their children), but rang later to say he was down in the shelter and their area was being badly bombarded. We could, in fact, hear it throughout the day. That evening, I went to an LIVF Bible study at another home in Ras Beirut on the western side of the city and again stayed away for the night. As I wrote home, "I managed very gratefully to have a hot shower." I added by way of explanation, "We've no water at the Blind School except very occasionally, and as there are frequent power cuts we often have to carry it up to the third floor in buckets." I did once wake at 6 am to the sound of water flowing through the pipes, having left the bath tap open overnight to catch any drips. Such a joy to shower and hair-wash in spite of the cold water!

Monday, October 2nd dawned warm and fresh. This was the day we had originally planned to open for the new school year, but it was not to be. At 3 am that morning, we woke to the heaviest shelling in East Beirut yet reported. Even though the bombardment was on the other side of the city, we could still hear it by early morning, though by then it was a little more spasmodic. Tension was high, and the night sky looked like a terrifying firework display. We prayed together during the night and read from Habakkuk: *"Destruction and violence are before me; there is strife, and conflict abounds."* The Lord replies, *"Look at the nations and watch – and be utterly amazed. For I am going to do something in your days that you would not believe…"*[1] Eventually, Habakkuk confesses, *"I stand in awe of Your deeds, LORD. Renew them in our day, in our time make them known; in wrath remember mercy."*[2] I wrote home, "Pray we'll have wisdom about opening the school and attempting to live a normal life in Kafarshima. The country is very unsettled owing to this latest outburst of fighting, which broke out almost the minute I arrived, yet the Lord keeps on reassuring my heart that I've

[1] Habakkuk 1:3,5
[2] Habakkuk 3:2

done the right thing in coming back just now." Later that day, we actually drove out to Eastwood with no difficulty, and it was a joy to be welcomed by Jusef and Asia and their six children. There was no sign of the Khoury family, as they had been unable to come down from the mountains to the north of the city. After a little unpacking, we were glad to drive back to the relative safety of West Beirut.

Rear of school, peppered with bullet holes, June 1979.

By the following week, Hazel and I had established a daily routine, spending most of the day working in Kafarshima and visiting in the surrounding villages to the south from where many of our children came. The severe fighting in the east and as far south as Hadeth, the adjoining village to Kafarshima, ceased on Saturday evening, October 7th, but as I wrote home, "People are still very frightened to come out of their houses because of the sniping. It's a tragic situation and a very dark prospect for schools." I continued, "However, there has been no fighting at all in Kafarshima in this latest round." We were puzzled as to why this should be until we were told that the ruling faction in Kafarshima had made an agreement with the Arab League peacekeeping force stationed on the boundary between the village and Hadeth. Each morning, a group of soldiers would go down to the checkpoint, chat to the Syrians, drink Arabic coffee and reaffirm the agreement that they would not fight. We simply praised God for this answer to prayer for the safety of the school building and indeed the village. I later wrote to praying friends, "To me, it was a wonderful picture of the Christian life. Our salvation is once and for all signed by the blood of Jesus, sealed by His Holy Spirit and settled with God the Father in heaven. But it is that daily recommitment of our lives, that daily feeding from His Word and drinking from the very fountain of life, that alone ensures the miracle of being hid in Christ, kept in Christ whatever the outward circumstances."

We continued to pray for an adequate settlement so that people could travel freely again. Furthermore, I asked friends "to pray that people will be released from the terrible fears and false rumours that grip their minds, and that the believers may be able to comfort those around them". Looking back, it was surely a miracle that our village was not hit during this particular spell of fighting. We praised God at that time for this sign that there was a purpose in the location of the building.

Hazel and I were still living in West Beirut and commuting daily to Eastwood. "What a joy it is to have electricity and running water at the school," I wrote home. "We've had no water in Beirut for over a week and the power is rationed – seven hours on and seven hours off – so we fetch and carry buckets of water from the school despite the distance. Electricity comes and goes there too, but we manage. Only once did the power fail, coming down in the lift with a few buckets of water. Praise God, the lift stopped just about a foot above the second floor, the door pushed open and we carried the buckets the rest of the way down and took them to Beirut in the car!" We always prayed as we approached the checkpoints that God would give us safe passage. It was imperative to draw to a halt in order to avoid angry shooting, but we gradually came to know where the checkpoints were and even to be friendly with the Syrian soldiers. There were some wonderful answers to prayer, even when the car was full of buckets of water! My stock phrase when asked where I was coming from was, *"Ana min Ingleterre."* ("I'm from England.") Amazingly, no one seemed to get suspicious of my frequent arrivals from England!

On Sunday, October 15th, having stayed with Afaf and her mother the previous night, I went straight to the Alliance Church to practise the hymns on the piano. "I'm just hoping Pastor Taylor doesn't choose any strange American hymns that I don't know!" I wrote home. I was expecting to meet Hazel there but she never came. That afternoon, a message came through that, having found a parking space near the church, Hazel was walking along the pavement and had somehow lost her balance. Having slipped, she had toppled over onto her left side and fractured her hipbone. "She's a tall woman," I wrote home, "and really fell hard, with terrible bruising right down the left side of her body – a real shock to the system." It appeared that she was spotted by two armed teenage boys, who carefully lifted her to her car parked nearby and drove to the home of Colin and Anne, the nearest people she knew. Colin lost no time in driving her to the American University Hospital (AUH) in Beirut.

There followed nine hours on an iron bed, lifted on and off twice for X-rays to hip and chest, until she was taken to theatre at 8.30 pm for the bone to be pinned. Such a brave lady! I called to visit the following morning and then miraculously managed to phone Eastwood from the LIVF centre to let Amine and his family know. The whole Khoury family descended upon AUH to visit Hazel the next day! I found myself the temporary possessor of an extremely old and tattered VW Beetle in which to drive there and back to the hospital every day. I wrote home, "I won't describe the driving in Beirut any more – maybe you remember the dodgems at Belle Vue? Well, something like that, though not quite so many bumps!" In a further letter, however, I wrote, "I trundle along in Hazel's VW, trying to drive a smooth course through the pell-mell of traffic all hooting their horns at various tones and pitches and totally disregarding any form of Highway Code. I never even look at the traffic lights, let alone try to obey them. I tell you, there's never a dull moment in this country, and as you know, I love it!"

A week after her fall, Hazel was discharged from hospital and learnt rapidly how to move around on crutches. In the meantime, I had been able to sign up as a mission associate in accordance with David Bentley-Taylor's recommendation and was starting to pack up both Hazel's belongings and mine at the flat where we had been staying at the Blind School. Hazel was staying *pro tem* with a missionary friend in Beirut to help regain her strength. I was longing to be able to move in to my fourth-floor flat at Eastwood and, in due course, open the school. It was now nearly four weeks since my return to the country and, as I wrote home, "My belongings are still scattered all over the place, including stuff in Jordan!" The latter were boxes of educational equipment for the kindergarten that some kind friends, who worked with a radio ministry that had a studio in nearby Hadeth, had brought with them from the UK. They were staying in Amman until it was deemed safe enough to return to Lebanon.

Hazel too was keen to get settled at Eastwood, and it was decided we would attempt to open on Monday, November 6th. This would allow her a little more recovery time following the fall and for life to begin to return to some sort of normality. I wrote home, "Hadeth to the north of us is beginning to open up a little, but many have fled. Those in villages to the south are tentatively watching the security situation. The Lord has kept this building in the position where it is, and so we pray He will bring the children He wants to be here." A few days later, the news was even more encouraging; I wrote, "Things are more settled. Hadeth in particular is recovering, but the devastation is far, far worse than the Civil War destruction of 1975/76. People are slowly beginning to return to their homes and gather up what's left after the looting. Soldiers from the Lebanese army are patrolling the streets."

By the end of October, I was living in my flat again and trying to make it habitable. "I've just finished mending my duvet before sleeping under it tonight," I wrote home. "A bullet hole around one-and-a-half inches long burnt through it, and you can imagine the fluff all inside the cover! I also chased mosquitoes, bedbugs, cockroaches and a lizard out of the flat and finally settled down to sleep." In spite of all this, the next morning I wrote, "It brings back so many memories waking up here again, and I'm full of praise." It was a joy to have running water, proper sanitation and a reasonable supply of electricity as we prepared to open the school. I was very conscious of prayer backing from so many friends and particularly those at All Saints, Marple, who in turn were supporting my own family. *"Yes, and I will continue to rejoice, for I know that through your prayers and the help given by the Spirit of Jesus Christ what has happened to me will turn out for my deliverance."*[3]

Each evening, as before, those of us living in the building gathered together on the fifth floor and sought the Lord for His Word of encouragement and affirmation. We were conscious that, though the village was unharmed in this latest upsurge in factional fighting, there was much fear in people's hearts. Would they be willing not only to register the children but also to risk their safety on the roads? Hazel had a vision similar to the prophet Haggai of the school once again being the place where God's Presence would be known and His Name honoured. This was to be a time of rebuilding. *"'Give careful thought to your ways. ... build my house, so that I might take pleasure in it and be honoured,' says the LORD. ... 'I am with you,' declares the LORD. So the LORD stirred up the spirit of Zerubbabel ... of Joshua ... and the spirit of the whole remnant of the people. They came and began to work on the house of the LORD Almighty, their God."*[4]

These words from the Lord were particularly pertinent to me as I sought to take the lead in the rebuilding of trust amongst the staff and in fostering a happy working atmosphere. Everyone had been affected by the warfare and lawlessness, and many were still grieving the tragic loss of Hélène Mansour, who had led the department so well. The chaos I found on the ground floor was overwhelming, in spite of having been warned, and there was much to face before we could reopen to the children. Yet

[3] Philippians 1:18b,19
[4] Haggai 1:7,8,13,14

with the task of rebuilding came the Lord's encouragement: *"'...be strong, Zerubbabel,' declares the LORD. 'Be strong, Joshua ... Be strong, all you people of the land,' declares the LORD, 'and work. For I am with you,' declares the LORD Almighty. ... '...my Spirit remains among you. Do not fear.'"*[5] Furthermore, there was a staggering promise: *"'The glory of this present house will be greater than the glory of the former house,' says the LORD Almighty. 'And in this place I will grant peace,' declares the LORD Almighty."*[6]

For me personally, there was further encouragement and a word to my heart from the prophet Jeremiah: *"Before I formed you in the womb I knew you, before you were born I set you apart; I appointed you..."*[7] When Jeremiah remonstrated with his feelings of inferiority and inadequacy, the Lord said, *"Do not say, 'I am too young.' You must go to everyone I send you to and say whatever I command you. Do not be afraid of them, for I am with you and will rescue you."*[8] With these promises in mind and the help of Jusef the caretaker and five of his children, we started to prepare for just four classes on the ground floor, one for each age group from three- to seven-year-olds. The furniture was all over the school building! Many of the cupboards were an absolute tip, books were torn and destroyed, and whole generations of cockroaches and lizards were dwelling in various rooms, including the children's cloakroom. Moving the piano was problematic, but when we did we were horrified to find all manner of creatures, including mice, scurrying about and gorging themselves on its inner workings. I wrote home, "Jusef went off into a great spate of Arabic and gave me such a look – a sort of 'now she's back and it all happens and things get moving' look! Anyway, he seemed to approve, and I was glad to be accepted back again." For once, I was grateful for the influence of a tidy-minded mother!

Having duly advertised the school reopening, at 8.30 am on Monday, November 6th, the children started to arrive with their parents. By midday, we had just over a hundred children in school, of which forty were seven years old and under and in my department. We were thankful to have small classes in those early days, as each day the numbers increased. Four weeks later, there were some seventy children in the four classes on the ground floor, and most of the children were new to the school and spoke only Arabic. I wrote home, "The Lebanese teachers are as helpful as ever,

5   Haggai 2:4,5
6   Haggai 2:9
7   Jeremiah 1:5
8   Jeremiah 1:7,8

and I just praise the Lord for the spirit of hard work and cooperation. Truly, He is with us in every minute of every day." Staff-wise in the department, there were three Lebanese teachers plus one part-time, along with two mother-tongue English teachers and me. I was thankful to be working alongside a number of teachers whom I knew from previous years, including Jill, who worked with Mary Margaret in the pre-school. Lamia, who was in charge of the Arabic curriculum in the department and taught the six- and seven-year-olds, had joined the staff in Hélène Mansour's time. She was an excellent teacher, deeply committed to providing the children with a thorough grounding in the Arabic language and keen to establish a sound curriculum across the department.

One lunchtime, a meeting was convened in Amine's office on the first floor to which all the Lebanese teachers who taught Arabic were invited, along with Georgette, who was in charge of Arabic in the junior and senior schools. Lamia invited me to this meeting, which I opened and then felt it was appropriate to give full permission for the meeting to continue in Arabic. For the rest of the time, I prayerfully nodded and smiled around the circle until it was clear that Lamia was happy with the conclusions reached, and then thanked everyone for surrendering their precious lunch break. After each teacher had left the room, Lamia turned and said to me, "Thank you so much, Wendy – it made such a difference having you with us." "But I didn't say a word," I remonstrated. "It was just your calm presence," she replied. This was such an encouragement to me that the Lord had brought me back to Eastwood for a purpose and that He was truly with us. *"...the LORD, is in your midst; you shall fear evil no more."*[9]

The new English teacher, Heather, had only arrived the weekend before school reopened, and was living on the fifth floor with Hazel and six other teachers. Heather adapted well and was full of ideas for making English language learning an enjoyable part of the curriculum for five- and six-year-olds. There were stories and puppet shows along with plenty of hands-on activities in her classroom. I did miss Bahia, who by this time had found a teaching post in a kindergarten near her home in Beirut. As travelling from West Beirut could still be dangerous, it seemed wise for her to remain in her current post. René, a mother of two from Bsaba, near Kafarshima, had approached Amine and was available to take Bahia's class for Arabic. René was full of enthusiasm and good humour, and took her part in morning Assembly and telling Bible stories to her class, as indeed

[9] Zephaniah 3:15 (RSV)

did all the teachers. Once again, we organised daily Assembly, with the little ones sitting on *haseri* (roll up mats) and the rest on chairs, singing, praying and storytelling in both Arabic and English. This was a vital part of the school day, usually mid morning before break. Just before Christmas, I wrote to friends and family, "Many in this lawless land are gripped by fears and rumours, many are just longing and thirsting for an end and an answer to it all. Pray that by our lives, we may uplift Jesus and draw others to Him. In school we are finding a real openness to the Word of God." Furthermore I wrote, "Pray that even with such little ones, we may be able to portray such a picture of the character of God in Assembly and Bible lessons and in all our dealings with them, that they will be drawn to trust in the One in whom perfect love and perfect justice meet."

Those early days were challenging and especially with regard to issues of behaviour. Many of the older boys were involved in political groups and were threatening to defend their little siblings with their guns. I felt so strongly about this that I totally banned toy guns from the department! For me, it was the kindergarten class, the four-year-olds, none of whom spoke any English, who taxed my patience the most. I longed for these children to experience some sort of normality in their little lives, as they had all been born into the wartime chaos that was Lebanon from early 1975. I wrote home for prayer. "Please pray I'll have patience with myself and patience with undisciplined children. Pray the Lord will give me His love for them. Nearly all are products of a war-torn country and many have widowed, fearful mothers trying to cope in damaged houses and apartments." And those prayers were answered. Only a week later, I wrote, "The political situation is far from settled, but praise the Lord for the semblance of discipline and normality we have here in school, with one or two new children coming every few days." As a staff team, we managed short times of prayer and sharing together, reassuring and encouraging one another.

I discovered that there are so many incidences in Scripture when the prophets remind God's people that the Lord is in the midst of them, working to heal and restore. *"I will repay you for the years the locusts have eaten … you will know that I am in Israel … never again will my people be shamed."*[10] There were promises of protection too. *"…I will be to her a wall of fire round about, says the LORD, and I will be the glory within her. … I come and I will dwell in the midst of you, says the LORD."*[11] For me, the most precious

[10] Joel 2:25,27 (RSV)
[11] Zechariah 2:5,10 (RSV)

promise from the Lord at this time was from Zephaniah: *"Do not fear, O Zion; let not your hands grow weak. The LORD your God is in your midst, a warrior who gives victory; he will rejoice over you with gladness, he will renew you in his love."*[12] I sensed that this was such a deep love that it could not be expressed in words, only in the silence of quiet prayer.

As the school numbers increased and with it the workload, I was so thankful for my privacy on the fourth floor. I was in no way isolated, as there was a Lebanese family of four living in the large room next door to my bathroom, the father of whom taught Arabic in the senior school. Their house in Beirut had suffered much destruction by shell and mortar fire, and it was good to have them with us in the building and the two boys in school. Furthermore, it was a huge help that Madame Khoury cooked a Lebanese meal for us every day in school time that we ate in the evenings.

Most Saturdays, I was able to borrow a car from Monsieur Khoury, who owned a garage in the city – sometimes a little blue Datsun, sometimes an orange Fiat 127 – and drive south down the Sidon Road and back north towards Beirut via the airport road. This was not the shortest but it was certainly the safest route into West Beirut. I looked forward to the break, staying overnight with Afaf and her mother. This became a safe haven for me where I could enjoy home life and an escape from living on top of the job. I wrote to my parents, "I praise the Lord so much for the acceptance I receive in Afaf's home. Being in Beirut, it's easier to get to church on Sunday mornings, where I still play the piano for the services." Hazel was restricted to her crutches, so we were thankful to have her younger sister Patricia staying with us on the fifth floor at that time. As my birthday approached at the end of November, one of the Khoury family, Armande, who had helped me on the ground floor from time to time, made a cake for me. I was glad to be able to share it with Patricia and Hazel, along with Joy and Sami and their children when they happily came to meet Patricia on my birthday.

By early December, the weather was changing. "The rains seem to have come with a vengeance," I wrote home, "and as usual, the roads are flooded. As I look out now, I can see a most beautiful sunset over the sea and a huge rainbow – always a sign of God's promise of blessing." Our numbers in the department were steady and we turned our thoughts towards Christmas. We would love to have prepared the children to perform a Nativity for their families as at previous Christmases, but there

---

[12] Zephaniah 3:16,17 (RSV)

236

was simply no time to practise. We did, however, place a special emphasis upon the Christmas story in daily assemblies during the last three weeks of term by using a 'Surprise Box'.

Each morning, we brought a different flannelgraph character out of the box whom God surprised as He prepared the way for the coming of Jesus as a babe in Bethlehem. The very first surprise in God's special book came from the prophet Isaiah to King Ahaz many years before Jesus was born. *"For to us a child is born, to us a son is given..."*[13] A baby King? To fight the enemy? What a surprise! He would be kind and loving, good and wise, and He

Christmas parties.
Top: Rene with kindergarten, 1978.
Bottom: Jill with pre-school, 1979.

would save the people from their enemies. Next came Zechariah and Elizabeth. They knew Isaiah's news that God would send a baby King, but they were sad because they had no children of their own. One day, Zechariah was praying quietly in the Temple, when suddenly an angel appeared in front of him to bring a special message from God. What a surprise! Elizabeth, though she was old, was to have a baby who would prepare the way for the baby King. Every couple of days, we brought a new character out of the box and marvelled at their surprise as the angel of God appeared to them. After Elizabeth came her younger cousin Mary, then Joseph, and then the biggest surprise of all when the baby Jesus was born to Mary. In a palace? No – in a manger, along with the animals where the shepherds found Him warm and cosy, wrapped in cloths. One of our favourite songs reminded us of the love of God, who sent Jesus to be our friend.

> *God gave us a baby, how good is the Lord!*
> *He sent the Lord Jesus, how good is the Lord!*

[13] Isaiah 9:6

237

He sent the Lord Jesus, how good is the Lord!
I never will forget what He has done for me.

René suggested we give the children a surprise party the day before the term ended. "I spent last evening stringing up streamers the children had made all round the kindergarten and down the corridors," I wrote home. We all made paper hats too, and some of the parents sent cakes and sweets for the party. Father Christmas (one of the senior Arabic teachers) surprised us with presents, the sun shone, and the term ended happily with party games and a group photo of us all out in the playground. "It's so wonderful how the Lord overrules in all the little details," I wrote home, "and helps me to cope with the high-powered emotionalism of the Lebanese teachers and children alike, especially at a time of excitement like this."

I had already mentioned to my parents that it was doubtful I would be able to come home for Christmas, even though my father had offered to pay the fare. Term had started late due to the fighting, and we were allocated just ten days' holiday. I knew there was still a deal to do in the department in order to be ready for the spring term. But I too was due for a surprise.

CHAPTER TWENTY

Damascene Adventure

T hough the rains had come just before our Christmas party, the last week of term was fine, cooler in the evenings, but gloriously sunny during the day. I reflected in the letter I sent home, "The dry weather has been a blessing and made things so much easier this last week. The oranges, grapefruits and tangerines in the garden are at their best right now, so I'm bubbling over with Vitamin C!"

Term finished on Friday, December 22nd, and I drove into Beirut to stay with Afaf and her mother as usual over the weekend. They were spending Christmas Day with relatives, "so it seemed appropriate for me to come back to Eastwood with Bahia, who used to teach here in the kindergarten," I wrote home. "She has no Christmas celebration at all if she stays surrounded by her Muslim family." I was hoping that her three children would be allowed to come too. The plan thereafter was for me to spend a few days sorting books in the library on the ground floor and be ready for school to reopen on Tuesday, January 2nd, 1979.

Christmas Eve was a Sunday, and I was happy playing all the favourite carols in church. Gordon Gale was taking the service, and the focus of his teaching was on the words of the angels to the shepherds. *"Glory to God in the highest heaven, and on earth peace to those on whom his favour rests."*[1] How can we know the Lord's peace in the midst of such uncertain and potentially dangerous times? *"For he himself is our peace..."*[2] How can it be then that Jesus taught, *"I did not come to bring peace, but a sword"*[3]? Gordon expounded the passage in terms of our personal relationship with the

---

[1] Luke 2:14
[2] Ephesians 2:14
[3] Matthew 10:34

Bahia and family, and Rosa, one of the caretaker's daughters.

Saviour who is our peace. Whenever the old sinful nature of selfish desires and resentments rears its head, then the believer loses his peace. The only answer lies, suggested Gordon, in the daily surrendering to the One who went to the Cross in order to bring us peace. *"I have told you these things, so that in me you may have peace. In this world you will have trouble. But take heart! I have overcome the world."*[4] During the previous evening, I had woken up feeling somewhat bereft, possibly homesick, and Afaf had prayed with me and for my family back home in England. Gordon's teaching brought such a reassurance to my heart that when we walk in obedience to God's loving will, we will know His peace, whatever our circumstances. *"Peace I leave with you; my peace I give you. I do not give to you as the world gives. Do not let your hearts be troubled and do not be afraid."*[5]

Christmas Day dawned bright and sunny, and I drove into Beirut to collect Bahia along with her children, Mona, Nadim and Nabil, to celebrate the day with Hazel and me at Eastwood. The children played outside and we had a precious time together. Boxing Day was spent with other missionaries at the home of the field leader in nearby Hadeth. I wrote home, "It's lovely they've welcomed me as an associate." It was during the following few days when I was working on the ground floor that Afaf heard of the possibility of a lift with an English couple *en route* to Jordan via Syria. Would we like to travel with them, perhaps, as far as Damascus and spend the New Year there? Such an unexpected surprise! We most certainly would!

We had driven through and around Damascus ourselves *en route* for Amman in previous years but had never paused to explore. This seemed an excellent opportunity to wander round the Old City and visit some of the places I had read about in the Acts of the Apostles. I knew that Damascus had been founded in Roman times. Might I be able to walk

4 John 16:33
5 John 14:27

down the street called Straight where Saul stayed after his dramatic meeting with Jesus as he neared the city? Might there be evidence of the house where Ananias laid hands on him to restore his sight? Would I be able to stand and look up to the opening in the city wall where the early Christian believers took Saul by night, lowering him in a basket so that he could escape to Jerusalem? My head was full of questions as we set off in the back seat of our friends' spacious vehicle up the Damascus road out of Beirut, twisting and turning through the mountains, across the Beka'a Valley alley and towards the Syrian border.

On arrival, we booked for a couple of nights at Al Raja Hotel. It was not the most salubrious establishment, but it was central to the Biblical sites I was longing to see. We soon found our way into the ancient Souk Al-Hamidiyah, an enormous covered market teeming with life. Built around 1780, it boasts an unusually tall, arched metal roof, dotted with holes to let in the light. As well as numerous cafés and ice cream parlours, the Souk is full of artisans plying their traditional handicrafts, such as beaten copperware and wooden mosaic artwork. We wandered past scores of shops on either side of the central walkway, each with a separate doorway; clothes and textile shops, jewellers, perfumeries, grocery stores, spice merchants, confectioners selling sugared Syrian fruits, *baklava* and much more. The colours, the noise and the aromas were almost overwhelming. As we emerged from the covered Souk, we found ourselves amidst open market stalls and, as I wrote home, "had great fun bartering for bargains". I had not forgotten my bartering skills or the necessary Arabic phrases and was amazed to find myself mistaken for an Arab, even with my fair skin! This caused much amusement to Afaf, who was, of course, fluent in Arabic, and to the stall holder too when I confessed that I was *"inglezi*[6]*"*.

After a somewhat uncomfortable night at the hotel, we made our way to an evangelical church known to Afaf, to meet with the believers and share fellowship with them. "The believers have done everything they could to make us feel welcome," I wrote home. "This afternoon, we were taken by car for an amazing trip all over the city and around, including Straight Street where Saul was staying and the spot in the city wall from where it is reputed he escaped in a basket."

We paused to spend time wandering along Straight Street, the main Roman road running from east to west through the old city. It seemed narrow in the most part, with overhanging enclosed balconies and still

---

[6] English

more oriental craft workshops in front of houses with ornate courtyards. I was particularly fascinated to watch expert mosaic craftsmen at work by the side of the street. They were surrounded by bundles of tiny thin straw-like pieces of wood in a multitude of colours that were glued together in geometric patterns. Once secure, the bundles were sawn into delicate mosaics and used to inlay all manner of goods, from mirror and clock frames, chessboards and wooden boxes of varying sizes, to oriental tables, armchairs and larger pieces of furniture. Some items literally shone with tiny pieces of mother-of-pearl encrusted in and amongst the wooden mosaic. I had seen these inlaid wooden items in artisan stores in Beirut; to actually watch master craftsmen at work was a joy.

As we continued our tour, it was as if the words from the Acts of the Apostles were coming alive before my very eyes: *"The Lord told [Ananias], 'Go to the house of Judas on Straight Street and ask for a man from Tarsus named Saul, for he is praying. In a vision he has seen a man named Ananias come and place his hands on him to restore his sight.'"*[7] We were taken through a Roman triumphal arch and into the old city. Here we were shown the traditional site of the house of Judas where Saul was praying. From there, we were taken to an ancient gate to the southeast of the city. Our Syrian guide pointed to a small opening high up in the wall, from which it is reputed Saul was lowered in a basket to escape the evil intent of the Jews. *"...his followers took him by night and lowered him in a basket through an opening in the wall."*[8]

Following the tour, we were taken to visit another family from the church and plied with cold drinks and *baklava*, followed by sweet Arabic coffee in tiny cups, and then delivered back to our hotel with much to reflect upon. But the day was not over! At 8 pm, we were collected again, driven back to the church, and there we stayed to celebrate New Year's Eve. Adults and children mingled together enjoying short plays, games and delicious food until just before midnight. At this point, quiet descended and the pastor gave a new year's message in Arabic. This was followed by prayer together as we gave thanks for the old year and welcomed in the new with worship and much hugging and embracing. On the way back to the hotel by taxi, we were surrounded by a cacophony of blaring and hooting of horns, the usual custom on New Year's Eve, along with joyous shouting, singing and whistling as folks drove through the city

[7] Acts 9:11,12
[8] Acts 9:25

242

flashing their headlights and sitting on top of their cars! Afaf and I were seated in the back seat marvelling at the experience, when the Syrian believer who was escorting us turned round and declared from the front, "Jesus is coming!" As I later wrote to my parents, "I shall never forget our weekend in Damascus!"

We travelled back to Beirut by *servis* car that afternoon, and I was pleased to be back at Eastwood by 5 pm, ready to welcome the children once again on Tuesday, January 2nd. Letters from home awaited me, including one from Amine to my parents, the owner of the school, whom they had met the previous Easter when he was studying in Cambridge. He had sent them a circular letter with handwritten words at the end. "We are thrilled to have Wendy back. She is a really precious person, and her love and devotion to the Lord's work through her responsibility at Eastwood is a great example and witness. The whole department of the young ones is a different world with Wendy around. I cannot express enough how grateful to God we all are for sending us Wendy again." He closed with some words of reassurance. "Don't worry at all; we are looking after her and it is quite safe in Kafarshima."

This was a huge encouragement to me, especially as Amine and I did not always see eye to eye when parents were pushing their children towards academic achievement at what I considered far too young an age. The spring term presented us with yet more new children and more domineering parents. On just the second day of term, Amine was struggling with a couple who were demanding that their daughter of five years and four months should be placed in the seven-year-old class because she was so intelligent. The more we explained our child-centred policies and group learning, the more they pushed. Eventually they left, and I felt sad that we had seemingly failed to convince them. About twenty minutes later, another new family appeared, and this mother could not have been more in favour and immediately registered her child with us. I wrote home, "Praise the Lord for such an encouragement!" and added, "I'm just so thankful, too, for the way the teachers react and their general support. The Lord truly has given me wonderful teachers. I'm thrilled at the way they support each other, their conscientious approach and the way they support me too." New pupils were being admitted almost daily, and settling them in with the other children required God-given patience from us all.

Towards the end of January, I found myself to be more physically tired at the end of each school day than ever. Afaf suggested I should stay with her and her mother for the whole weekend, rather than just overnight on Saturday. It was good to have the break away from the school. I wrote to my parents, "We had a wonderful reminder in church this morning, not only of the faithfulness of God, the Governor of the Nations, working out His will even in this situation here, but also from the Book of Job. Job's trust in God was tested no matter how extreme or difficult the circumstances were." "...for dominion belongs to the LORD and he rules over the nations."[9] "But he knows the way that I take; when he has tested me, I shall come forth as gold."[10] I continued in my letter home, "Praise God for daily renewal in His Spirit to face each day, and pray please that I might have more patience with the children at times when it seems such a battle." I certainly sensed the power of prayer; as if there were a wall of protection round about us as we faced each new day with all its uncertainties.

Back at Eastwood, we continued our prayer and Bible study together on Sunday evenings. God's Word was always uncannily appropriate to our needs. When tempted to feel resentful or misunderstood, His Word was clear in its simplicity. "Above all, love each other deeply, because love covers over a multitude of sins."[11] Chapter 5 is even more specific with Peter's teaching: "All of you, clothe yourselves with humility towards one another, because, 'God opposes the proud but shows favour to the humble.'"[12] On the evening I returned from my weekend at Afaf's home, we were meeting in my sitting room on the fourth floor and studying 2 Timothy together, especially Paul's encouragement to Timothy to be faithful to his calling: "...for God did not give us a spirit of timidity but a spirit of power and love and self-control."[13] How I needed to take these words to heart as I prepared for a new school week, claiming God's grace and humility.

The continuing political uncertainties and the winter rains were taking their toll on the health of the staff in the department, particularly Heather, recently arrived from England. I wrote home in early February, "Heather has been off sick for two weeks now with a very bad attack of flu and the resulting side effects, weakness and dizziness." I continued, "So I've been teaching her five-year-olds along with my four-year-olds for one-and-a-

9 Psalm 22:28
10 Job 23:10
11 1 Peter 4:8
12 1 Peter 5:5, quoting from Proverbs 3:34
13 2 Timothy 1:7 (RSV)

half hours every morning – forty-three children – and it has been a bit of a strain." We also had to double up classes in the after-noons, and I was glad to have an hour-long *siesta* as soon as school finished for the day. I too went down with a bout of 'Beirut tummy', but managed to sleep it off on a diet of bananas and yoghurt!

David, Hussein and Carol in the
sand, June 1979.

By mid February, spring was well on its way, with wild cyclamen and anemones filling the fields and hedgerows with colour. There was a national holiday to celebrate the prophet Mohammed's birthday, and I was well enough to go with Afaf and her mother for a drive in the mountains above the school. The roads were safe, and it was a joy to visit the potter at work in Jisr-el-Qadi, a pretty village on the Damour River between Beiteddine and Souk el-Gharb. Later I wrote home, "It's such a breakthrough to be able to drive around a little, especially in the hills to the north and east where there has been so much fighting. Now the whole area is patrolled by Syrian soldiers of the Arab League peacekeeping force. They tell you if there is any sniping and turn you back." It was encouraging to see life returning to normal, but how we longed and prayed for a peaceful settlement and real stability. Other blessings at that time included post from home that had been delayed by up to three months because of the earlier unrest. It did seem as if the Lebanese ability to bounce back and rebuild was taking effect, even if caution was necessary when travelling from one side of Beirut to the other.

Life at school continued, and I was so thankful for all the prayerful support I was receiving. I wrote home, "I know this is God's place for me right now. True, it's not easy. We're in a battle, and the more intense the battle, the greater we prove the weapon of prayer against all Satan's attacks. God's Spirit is moving and prayer is being answered, and I praise Him for the strength, the wisdom and the patience He is giving me." I felt like the Colossian believers as Paul prayed for them to be *"strengthened with all power according to his glorious might so that you may have great endurance and patience."*[14]

---

[14] Colossians 1:11

Mary Margaret on playground
duty, March 1979.

Discipline did not get any easier as term went on, and I solicited concerted prayer from friends at home. "Please pray for the discipline within the department. The seven-year-old boys are becoming quite tough, and integrating new children has not made matters any easier." I once resorted to sticking a six-year-old boy down on his chair with sticky tape because he was interfering so much with other children. Unfortunately, when it was his turn to come to my table to read from his book and show me his work, in the busyness of the classroom activities I had forgotten about the sticky tape! A little girl, Anna, spoke up on his behalf: "Miss Radcliffe, Wa'el can't move." And so I literally carried him on his chair to read to me. I hated having to humiliate him in this way, but he did say "thank you" when I released him at home time, and his parents made no complaints. Great patience was needed when dealing with children who had become accustomed to the prevailing atmosphere of guns and stick-up-for-your-rights while we were seeking to exercise control in a firm but lovingly consistent way.

All the teachers were sharing in our daily times of Assembly with the three- to seven-year-olds, now numbering eighty in the department. The school buses arrived each day with their precious cargo, and some would go out into the surrounding area for a second load of children. From my fourth-floor balcony, I would often see the little ones playing on the swings and seesaws in the garden, which was bathed in early morning sunshine. Early one day, I wrote home, "I thank the Lord that He renews my love for these children, and I'm so grateful for all that the teachers contribute daily. I wonder what this day will hold for all of us. He knows."

Such was our confidence that life was returning to normal, that I suggested to my parents that my sixteen-year-old brother Robin might like to come and visit as soon as he finished his O level and CSE exams. The invitation came with a warning that we may have to abandon the idea if there were any hint of full-scale fighting breaking out again. The excursion ticket for a youth fare with BA or MEA would last a full thirty days, so I suggested he come mid June to mid July. School was expected to remain open until the third week of July to make up for time lost at the beginning of the school year. I wrote home, "I would love him to have the full benefit of living in another culture." The Lebanese family who lived with Hazel on the fifth floor had a fifteen-year-old son who spoke good English, and I knew there would be others who would befriend Robin. I bombarded my father with details of passport, visa and vaccinations that would be necessary and warned him about the heat. "It will be hot by June / July, and no doubt Robin will spend a good deal of time in the school swimming pool. And there's always the Med!"

Writing to friends at home, I thanked those who were praying for our safety. "I watch the children bounce into school morning by morning, and I just praise Him that He's enabling us to give them as near to normal a school life and education as is possible in this country in the melting pot – a land still fraught apart by the strifes and ambitions of the different political party leaders." The freedom to take Assembly as an act of Christian worship with children from Christian, Muslim and Druze backgrounds was not to be taken for granted. One day in a Junior 1 (six- and seven-year-olds) English lesson, Carol from a nominal Christian family in nearby Hadeth (they had two rooms left in which to live) wrote in her writing book, "I like Jesus," and then drew a picture of the story we had been sharing in Assembly that week about the raising of Jairus' daughter by Jesus. I wrote home, "Isn't this just what we are praying for? That from an early age the children will be secure in His love for them and respond in simple childlike faith and love towards Jesus Himself?" I continued, "You should hear them singing *Jesus loves me, this I know* and many other songs in English and in Arabic."

Parents often told us how their children loved Assembly. "What do you do?" asked a Muslim mother to the kindergarten Arabic teacher. "Well, you come and see," replied René. "Ten past ten every morning." And she did! Another mother came to tell me that Lina, aged five years, now tells her grandmother that when you pray, you put your hands together so, and you don't have to go down on your knees and kiss the ground. God always hears us when we talk to Him because He wants to be our friend. We often sang our prayer song to remind the children.

Talk to God, talk to God,
He hears what we say.
Talk to God, talk to God,

Every, every day.

David's mother told me that she heard her five-year-old son by his bedside at night praying in English – "just fank you in my heart" – from words we always prayed at the beginning of Assembly that I learnt when I first started teaching at Kingsmead School in Hoylake.

When I'm very quiet and still,
I think how loving God must be.
I just say thank You in my heart
For all His love and care for me.

What a privilege it was to share God's love so openly with these children at such a time of national suffering and uncertainty.

Early in March, a heavy head cold descended upon me, probably due to unexpected torrential rain and a drop in temperatures. Heather was off sick again with bronchitis, and so we were particularly busy in the department. After a few days and many hot lemon drinks, I rang our doctor in East Beirut, who prescribed an antibiotic that left me feeling sick and dizzy. Afaf kindly brought me to her flat in Beirut at the weekend so that I could take a break, and all I could do was sleep! I was completely drained of energy and could not even manage to stand up to sing the hymns at church on Sunday morning. That night, I had severe abdominal pains and rang the doctor and then the school to explain that Dr Manoogian had signed me off sick and ordered a couple of days' complete rest. Furthermore, I was asked to attend at the hospital as soon as possible for tests. "I hardly dare tell you," I wrote to my parents, "what Dr Manoogian suspects from the symptoms I've described to him. He asked me to go out onto the balcony and look at the whites of my eyes in a mirror. Guess what? They are a delicate shade of yellow!"

CHAPTER TWENTY-ONE

Hammana

D
r Manoogian clearly wanted to check me out as soon as possible, so I was thankful for a lift back to Eastwood with Amine as we were expecting a visit from the British Ambassador the next day. As I explained in my letter home, "I'm hoping someone from Eastwood will be able to take me through to see Dr Manoogian after school one day this week in order to have some tests. He's in Ashrafieh in East Beirut at the Christian Medical Centre (CMC) and you have to know which are the safe roads to take." I was longing to be physically fit again and yet so thankful that Heather was feeling better and that a trained teacher from the village had contacted the school and was willing to teach the kindergarten. What provision for such a time as this! And God spoke to me through His Word, nourishing me with His promises. *"Surely it is you who love the people; all the holy ones are in your hand."*[1] As I continued reading this chapter of blessings, I was struck by more promises. *"...your strength will equal your days,"* and, *"The eternal God is your refuge, and underneath are the everlasting arms."*[2] "He's there," I wrote home. "I'm not only in His hands, but His arms are underneath, supporting and strengthening."

On Wednesday, March 14th, Edmond Khoury, the younger brother of Amine, offered to drive me to the hospital in Ashrafieh. I had been well treated there in 1974 when admitted for a few days with a severe viral infection. Edmond was an excellent driver, and we took a roundabout route to avoid unsafe areas. During the journey, he explained he was travelling to London two days later and was more than willing to take letters to post at Heathrow. Furthermore, he suggested I might like to make

[1] Deuteronomy 33:3
[2] Deuteronomy 33:25,27

249

a cassette tape that he would post to my parents to explain to them what was happening, including Hazel's plans for my subsequent care. I warmed to his suggestion.

Dr Manoogian took one look at me and declared, "Jaundice. Have you heard of jaundice?" I explained I had suffered from jaundice as a small child and could still remember my skin becoming yellow and the need to eat little and often and drink lots of water. "Infective hepatitis is much more serious than childhood jaundice," he said, and proceeded to prod around my liver region and explain how inflamed it was. I was certainly in pain, and mentioned how nauseous I felt and the yellowness of the skin all over my body. The tests revealed low blood pressure and a high level of bilirubin, a bile pigment secreted by the liver. The doctor's diagnosis was clear. "This will take longer to recover from than your childhood jaundice, and you are infectious. I suggest one to two months without work and be careful for up to twelve months." As I absorbed this information, he continued, "You will need a low-fat diet with high carbohydrate and plenty of lean protein, especially fish." He prescribed a cortisone drug to relieve the pain initially and a tablet to take before meals to regulate the bile.

Hazel, who from her many years of life in Lebanon was experienced in dealing with Westerners who contracted hepatitis, was soon making arrangements for my recovery. I was able to share these with my parents on the cassette tape I made that evening for Edmond to post on his arrival in England. Speaking into my portable tape recorder felt like a one-sided telephone call. "I now know where my liver is," I said with feeling, "but Dr Manoogian was very good, and though in pain and utterly exhausted, I am just so thankful for a clear diagnosis and treatment plan. I know I'm not indispensable in school and I know the teachers will cope, as it's only four weeks until the Easter break. In fact, I do praise the Lord for giving me this time and a sense of peace that all will be well." "*Peace I leave with you; my peace I give you. I do not give to you as the world gives. Do not let your hearts be troubled and do not be afraid.*"[3]

It was clear that I could not stay in my fourth-floor flat in the school building. Isolation would have been impossible with people coming and going. Equally difficult would have been keeping to a low-fat, high-carbohydrate diet. I certainly was in no fit state to fly home to England, and admittance to the CMC in Ashrafieh was risky because of the factional

[3] John 14:27

fighting in that area. Hazel suggested a Christian hospital situated about thirty kilometres east of Beirut in the mountain village of Hammana, about a ninety-minute drive from Kafarshima.

Hamlin Hospital was founded in 1907 by an enterprising young doctor, Mary Eddy, in order to care for patients suffering from tuberculosis, who at that time were treated as outcasts. The original hospital, built in memory of Rev. T. Hamlin, was near the Mediterranean coast, but this proved to be too hot and humid in the summer months and unsuitable for TB patients. The decision was taken to organise a summer resort in the beautiful valley of Hammana. After a few years of transporting patients by mule to the camp in Hammana at nine hundred metres for the summer and back down again for the winter months, an old school building on the edge of the village was purchased for use by the patients. When war broke out in 1914, it became impossible to transport them in safety, and from then on, the TB Sanatorium was established in Hammana as a hospital for chest diseases. From the very beginning, Dr Eddy, inspired by Jesus Christ and His love, committed to caring for the patients in body and soul.

By the present time, and four years into the Civil War, many sick and wounded people had come for help when roads were blocked and there was no other way of reaching another hospital. Doctors and other physicians, including nurses and midwives, were offering help. Hamlin had become a small general hospital, which included wards dedicated to care of the elderly, infirm and chronically ill patients, as well as a small operating theatre, maternity ward, children's TB ward and pharmacy. There was even a room dedicated for use as a chapel, with regular visits from local pastors.

Hazel encouraged me to pack winter clothes and a hot water bottle, as she knew it would be cooler in the mountains, and then left to attempt a phone call to ensure there was a room available for me. Unfortunately, she was unable to catch the line, but undaunted, she decided we would go the next day in the hope that I could be admitted! "Please pray I'll know how to use the time," I said on the cassette tape to my parents that evening. "It's a gift! Pray I'll have the energy to plan Assemblies and the work for my classes and make the best use of this time of rest."

Thursday, March 15th dawned bright and sunny, and after a whirlwind tour of saying goodbyes to the teachers, I was ready to leave at 1 pm. Hazel's car was in use, so we packed mine and set off with me in the driving seat, feeling somewhat queasy and distinctly yellowish in colour.

Hamlin Hospital, 1979.

I had perhaps unwisely volunteered to drive, as Hazel was still using her crutches, which were tucked down the passenger side of the car. Into the Lebanese mountains we drove, soon to be stopped at a checkpoint manned by Syrian soldiers of the Arab League peacekeeping force. They were friendly enough as I explained in my broken Arabic that we were on our way to the hospital in Hammana, but it took a while to deliberate on the state of the road and whether it was safe enough to continue. Hazel grew a little impatient and tapped her crutches, whereupon we were waved on without further ado! "Hazel," I said, trying not to explode, "whatever will you say when the soldiers on the other side of the road see you driving back again?" I never did find out.

We continued along eerily quiet mountain roads with beautiful views, passing several villages scattered along the mountain ridge. Some of the houses had pitched red-tiled roofs for warmth and protection from the elements in the winter. Ahead of us loomed an oasis of a thousand pine trees, planted many years previously to provide shade on the driveway and in the hospital grounds. Somewhat apprehensively, I drove down the road passing the house of Dr and Mrs Nucho who worked at Hamlin. As we approached the gate, it was opened by the gateman, and we drove into the main courtyard. It was late afternoon, and we were met by Nans, one of the hospital staff, who lived in a small flat near the gate. As Hazel explained my need for rehabilitation and care, I awaited a decision, sincerely trusting that a suitable room would be available. After barely half an hour, I was admitted, and so it was that in just over twenty-four hours from my diagnosis, I found myself tucking into a chicken supper in my room in the Lebanese mountains!

My first full day at Hamlin was decidedly eventful. I woke that morning needing to orientate myself and discovered I was in a private room on a first-floor corridor. There was a double-glazed door out onto a large balcony with an overhanging roof for shade, that was shared with three other rooms. As I was the only patient at that time, I had the joy of the balcony to myself. The view from the window was not expansive but very beautiful. As I stood on the balcony, an image of Switzerland lay before me: a rocky outcrop covered with evergreens – pines, firs and spruce, as well as the cedar trees for which Lebanon is famous – and little houses nestled against the rock, all set against an azure blue sky. "I have a rather forbidding notice on the door into the corridor which says 'ISO-LATION' in large red capital let-

On my balcony at Hamlin Hospital, March 1979.

ters and has instructions about the disposal of linen and eating utensils," I informed my parents in my letter home. Leading from the room was a tiny bathroom with shower, toilet and handbasin. "So since arrival on Thursday afternoon, I've been restricted to the room, the bathroom and the balcony, but I assure you, there's never a dull moment!"

Even before breakfast, I had temperature and blood checks, and around 9 am, a plumber arrived to fix the toilet that refused to flush. It was a high-level cistern that had clearly not functioned for some time. However, with the help of his mate and much tinkering, he finally announced success, and they both departed along with their ladder and toolkits. I had been sitting in bed preparing some kindergarten books for Nada, the teacher who had offered to stand in for me, and was thankful to have access to the bathroom. Having pulled the flush, I returned to my books and later described what happened in my letter. "The water settled down in the tank and then *whoosh* – the whole procedure started again, and again, and again. And there was nothing I could do to stop it!" Two nurses appeared to straighten the bed and quickly called the plumbers to fix the continuous flushing. The whole incident reminded me of an episode from *Steptoe & Son*[4], as just as the men arrived with all their paraphernalia and were debating the situation, in came the doctor and sister. Dr Nucho promptly ordered me back into bed! Marching into the bathroom, I heard him say, *"Automatique? Bravo aleki...*[5] *lakin...*[6]*"* I didn't catch the rest as I was choking with laughter on my bed.

[4] BBC sitcom of the 1970s
[5] Well done...
[6] but...

I was pleased to meet Dr Nucho, the medical director of the hospital. He had taken over the responsibility from his father in 1955, aged thirty-nine, following a shooting by an angry patient that killed Dr Nucho Senior and shot his son in the right hand. The main hospital building, the former school, was named the Nucho building in memory of him. Because of the shot in his hand, Dr Nucho Junior could no longer perform operations, but his other skills were well used in general practice. Mrs Nucho was an American nurse who helped in the operating theatre and taught in the nursing school. It was clear that they were both devoted to the work God had given them at Hamlin, and I certainly felt in safe hands. Following an examination and an injunction to rest and not to fight the exhaustion, I was thankful to eat my chicken lunch and fall asleep. Thereafter, Dr Nucho included me in his daily rounds.

A regular visitor from the hospital staff was Nans, who had met us as we arrived at Hamlin in mid March. She had come to work at the hospital in January 1976, early in the Civil War, just three years previously. She was a Dutch missionary with a heart to serve in any way she could. Evangelistic work and pastoral visiting were high on the list, and she ran a Sunday school for the children in the hospital. Nans had worked for many years in the Beka'a Valley alongside the churches and schools of the National Evangelical Church. In 1975, when the 'troubles' began, travel through the villages became too dangerous and the work ceased. She told me how Dr Nucho had contacted her with a request for help as so many sick and wounded were coming to Hamlin at that time. Nans said that she was willing but was neither a doctor nor a nurse. "Dr Nucho replied that I had two hands," she told me, "and that was true." And so Nans settled in the hospital and applied her desire to serve in a myriad of ways. She was more than happy to help on the wards, distributing trays of food and giving the elderly TB patients extra attention. Most mornings, she was busy in the children's ward, telling the young TB patients Bible stories, singing and offering help with schoolwork and craft activities. Visiting the adult inpatients and their families in the villages offered unique opportunities to show the love of Jesus. Bible Society produced tracts in Arabic, and patients of all faiths would often accept these and ask for prayer.

I looked forward to Nans popping in to see me with news, and enjoyed times of prayer together. Her Syrian colleague, Amal, would visit too and share about her work in the hospital with the young TB patients. I had been watching Amal with the children from my balcony, as their ward was positioned at right angles to my part of the building. These children had experienced a lot of fear in their young lives. Even during their time in hospital, they had taken shelter in the basement more than once for safety from rocket blasts and nearby shooting. Amal shared with me a favourite verse that she would teach the children to memorise. *"The LORD is my light and my salvation – whom shall I fear? The LORD is the stronghold of my life – of whom shall I be afraid?"*[7]

Amal and Nans at Hamlin.

Nans and Amal organised Sunday morning services in the hospital chapel and invited local pastors to lead and preach. If roads to Hammana were unsafe, cassette tapes would be used with worship and teaching recorded from Trans World Radio. For Easter Sunday, a sunrise service was planned to be held on the rooftop above the chapel, and I longed to be well enough to take part. On my second Sunday at Hamlin, when I was still restricted to my room, a Syrian pastor tapped on the door. Rev. Kareem Khasha had been to speak at the 10 am chapel service and had been asked to visit me. "How are you?" he said. "Fine," said I, "every day a little better." "Every day with Jesus is sweeter than the day before," was his rejoinder. As he left, Pastor Kareem stood at the foot of the bed, almost as though he were leading the prayers in a service of worship, and I felt greatly humbled to be prayed over in this way. Later I was able to join the Sunday services myself and worship in my broken Arabic. Till then, I relished my own times of worship on Sunday mornings using two cassette tapes given me by my dear friend and Sunday school teacher from All Saints Marple, Edith Bowyer: 'Celebrate the Feast' with the Fisherfolk[8] and the Series 3 setting of the holy communion service.[9]

---

[7] Psalm 27:1

[8] a celebration of the Eucharist recorded live in St John's College, Oxford and released in 1975

[9] a musical setting to the alternative service of Holy Communion which was trialled by the Church of England in the 1970s and later incorporated into the Alternative Service Book (1980)

My nurse, Elise, and the view from the balcony, April 1979.

One Sunday afternoon, I was listening to a sermon on tape by Rev. John Stott from All Souls, Langham Place, London. I was lying back in bed, when there was a tap on the door. One of the Lebanese nurses entered, and I was puzzled because Nazlat, the staff nurse, had already checked my temperature, pulse and blood pressure. John Stott continued, and I turned over to switch the tape off. Acutely embarrassed, the nurse blurted out, *"Fie shee ta-ni?*[10]*"* and then disappeared like a flash! I felt sure that John Stott would be most flattered!

In spite of the isolation, I was never alone. "The presence of the Lord has become increasingly real this week," I wrote home. "I couldn't even count the number of folks who come in and out. Some give me mini Arabic lessons whilst bringing meals, making the bed or cleaning the bathroom. Others who know more English just come to chat, take my temperature and blood pressure." Amongst the hospital workers were Drs Victor and Huda, a married couple from Egypt, and Marguerite, an English midwife and MECO associate like me, who was in charge of the maternity unit. I asked my parents to pray especially for Élise, a Dutch nurse who came every afternoon to take my temperature and always stayed to chat. "It's such an enormous privilege and responsibility," I wrote home, "to see God at work through all these contacts."

God was at work in my heart too, even as I rested in these beautiful surroundings. Each evening, as I settled to sleep with the Psalms, I found verse after verse that echoed the gratitude I was feeling. "*...you, LORD, are a shield around me, my glory, the One who lifts my head high. ... I lie down and sleep; I wake again, because the LORD sustains me.*"[11] I really felt the truth of these words, as I was rarely able to sleep right through the night because of the ache behind the ribs on my right-hand side. "*I will lie down and sleep,*

[10] Do you need anything?
[11] Psalm 3:3,5

for you alone, LORD, make me dwell in safety."[12] If I had any doubt at all about deserting the school and the children, God spoke through the Psalms to reassure me. *"Know that the LORD has set apart his faithful servant for himself; the LORD hears when I call to him."*[13]

I was fascinated to find that Solomon's Song of Songs was full of references to Lebanon. *"King Solomon made for himself the carriage; he made it of wood from Lebanon."*[14] More precious reassurances came from these songs that touched my heart. *"I belong to my beloved, and his desire is for me."*[15] As I shared with my parents, I wrote, "I've never been so happy in my life – what a privilege to be given this time." In my newsletter to praying friends, I found the following verse to share:

> *In Thy strong hand I lay me down,*
> *So shall the work be done;*
> *For who can work so wondrously*
> *As the Almighty One?*[16]

My time in isolation was drawing to a close, and after three weeks of being confined to my room and balcony, I was determined to make the effort to get dressed. It was Palm Sunday, and when Victor and Huda, the Egyptian doctors working at the hospital, came to escort me to the chapel, I felt quite a sense of achievement. The Arabic was familiar and especially so the children's talk, as I was used to having my own storytelling in English translated into Arabic during Assembly at school. I wrote home to share with my parents. "It was quite an experience to be worshipping with TB patients in wheelchairs and children who are admitted here in the early stages of TB." On returning to my room with not a little pain behind the ribs, I discovered a dear friend from the LIVF group in Beirut had arrived, Lina, and we enjoyed a time of sharing and praying together. After lunch, I slept for three hours! The following day, yet more visitors from Beirut found their way through the mountains to Hamlin and my room. This time, it was the pastor and his wife from the Alliance Church, along with Gordon Gale whose sermons I had always found so inspiring. They came bearing a bunch of carnations and news from the church. "Fortunately, the piano-playing has been taken over by a girl who can play the organ. Praise

12 Psalm 4:8
13 Psalm 4:3
14 Song of Songs 3:9
15 Song of Songs 7:10
16 Eliza H. Hamilton (published 1869)

the Lord!" I wrote home. Pastor Taylor read from a psalm and Mr Gale prayed before they left, and I was greatly blessed.

The Taylors were not the only visitors to bring flowers. I had been at Hamlin for only three days when a delegation from Eastwood arrived. Thankfully, I had just finished preparing a syllabus and lesson plans for Nada, the teacher from Kafarshima who had taken over the kindergarten. It was a joy to see Hazel along with two other teachers from the school, Heather and Faith. Hazel reckoned she was immune from the hepatitis virus as she had lived in Lebanon for so long, and the others hovered in the doorway, amused by the "ISOLATION" sign. They were loaded with grapefruit from the citrus trees at Eastwood; jam, honey and sweets to pep up my carbohydrate intake; my own cups, plates and Thermos flask; and bunches of wild flowers – cyclamen, freesia and wild orange blossom – picked and sent from the staff and children. "So there's a lovely fresh scent in the room now," I wrote home. "Truly, I couldn't be more at home. Where the Lord makes His residence, there is such a fulness of His presence – it's really indescribable."

Hazel loved driving up to Hammana and visited the hospital as often as she could, regularly bearing fruit and flowers and letters from England. *"Like cold water to a weary soul is good news from a distant land."*[17] Her sister Patricia, who had stayed with us the previous November, sent an Easter greeting card with a message that touched me deeply. "Dear Wendy, a little early for Easter but so sorry to hear about your jaundice. I can picture you in that beautiful Hamlin Hospital, but how your babies will miss you! I always remember that little one suddenly overcome by an irresistible desire to kiss you in the middle of class. God bless and heal you. *'...unto you that fear my name shall the Sun of righteousness arise with healing in his wings.'*[18] Much love, Patricia."

When visiting at Hamlin, Hazel would always seek out an elderly resident for whom she had a particular affection. Many years previously, Sitt Saada had been abandoned as a baby at the door of the English mission in Beirut. She was blind and her feet were deformed, but the missionaries took her in, loved and cared for her. Little Saada learnt quickly to speak both Arabic and English and, with braille, studied to become a teacher. When her working life was over, there was a room for her at Hamlin that she filled with all her braille Bible books. Saada took a full part in morning

17 Proverbs 25:25
18 Malachi 4:2 (AV)

devotions on the ward, and would read and sing lustily the hymns she had learnt by heart. Most of all, she loved helping others on the ward and cheerfully greeting visitors.

As time passed, others came to visit from Eastwood. I was delighted when Amine came one afternoon with his mother, who had been so kind to me. "It was a joy to testify to the Lord's goodness and to share my little Switzerland from the balcony here," I wrote home. Amine brought a huge bag of *akedinia*[19], freshly picked from the trees in the school garden. These were a delicious juicy fruit, orange in colour, with shiny brown stones in the centre of each fruit, tasting to me more like an apricot than a plum. On another occasion, he came with two other teachers: Georgette, who headed up the Arabic teaching in the senior school; and Mary Margaret, who worked with Jill in the pre-school. This time, he brought grapefruit and beautiful pink roses. "There were thirteen," I wrote home, "a baker's dozen, but now only nine because I gave one to each of the four nurses who bring my meals by turn!" He also paid my salary for March. I remonstrated profusely that I did not deserve full salary, to which he responded, saying, "Oh yes, you do deserve it – you're praying." I was speechless. "I don't think I've ever been paid for praying before!" I wrote home.

In addition to flowers and plants, visitors came bearing other gifts, which were great to share with whoever popped into the room. One Sunday afternoon, I was sitting in bed when Antoine came from Aley with his mother, along with Brenda and Mary, friends from the LIVF Graduates Fellowship. They brought a tin of Blue Band chocolate-coated toffees, and we duly passed them round. The room was full of flowers – carnations, roses and wild flowers from the hospital grounds – so the toffees were very acceptable. As we were chatting, Mary's brother came to see her. "He is doing his national conscription," I wrote home, "and is at present serving with the Syrian Deterrent Forces at a camp just near here." It seems he had heard his sister was visiting the hospital and wanted to say *marhaba*[20]. Neither Mrs Haddad nor Mary's brother spoke English, so my poor Arabic was stretched to the limit. By the time the five of them left, I was happy to enjoy a nap!

The very next day, another party of visitors arrived, comprising Hazel with Mona from the school, Ruth who had taken over the Sunday school

[19] loquat
[20] hello

My nurses at Hamlin Hospital.

at the church and Joan who taught at the mission school. All came bearing gifts. Ruth brought an unusual exotic plant from the church, a deep red flamingo flower. Joan brought grapefruit, and Mona brought a kilo of *lokum*[21] in a variety of flavours: rosewater, bergamot and lemon. Hazel topped up my honey supply! No flowers, but Amine's roses and a cyclamen plant from Nans still graced my room. Once again, I was glad to rest after their visit.

It was now early April, and I was taking a little walk round the hospital grounds every day, enjoying the *khamseen*[22] and marvelling at the view across the wide valley and, beyond that, the Mediterranean coast and Beirut headland. One day, after a quieter morning, I had just returned to my room following my daily constitutional, when who should come to visit but Mary's brother, attired in his full Syrian army uniform! Fortunately, he came with Amal, Nans' co-worker, who spoke a little English, so I asked her to stay. "He walked in clutching some flowers," I wrote home, "a posy about six inches in diameter, consisting of carnations of every shade of orange through pink through red that you could imagine, with a few white blooms." It was a beautiful offering, wrapped round with orange tissue and a bright pink narrow ribbon. "It was all I could do to prevent myself from crying on the spot," I continued in my letter home. With dictionary to hand, we conversed in my halting Arabic, and my new soldier friend was clearly doing his best to speak in simple terms. I was thankful to have Amal to help as I spoke of my recent visit to Damascus following the steps of St Paul.

After they left, I put the posy in a narrow-necked jam jar full of water and wept, marvelling at this beautiful picture of God's love for me. I felt just like one of the four-year-olds in my class, stumbling into school with a rose or a little bunch of drooping field poppies in a hot, sticky hand and presenting it, knowing they would receive a kiss and "You know how I

[21] Turkish Delight
[22] warm winds

love flowers" in response. I reflected that this must be how God desires His children to approach Him, and wrote home, "My children, however naughty, know that they can melt my heart with their little offerings like a flower. God wants us to offer ourselves just as we are and – joy, oh joy! – He accepts us." Later I found verses that expressed why I found myself weeping with such gratitude. *"For I am the LORD your God, the Holy One of Israel, your Saviour; I give ... since you are precious and honoured in my sight, and because I love you ... everyone who is called by my name, whom I created for my glory, whom I formed and made."*[23]

In addition to visits from friends from the LIVF Bible study group, I looked forward to a visit from Afaf with whom I had been to Damascus earlier in the year. I had heard she had been unwell after I was admitted to Hamlin and was concerned she may have contracted the hepatitis, since I had stayed with her and her mother the weekend before. "One afternoon, I heard shuffling outside the door," I wrote home, "and realised that someone was laughing at the details of the 'ISOLATION' notice still writ large on my door." Still chuckling, in walked Afaf with Alison, who was studying Arabic at the university in Beirut and working at the student centre. I was thankful Afaf was well and shared God's goodness to me at Hamlin, including the excellent medical attention I was receiving.

Dr Nucho visited every day and from time to time repeated the importance of the low-fat, high-protein, high-carbohydrate diet in order to regulate the bile and reduce the nausea. "My high-protein diet is of a five-star hotel standard and too much really," I wrote home. "Chicken at lunchtime today with boiled vegetables, salad, spinach, *laban*[24], jam and fruit. It was more or less a repeat of this at 6 pm, and I'm determined to make the most of it!" And so, in addition to the medical checks and blood tests, my days were punctuated by the regular arrival of trays of low-fat / high-protein meals. There was very little medication, as I was taking decreasing amounts of cortisone tablets to reduce the pain in the liver region. Dr Nucho was insistent upon the benefits of sheer rest as the greatest aid to full recovery. I do, however, recall some huge, two-centimetre-long, dark green vitamin capsules with "Essential Forte" written on the bottle alongside my name, "Mrs Windi", and duly swallowed one of these monsters with each meal, hoping it would do me good!

[23] Isaiah 43:3,4,7
[24] yoghurt

Breakfast appeared each morning at 7.45 am and comprised tea, *laban*, apricot jam, a very small piece of cheese, Arabic bread and grapefruit that Hazel had brought from the citrus grove at Eastwood. "You can't believe how much I'm enjoying my meals, and you'd laugh to see me eating spoonfuls of honey, even in the middle of the night!" I wrote home. Boiled chicken featured regularly in the main meals along with *kafta*, a grilled oval-shaped Lebanese burger made from ground beef, onion, parsley and mild spices, and served on a bed of rice with salad. It was delicious and reminded me of Madame Khoury's meals, which we had enjoyed so much, especially in the early days of reopening the school the previous November. By far the most exciting meal appeared one lunchtime. "I have just finished an amazing meal," I wrote home. "Staring at me from the plate was a fish about eight inches long, similar to a small sea bream, complete with head, eyes, tail and teeth, very delicious with squeezed lemon!"

By this time, I was able to walk around the hospital grounds even more and visit Marguerite, who kindly plied me with cups of tea from her ground-floor flat. After a nap in the afternoon on this particular day, I made my way along the corridor and entered the hospital lift to descend. But disaster struck! On reaching the ground floor, the doors refused to open and I was stuck. Owing to power cuts, this was not the first time this had happened to me, and I was thankful that at least this lift was spacious enough for me to lie down if necessary! "Twenty minutes later, when I was released," I wrote home, "I felt just like Lazarus walking out of the tomb." On returning to my room, there was another fish lying on the plate for my supper! "I couldn't believe my eyes. So, nothing daunted, off came the head and the tail, and I proceeded to dismember this one and thoroughly enjoy it!"

Other than the pain in my side and the need for regular naps on and off during the day, it was a privilege to have more time to spend in prayer. On one of Hazel's visits, she came with Heather, who mentioned Assemblies, the daily acts of worship with the three- to seven-year-olds in the department. I had prepared outlines for telling the Easter story and was confident that each of the five teachers was well able to share these precious truths of the last week of the life of Jesus here on earth. My longing was that they would tell the events of Palm Sunday, the Last Supper, the Crucifixion and the Easter joy to follow in a way that would touch the heart of each child with God's love. Heather was particularly burdened about Assemblies and asked that I would pray, especially at this time of the morning. Assembly took place from 10.10 to 10.25 am, and at that time my room was nearly always quiet. "Breakfast comes at 7.30ish, and by 10 am the cleaning has all been done, I make a cup of tea from my Thermos flask and settle down for my quiet time with the Lord," I

Heather storytelling in Assembly and Lamia translating into Arabic.

wrote home. "It's lovely to be able to think of the children and their teachers and pray right through this time. They all share with me the burden of making spiritual truth simple enough for even the three-year-olds to understand." I had even asked for prayer for the Assemblies in my latest letter to praying friends. "Please pray for the Assemblies from now till Easter. This is the most challenging part of the Christian faith, especially to the Muslims and Druze."

Even though I was out of isolation, I still loved the balcony, especially as the weather was becoming warmer by the day. I often sat with my table half in the room and half on the balcony, reading, writing letters and stitching away at my crochet. "I've just finished reading Edith Schaeffer's book *L'Abri*," I wrote home. "It's her story of how the work of L'Abri started in Switzerland." I had only to look up from my seat on the balcony, or even from the bed, to marvel at my own little Switzerland of snow on the high mountains and bright sunny days. When the nurses bobbed in and out, they would always take an interest in whatever I was doing and give me plenty of opportunities to fumble away in my broken Arabic. My crochet was of great interest too. It was a creative and not too taxing pastime throughout my weeks at Hamlin. I found it easier to work with the crochet hook one stitch at a time than with a row of stitches likely to fall off the knitting needle when sitting up in bed! Friends plied me with plenty of colourful yarn, and I graduated from stitching small 'granny squares' to make into kitchen pan holders, to larger blankets, cushion covers, a V-necked sweater for my father, a skirt for my mother and various hats, scarves and belts! I even attempted crochet matinée coats and bonnets to give to friends with newborn babies.

Huda, Victor and I with Dr Nucho,
April 30th, 1979.

The balcony was my little garden. Birds were making their nests in the guttering in the roof above and in the pine trees opposite. I loved to tend the geraniums that had been planted by Marguerite in concrete window boxes about two feet long. "It's surprising what pruning the dead wood and leaves and a little titivation of the soil with a teaspoon will do," I wrote home. A fortnight later, I wrote again. "Now they are beginning to flower – pink, white, crimson geraniums. I'm thrilled and water them every day!"

Writing letters was long overdue, and I was thankful for those visitors who were happy to carry letters and post them on arrival in their home countries. The Lebanese postal service was still somewhat erratic because of ongoing hostilities in parts of the country. My father generously provided me with stamps: seven pence second class and nine pence first. "Alison flies to England today," I wrote home, "so I trust my letters will be well on their way! I'm so thankful for the time to write personal notes to people who wrote to me before Christmas, as well as my newsletter to praying friends." When George came to view the school with a view towards teaching in the senior school the following term, Hazel brought him to visit. Amazingly, he offered to carry not only letters but also some of my crochet items for friends and family in England as he had very little luggage.

I was sitting on the balcony on the morning of Good Friday, April 13th, and was ready for the communion service in the chapel that afternoon. This was a sombre service of remembrance and, though unusual for me to share in bread and wine on Good Friday, I was pondering Paul's words to the Corinthian believers: *"For whenever you eat this bread and drink this cup, you proclaim the Lord's death until he comes."*[25] Not long after the service, Hazel and Heather came to visit. I was very moved as Heather explained how she had arranged for the whole department to speak to me on a cassette tape, teachers and children alike. "Every child in kindergarten and

[25] 1 Corinthians 11:26

Junior 1 has spoken individually and others have sung," I wrote home later, "and every teacher has spoken greetings for Easter and news about the children. It was really very touching." Listening to the tape made me realise how much I was missing them all and trusting that I would soon be well enough to resume teaching again. Dr Nucho had taken blood tests, and we awaited the results, praying for guidance concerning how much I would be able to do in the department once I was discharged.

Happy Easter note on my breakfast tray.

That evening, the heavens opened and the skies were lit with streaks of lightning as the thunder echoed through the mountains. Afaf had arrived to stay for Easter weekend in the nurses' home and she came to my room for lunch. The sun had broken through and we were chatting on the balcony, when two visitors arrived unexpectedly: Faith from Eastwood, bearing roses from the garden; and Katie, the headteacher of the girls' mission school in Beirut, who brought yet more honey, my fifth jar. This was honey on the comb, a great childhood treat, and I was reassured its properties would contribute to a healthier liver. "It's delicious in *laban* and I eat it in *khubz arabieh*[26], as well as just as it is from a teaspoon!" I explained in my letter home. Afaf braved the rain to shop in the village for a box of little Easter eggs for me to give to the nurses and visitors on Easter Day. We were ready to celebrate the feast.

It was a joyful Easter service in the chapel in spite of overcast weather. "I knew the tunes of all the hymns, so I hummed along and joined in for the hallelujahs! They're the same in every language," I wrote to my parents. It was a day to remember, as virtually everyone in the hospital came to visit at some stage during the day. When Dr and Mrs Nucho came with a spray of lilac from their garden and an Easter card, Afaf was with me and the four of us prayed together for the hospital. Breakfast that day was memorable. On the beautifully presented tray there was a sweetbread baked in Hammana and a coloured hard-boiled egg with a handwritten

26 Arabic unleavened bread

note alongside which read, "Happy Easter [in English and Arabic]. Please don't eat it. Thank you," and signed by Nazlat, the Lebanese staff nurse who was responsible for my diet. I knew that eggs were prohibited in my diet but felt so blessed and gave Nazlat a hug as we left the chapel. The afternoon was very busy, with visitors galore, and I was glad Afaf was with me to welcome them all and pass round the Easter eggs.

A few days after Easter, when I had been staying at Hamlin for just five weeks, Dr Nucho took a final blood test with a view to discharge on condition that I promised not to attempt full-time teaching on my return to Eastwood. School was due to restart after the Easter break on Tuesday, April 24th, and I was longing to be there, if only to see the staff and children again and take Assembly. I loved recounting the stories of Jesus' appearances to His friends and sharing the joy of the resurrection. But it was not to be.

After lunch on Friday, April 20th, I walked to the chapel to play the harmonium for a little while and then for my very first walk outside the hospital gates with Victor and Huda. "Oh dear," I wrote home, "I was absolutely exhausted with plenty of pain and strain in the liver area. This is what everyone has warned me about. I could hardly stand on my return to the room." The next day brought news of the blood test results. "Dr Nucho is pleased with the results, though I'm not one hundred per cent clear by any means," I wrote. "I'm what he terms 'a classic case' of hepatitis and it's going to take time." We were to aim for discharge not before Monday, April 30th and then very little teaching on my return to the school. I was disappointed, and yet thankful that Nada had agreed to stay on and teach my classes until at least the end of May. I asked my parents to pray that we would have God's wisdom regarding how much I should attempt during May. "I do still have pain in the liver area," I confessed in my letter home, "so I'm sure it's right to be here for another week. Dr Nucho reckons I'm on *rodag*[27] and you often see it on the back windows of cars!"

On the day school reopened, Nans appeared with a suggestion. "Do you think Dr Nucho would let you come out to Hammana for a short while?" It transpired she had some shopping to do and offered to take me for my first drive out since my admittance nearly six weeks previously. "I think Nans was so taken with my excitement," I wrote home, "that she was inspired to drive around for fifteen minutes or so, and I was thrilled. The

[27] French: running-in

countryside is beautiful; fresh, green, wild flowers, gorse, rhododendrons. I just don't know this part of Lebanon at all, so I was like a child in my excitement!" The following day, I was still feeling a little disheartened about school, when in walked Colin from the LIVF office, announcing he would like to take me out for a picnic lunch nearby. He introduced me to a visiting couple who knew people from Kingsmead School in Hoylake, including David Watts, the headmaster. It was such a joy to have another outing, share memories and hear news of friends.

There was one more experience of life at Hamlin which I cherished as I prepared to leave. Nans had invited me to the nurses' Bible study in Arabic. "With my English Bible, I could at least follow the text," I wrote home. "It was a joy to see two of the Muslim nurses present, but oh how difficult it is for them to break from their families and make a clear stand as believers." I had already decided to wrap up small gifts for the nurses and cleaners. I had a little bottle of perfume and a copy of Today's Arabic Version of the New Testament, recently published by the Lebanese Bible Society, for each one, along with a note of thanks for all their care for me. I knew I would miss their loving attention, and had been in prayer about readjustment to life at Eastwood – living in my own flat, cooking and cleaning, not to mention the sheer physical energy needed with four- and five-year-olds. "I feel the Lord is telling me something concerning the future and kindergarten teaching," I wrote home, "but I obviously need to discuss the whole thing with Hazel and then with Amine. Please pray for God's overruling and guidance. I so need wisdom to discern His will for my future work here."

The following day, just two days before discharge, I had an unexpected visit from Neville, one of the South African members of MECO, whose wife Noreen lectured at the Hamlin nurses' school. "He is an extremely forthright man," I wrote later, "and I believe the Lord sent him to me this morning a few minutes after I'd finished my quiet time and was just resting." Neville had a friendly and caring manner as he posed an important question: "How has the time here been for you spiritually?" I felt completely at ease as I shared the joy of the near presence of the Lord during this time of being set apart from the normal busyness of day-to-day life. Furthermore, I was able to share my apprehension regarding full-time teaching, post hepatitis. This in spite of having being so sure of God's call back to Eastwood the previous year in the uncertain wartime conditions in Lebanon. "*You are my hiding place; you will protect me from trouble and surround me with songs of deliverance."*[28] This had been true for me time after time in the years since the Civil War had started in 1975. I was assured that the Lord would continue to fulfil His promise to me. *"I will instruct you and teach you in the way you should go; I will counsel you with my loving eye on you."*[29] My work might need to change, but my call and desire to serve the Lebanese people was undiminished.

---

[28] Psalm 32:7
[29] Psalm 32:8

CHAPTER TWENTY-TWO

Disappointments and Miracles

I had mixed feelings as I packed up to leave my room at Hamlin Hospital after a memorable six weeks' stay. My thousand pounds health insurance package, purchased for a premium of £23.50 only days before leaving England the previous September, more than covered the hospital costs and Dr Nucho's fees. This was a miracle of God's provision, and now I was trusting Him for just enough physical strength to bear me up as I entered the fray of school life again. I was sad to say goodbye to Nans and Amal, to Victor and Huda, to Marguerite, to Dr and Mrs Nucho, and to the many nurses and hospital staff who had been so kind to me. "I'm packing up from my little six-week-old home. It's quite sad in many ways," I wrote home, "but all mountain top experiences come to an end sometime and God never changes."

By 9 am on the morning of Monday, April 30th, I was dressed and surrounded by all the nurses on the balcony for a photo! It was quite an emotional moment as I handed each one their gift. I wanted to express my thanks to them for all their care and loving attention. Victor and Huda had offered to take me down to Eastwood, and once again I found myself with mixed feelings and huge apprehension as we drove into the school forecourt. "It's much, much warmer down here than in Hammana," I wrote home, "and mosquitoes abound!" I was encouraged by the warm welcome from Hazel and the Khoury family, and borne up on their good wishes.

The plan in the first instance was for me to take the daily act of worship in the department and possibly one or two lessons, gradually working my way back into full-time teaching. Disappointingly, it soon became clear that this was not going to be possible. Dr Nucho had warned me against

Rene and Nada in the playground
for a birthday, June 1979.

attempting too much too soon, especially as I was now living on the school premises. Resting after Assembly, upstairs in my fourth-floor flat, was not easy with playground noise and other distractions, including a visit one afternoon from one of the pre-school assistants. I woke to a knock on my bedroom door, and as I muttered, "Come in," there stood a delegation consisting of the assistant, a dear girl called Mary Margaret and a somewhat subdued small boy who had been fighting in the playground. From my bed, I duly reprimanded him!

I continued taking Assembly each day, but though I had peace of heart, the physical pain I had experienced previously on my right-hand side was recurring and I found myself needing to rest more and more. Just simple tasks like washing clothes had to be punctuated with periods of rest, especially if my heart started to pound at the slightest burst of energy. "I am certain that the school and the little ones are in His hands," I wrote to my parents. "He has provided for them in the past and will continue to do so in the future wherever He chooses to place me! I only wish to serve the national church, as and how God directs."

I was thankful that Nada was continuing to teach the kindergarten until the end of May, but as school was not due to close until July 11th, I did not want to worry Hazel with concerns regarding my health. "Please pray I'll have patience with myself and wisdom to know how much to do and not do," I wrote home. "It's not as easy as it sounds." I also asked my parents to pray for courage as I broached the subject of the future with Hazel, as I had no wish to add to the uncertainties we faced within a country still far from settled politically. "I had a chat with Hazel last week and to Amine earlier this week and just expressed to them how it seemed as if the Lord were closing the door on kindergarten teaching for me, at least for the time being," I wrote home. "Nor do I know for sure yet where the Lord is leading me, though Pastor and Mrs Taylor from the Alliance Church have offered me the use of a flat in Ras Beirut and I would be available to help in church work – women's Bible studies, book-keeping, Sunday school and visiting." In addition, the mission girls' school in Beirut was about to reopen for the first time since the Civil War began, and I had been offered part-time teaching at the training college by Katie, the principal. "Hazel has found it hard to accept that this is the way I'm thinking, but she is gracious and knows that He will provide for me and for Eastwood."

Pre-school with Jill and Mary Margaret, June 1979.

I was acutely aware that it was a real venture of faith to be leaving a full-time salaried job for church work and that I would need to depend solely on financial support from the Alliance Church and, hopefully, from All Saints, my home church in Marple, Cheshire. I continued leaning heavily on God's earlier promise to me, *"I will instruct you and teach you in the way you should go; I will counsel you with my loving eye on you."*[1]

I knew Hazel was keen to find a way forward for me to continue at least part-time in charge of the department, taking the daily Assemblies with minimum actual teaching. It was humbling to be so appreciated, especially when the day after our conversation she handed me a small card with words from *The Weaving*, a poem shared by Corrie Ten Boom:

> *He knows, He loves, He cares;*
> *Nothing this truth can dim.*
> *He gives the very best to those*
> *Who leave the choice to Him.*

In the meantime, I was trusting that I would have enough physical energy to keep going in school until the end of term, and was glad that my air ticket was now booked for July 13th. It was becoming increasingly difficult to judge how much I could do and still have stamina in reserve for any crises that might occur in the department. One morning, as I was preparing to take Assembly at 10 am, I received a message that René, my trusty kindergarten Arabic teacher, was sick with food poisoning and

[1]   Psalm 32:8

would be unable to come to school. Hurriedly, I made my way down to the classrooms on the ground floor, only to find the four- and five-year-olds were still playing outside, waiting to be called in. Inwardly, I was crying to the Lord for just enough strength to cope, as I lined the children up on the balcony and brought them into the classroom. Just at that moment, I heard one of the little girls say, "Good morning, miss!" in her best English, as Nada appeared from nowhere to take the class! Only that morning, I had been reading, *"I relieved your shoulder of the burden; your hands were freed from the basket. In distress you called, and I delivered you; I answered you..."*[2]

The following week, we held two parents' open days that had been postponed since March. "It just brought tears to my heart to realise how much parents care," I wrote home, "and also how hard my teachers have worked to keep up the standards in Arabic, English and maths that we aim for."

In spite of such wonderful reassurances from the Lord that He would never leave me without support in the classroom, it was certainly a battle against depression, especially first thing in the mornings. I was so encouraged by the help of friends and staff, and very aware of the power of the prayers of family and friends at home in England. I often asked for prayer for our daily Assemblies as well as personal prayer. If any of the teachers were in distress, it was a privilege to invite them up to my fourth-floor flat for prayer about their personal lives as well as our work together in the school. One day, I discovered that René would set her alarm every morning at 5 am in order to snatch some moments of quiet to read her Bible and pray before the busyness of the day took over her life with two small children. Sadness had crept into René's life, as her husband had become increasingly involved in the right-wing militia that ostensibly 'guarded' the village of Kafarshima. My heart went out to her as she shared some of the consequences on family life of his addiction to cocaine and how she trusted the Lord to enable her to be strong for the sake of her family. So much sadness and loss had entered people's lives as a result of the ravages of the Civil War. Sharing the grief and visiting in the homes, listening and praying, became an ever more important part of the work of the school.

Into Lamia's class, Junior 1, we had admitted a rather tall, lanky six-year-old boy in the previous November, when Eastwood had reopened. Edmond had been educated at a French school prior to the onset of civil

[2] Psalm 81:6,7 (RSV)

strife but had made little progress due to school closures. He had multiple learning difficulties but was a cheerful child and well liked by the other children. His mother described him as mentally retarded and was clearly desperate to find a school that would accept him. She told us that the doctor had assured her that her son would be 'normal' by the time he was ten years old. So Edmond came to Eastwood and, in return for love and patient teaching, he began to respond. One of his favourite times in the day was Assembly, our daily act of worship – prayer, story, songs and an opportunity for children to ask questions and be awakened spiritually. His favourite song was *One, two, three, Jesus loves me*, and he always joined in the actions with great enthusiasm.

> *One, two, three, Jesus loves me.*
> *One, two, Jesus loves you.*
> *Three, four, He loves you more*
> *Than you've ever been loved before.*
> *Five, six, seven, we're going to heav'n.*
> *Seven, eight, won't it be great!*
> *Eight, nine, Jesus is mine.*
> *Nine, ten, we'll sing it again.*
> *(Nine, ten, we'll all say amen.) [second time]*[3]

One Saturday afternoon towards the end of May, Edmond was playing in Kafarshima and failed to come home. After much anxious searching, his body was eventually found down an open manhole, four metres deep, in a pathway not far from his home on the side of the hill. The family was devastated and gathered together to comfort each other. On Sunday evening, those of us who lived in the school building and knew him came together in my flat. We prayed for the family, and I especially asked the Lord to show me what to say to the children the following day in Assembly. As I prayed, the Lord led me to that perfect picture of heaven in Revelation: *"He will wipe every tear from their eyes. There will be no more death or ... crying or pain..."*[4] I was convinced that Edmond was now free from his disabilities and with Jesus forever. The next day, I spoke with the children about heaven and what a beautiful place it is, and reminded them

---

[3] Adapted for singing in English by Arabic speakers from the song by Lisa Mazak (age 9). Copyright 1974, The Fishermen, Inc. Assigned to Celebration Services (International) Ltd., 1975. All rights reserved. Used by permission.

[4] Revelation 21:4

of the words of the song Edmond loved to sing. "When we love Jesus, one day we will go to heaven where there are no tears, no falling over and hurting yourself, no fighting, no pain." As Lamia translated into Arabic phrase by phrase, I watched how the children's eyes lit up and one boy actually clapped for joy for Edmond!

After school that day, I changed into dark clothes and walked through the village with a group of Edmond's teachers to visit his family. They were seated round the edge of their shuttered sitting room weeping as they shared their shock and grief. We sat for a little while and drank the bitter Arabic coffee we were offered. I especially wanted to speak to Edmond's mother, who had been so pleased with his progress at school. I shall never forget how she shared with us Edmond's enjoyment of school life and how he had been singing his favourite song repeatedly, even on the day he died: "One, two, three, Jesus loves me. Five, six, seven, I'm going to heaven." She told us she was pregnant and was praying for a safe delivery. How we rejoiced with the family when a healthy baby was born a few months later.

As the days progressed, I was becoming aware that all was not well with my liver function and was looking forward to attending at the American University Hospital in Beirut for the blood test that had been requested by Dr Nucho. This was booked for Tuesday, May 29th along with a follow-up appointment at the Christian Medical Centre in Ashrafieh with Dr Manoogian, who had initially diagnosed the hepatitis two months previously. "I'm supposed to be resting, according to what Dr Manoogian told me yesterday," I wrote home, "but it has become increasingly clear that I am my own worst enemy. I just cannot rest while I'm still here in the school building." Friends at church and the LIVF centre were very supportive, as indeed were Amine and Hazel, when I made the decision to bring the date of my flight to England forward by four weeks and booked a flight home for Tuesday, June 12th. "Please pray I'll get priorities right in the coming ten days, get everything packed up here and moved into Beirut," I wrote home, "as well as leaving the department well organised for the teachers, as I'll be away for the end of term." It was a big decision, but I was very aware of the Lord's peace as I shared a modern paraphrase of verses in Philippians in my letter home: *"Don't worry about anything; instead pray about everything; tell God your needs and don't forget to thank him for his answers. If you do this, you will experience God's peace which is far more wonderful than the human mind can understand. His peace will keep your thoughts and your hearts quiet and at rest as you trust in Christ Jesus."*[5]

I was still uncertain how my health situation would resolve itself, but I knew that God had a plan for me to continue serving Him in Lebanon for the foreseeable future. On my return, I would be living rent-free in a sixth-floor flat in Ras Beirut, with-

Friends at the LIVF Centre in Beirut, June 1979.

in walking distance of the Alliance Church. This flat had been rented by the church for a number of years, and a room was currently vacant. It was fully furnished with sitting / dining room and balcony, two bedrooms, kitchen, washroom, bathroom and separate toilet. I would be sharing with Alison, who was studying Arabic and working as an LIVF staff worker alongside Afaf and the students. Eastwood would still be my main task, but I would be part time as from October, at least until I was fully recovered, possibly for a school year or more, and living in Beirut where I could help in the church. *"Therefore we do not lose heart. Though outwardly we are wasting away, yet inwardly we are being renewed day by day. For our light and momentary troubles are achieving for us an eternal glory that far outweighs them all. So we fix our eyes not on what is seen, but on what is unseen, since what is seen is temporary, but what is unseen is eternal."*[6] I shared my reflections with my parents: "Sometimes I shudder at the thought of all this change, but basically I know I must go on in faith. Who can tell what the future holds in this country, or any other? Praise Him that the future is all in His hands."

The time was short for packing and ferrying carloads of my belongings to the Alliance flat. After Nada left, Bahia came to help in the kindergarten until the end of term, and I continued to rejoice in the way the staff worked together so well. On Saturday, June 9th, I drove my Fiat to Beirut with the last suitcase and left all my plants with Afaf at the LIVF centre. Monday 11th was my last morning in school, and we sang *Trust and obey, for there's no other way to be happy in Jesus* in Assembly. I knew that God was in control,

[5] Philippians 4:6,7 (TLB)
[6] 2 Corinthians 4:16-18

weaving events together even when I was not consciously asking for His intervention. I knew He was silently planning in love for me, for the school and for Lebanon. My journey to the airport after an overnight stay with Afaf was uneventful and all the flights were on time. I had a mere forty-minute wait at Budapest airport for the onward Malév flight to Heathrow, and it seemed like no time at all that my father was meeting me at Ringway airport in Manchester. The sense of release from responsibility was overwhelming, and I slept for days!

England was refreshingly cool in mid June 1979 after the heat of Lebanon, and I was thankful. It was good to meet up with family and church friends, but I soon realised how often a headache would descend upon me unexpectedly and I would need to stop and rest. Home was a busy place. My eighty-nine-year-old grandmother was now living with us, and my fifteen-year-old brother Robin was taking external exams. My sister Hazel lived nearby with husband Neil and would often pop in to visit. Church friends were generous in their support and provided meals and other practical help.

The summer months were punctuated with frequent blood tests to check my liver function. I had been home for less than a week when our family doctor took a blood sample and cautioned me to take regular periods of rest throughout the day. By early August, I was referred to Manchester Royal Infirmary (MRI) for more blood tests and a strong suggestion that further investigation of the liver would be needed. My return to Lebanon in September was looking less and less likely. I was deeply disappointed when the liver specialist at MRI confirmed the need for a liver biopsy and a probable admission date of early October. Dr Harrison was adamant that I should stay in England until at least January 1980 and only consider flying back to Beirut if the prognosis for a return to full health were positive. In my head I knew this was realistic, as time after time in my efforts to keep in touch with friends and be supportive in the home, I would have to give in to extreme tiredness. Furthermore, the pain in the liver area was worsening in spite of my efforts to keep to the high-protein / low-fat diet.

Notwithstanding my sadness at not being well enough to return to Lebanon as planned, it was good to be at home during this period, and I remained convinced that God had a loving plan and would heal. *"'For my thoughts are not your thoughts, neither are your ways my ways,' declares the LORD. 'As the heavens are higher than the earth, so are my ways higher than your*

276

ways and my thoughts than your thoughts.'"[7] In between frequent pauses to rest during each day, life was busy. My elderly grandmother had only recently come to stay with us. She came initially for the weekend and was still with us a year later. I was glad to be able to help care for her and also assist in clearing out her house in Ashton-under-Lyne. It proved to be a mammoth task, sorting through years and years of accumulated household items, furniture and linens and sharing them amongst family members. The kitchen was full of a lifetime's collection of cooking paraphernalia, a deal of which was cracked and unusable. It was a healing process as I revisited childhood memories of the many happy times cooking with Granny in that very kitchen. Upstairs, the bedroom drawers and wardrobes were full not only of clothes but of other surprising items. One afternoon, after carrying downstairs the clothes that she needed, I decided to sort through a large chest of drawers in the front bedroom. As I opened one of the lower drawers, a fox's head jumped out at me and gave me such a shock that I decided to leave that particular drawer for when my father called on his way home from work! Granny's furs were her prized possessions and my aunt was asked to find new homes for them!

These months gave me opportunities to reconnect with friends at All Saints, Marple and to thank them for their prayerful support, not only for me but for my parents too. In addition to being able to worship in church on Sundays and attend some of the small groups that met informally in homes, I was asked to speak at a midweek meeting about the situation in Lebanon and illustrate with slides of the country and the school. The church missionary committee was already discussing the possibility of helping to support me financially on my return to Lebanon, as I would only be teaching part-time at Eastwood. I sought to be completely transparent as I spoke that evening in late August and shared what an uncertain year it had been for us all.

"In reopening the school last November, I praise God for how wonderfully we were upheld through all the tensions, the limitations and the disappointments. I have personally felt under great pressure at times, very limited in my ministry with individuals, because the uncertainty of school life burnt up all my nervous and spiritual energy. I've met many situations with which I couldn't cope and from which I simply had to withdraw and have felt a deep sense of personal failure." I wanted praying friends to know how valuable was their understanding prayer. "There

[7] Isaiah 55:8,9

were times," I shared, "when I actually felt the burden lift or the problem solve itself in a moment of particular need. Other times, when feelings were unreliable, it was good to count on your prayers and on God's response. And sometimes the amazing truth has flooded over me – particularly after I left our village for my six-week stay in hospital – that somehow, in spite of the failures and mistakes, the feelings of inadequacy in personal ministry, in spite of me, God's renewing power has been at work."

It was always a joy to show slides of Lebanon and groups of children in the school and the playground. I closed my talk that evening with some further reflections about the future. "There are still so many areas that I don't understand – the awful chaos and seeming unendingness of the political conflict in Lebanon, my own personal future and the bewilderment of the national church. Just recently, when I was told that my liver still wasn't functioning properly and there was no hope of returning in September, I was reading in the book of Job. His whole world had crashed around him, he had lost everything and yet he said to his wife, *'Shall we receive good at the hand of God, and shall we not receive evil?'[8]* He accepted completely that what God permits is good and he finally acknowledged to the Lord, *'I know that you can do all things; no purpose of yours can be thwarted.'[9]* *'…we live by faith, not by sight.'[10]* This is God's call to me now."

As I gradually came to terms with the delay in my return to Lebanon until at least January 1980, I began to appreciate what a miracle of God's healing provision it was for me and my family at this time. As I rested most afternoons, I reflected on just how perfectly God had timed my presence at home in Marple. One evening in early September, my parents were called to the home of my mother's parents, who also lived in Ashton. My grandfather was extremely unwell with emphysema and struggling for breath. One week later, he was taken to the local hospital, and from then on my parents went to visit virtually every evening. It was an emotionally exhausting time for my mother and she too needed time to rest, so we would often share the domestic duties as well as caring for my other grandmother, who was living with us. A friend in Lebanon wrote to me at that time, "You may find that you do not know clearly why God has kept

---

[8] Job 2:10 (RSV)
[9] Job 42:2
[10] 2 Corinthians 5:7

you at home just now, in the same way that Job did not know the reasons behind his suffering, but I do pray that you will be able to rest in the Lord and trust Him while you wait."

A few days after I had been due to return to Lebanon on September 21st, the vicar of All Saints rang to explain that the church would indeed be supporting me financially with one hundred pounds per month from September. I was humbled by their generosity and full of gratitude to the Lord for this encouragement. That same week, I received a notification from Dr Harrison, the liver specialist at MRI, of the admission date for my liver biopsy: Wednesday, October 10th. My father kindly drove me to the PIU (Programmed Investigation Unit) at the hospital on his way to work. I was to be an inpatient in Nightingale Ward and was allocated a bed in one corner, my own little cubicle lit by a very high narrow window. There followed a routine blood test, and I was then asked to spend the rest of the day in a waiting room at the far end of the ward as my bed was needed for a day patient.

Nothing daunted, I gathered my belongings, including a large pile of unanswered letters, and proceeded to settle for the day, reading and replying to friends near and far. Initially, my sense of euphoria was almost tangible as I wrote, "I've come for my holidays," and, "It's a few days' break from responsibility at home." The room was quiet, and gradually it dawned on me that the Lord was very present and was in the process of healing me from the infection that was threatening the full recovery of my liver function. This conviction grew in spite of the almost constant pain. I knew that many were praying for healing and I found myself writing to friends, "I truly believe that the Lord will use this medical test, this biopsy, to prove He has healed me completely from any further complications from the hepatitis. Thank you for your prayers." That evening, my parents visited and I was allowed back into my cubicle to face a plate of cooked liver for my evening meal!

On waking the next day, I re-read a verse I had been given on a bookmark by a friend at All Saints: "...do not fear, for I am with you; do not be dismayed, for I am your God. I will strengthen you and help you; I will uphold you with my righteous right hand."[11] At 10.45 am, my bed was wheeled into a side room and a local anaesthetic injected just below the rib cage on my right-hand side. Five, ten, fifteen minutes passed and Dr Harrison had still not appeared. "I will not fear" went through my mind a dozen times as I

[11] Isaiah 41:10

felt a further injection being administered. At that point he arrived, full of apologies, accompanied by a group of medical students who positioned themselves around the foot of the bed. I lifted my right arm on request and covered my face, picturing God's righteous right hand covering mine, and waited. "Have you done it?" I asked seconds later, having not felt even the slightest prick. "Oh yes," he replied, "would you like to see it?" In front of my eyes was a tiny sample of my liver tissue floating in a jar half full of some sort of solution. Showing my ignorance still further, I asked, "Is that all you need?" to which there was laughter from the foot of the bed! "Oh yes," he smiled, "this is plenty," seemingly pleased with the whole procedure.

That evening, as I settled in the hospital cubicle with my blood pressure being checked every fifteen minutes, I shared with my parents and marvelled at the whole experience. I was enormously grateful for the medical attention I was receiving, and looking forward to discharge the next day. My father came at 3.30 pm and we were home just after 4 pm. There followed a restful weekend, and on Monday morning, October 15th, as I helped my mother with the washing, I realised that I was completely without pain in my liver area. That evening, my parents resumed their visits to my ailing grandfather in hospital and I drove to my Arabic class in a nearby school, feeling so much better.

Wednesday 17th was the date of my first follow-up appointment at the Liver Clinic at MRI, one week after the biopsy. Sitting in the waiting room surrounded by some very sick people, I reflected upon the lack of pain and my conviction that the results of this biopsy would prove that God had healed completely. "All is clear," pronounced Dr Harrison. "We just need further blood tests to trace any infection." My appointments at the clinic continued throughout November until the specialist was convinced that the liver was functioning normally. "All we can find are the antibodies from your TABT (typhoid and tetanus) inoculations and so I see no reason why you should not return to Lebanon in January." There was a cautionary word about overworking for the next twelve months or so and a request for regular blood tests.

I was absolutely jubilant and so thankful to God and, indeed, to the medics at Manchester Royal for this miracle of healing. It was not until much later that I learnt from Afaf that on the very day I was writing letters in the ward waiting room, she and two other friends from LIVF had gathered to pray in her office in Beirut. "We pleaded with the Lord for Him to heal you," she said when I managed to contact her by phone with the news that I had been cleared to return after Christmas. *"I am the Lord, who heals you."*[12] My heart was full of praise. It was only two weeks later that we received a call to inform us that my mother's father had, as expected, died peacefully in his sleep. His funeral was a sombre yet moving service, and for the first time for many months, I was able to stand throughout the singing of every hymn.

December was a busy month, full of goodbyes to family and friends. I met with small contact groups of friends from All Saints in their homes and testified to the Lord's healing. I shared about the school and the church work that I hoped to be involved in on my return to Lebanon and thanked them again for their support in prayer and finance. A big surprise came in the form of a cheque from Suzette, the mother of Mac, whom I had taught in the kindergarten before the Civil War had begun. Suzette and I had shared weekly Bible study together after school, and though she and George with their son, Mac, had returned to her home country of South Africa in 1975, we had kept in touch by letter and prayer for each other. The monies had been collected at her hairdressing salon near Johannesburg as a contribution towards the church work I would be doing in Beirut. I was greatly encouraged by this loving gift and the note that came with it from the ladies in Afrikaans and English: "I pray for you. ... Hope you get better soon. ... May the Lord bless you for your faithful witness to Him. ... Wonderful to know that you trust Him in all your needs. ... God bless."

Christmas preparations at home were exciting as my mother and I baked cakes, puddings and mince pies. We even managed to make sweets – chocolate truffles and marzipan fruits, fudges and toffees – and wrap them as gifts in recycled chocolate boxes for the whole family. Alongside these preparations and the many farewells, I was so thankful to have more energy to think into what I would need to prepare for my return. There were boxes of school equipment for the kindergarten to pack and new cotton dresses to sew using my mother's manual Singer sewing machine. I even managed an overnight visit to see friends in the Wirral, including Gwyneth, who had encouraged me to follow God's call to Lebanon in 1973. On Christmas Eve, snow descended like a thick blanket, and by the end of the week we were completely snowed in. Packing continued after Christmas celebrations amidst the busyness of much shovelling of snow in order to back the car out of the drive! I was glad to seal the last box and

12 Exodus 15:26

bundle the thirty-five kilograms of kindergarten equipment into the boot of the car and drive through gritted roads to TMA (Terminal Manoeuvring Area) at Manchester Ringway airport.

My valedictory service at All Saints on Sunday, January 13th, 1980 was memorable. I was given an opportunity to reflect on my extended time at home during the summer and autumn and the wonder of God's healing from hepatitis. I spoke from Philippians 4 and Paul's gratitude to the church for their regular support for him in prayer and finance. I was convinced that God would supply all my needs, and indeed, as Paul said, *"...my God will meet all your needs according to the riches of his glory in Christ Jesus."*[13] What more wonderful promise could any of us ask for at the beginning of a new year? "You are my Philippi," I said to all those who had come to bid me farewell. One by one, my father and other friends laid hands upon me as I knelt, praying the power and presence of the Holy Spirit to equip and go before me into this new phase of my life and work in Lebanon. They prayed for the work of the school in the midst of the continuing civil strife, my developing work with the Alliance Church, and for God's help in living a balanced life as I continued to recover post hepatitis. The following verses[14] were given as a prayer of reassurance of God's faithfulness to me:

> Help me, dear Lord,
> To live from day to day.
> And leave to Thee the planning
> Of my way;
> Accepting what I cannot understand,
> Just knowing I am guided
> By Thy hand.
>
> Give me, dear Lord,
> The strength from day to day
> Closely to follow Thee
> Along life's way,
> Courageous, strong and steady
> In the fight,
> To keep my faith
> Till faith be turned to sight.

[13] Philippians 4:19
[14] I have been unable to trace the source of these verses.

Give me, dear Lord,
The strength to do Thy will,
In faithfulness and love
To serve Thee still
And, lifting up my eyes,
Help me to see
The way ahead is planned
In love by Thee.

CHAPTER TWENTY-THREE

The End of the Beginning

My journey back to Lebanon was far from uneventful. I drew the curtains on the morning of Tuesday, January 15th to a world of white, following a fresh heavy snowfall in the night. My father had parked the car on an even patch of ground near the main road, which had been well gritted the night before. Having bidden farewell to Granny, my mother and brother Robin the previous evening, Dad and I trudged our way to the car in the early hours laden with luggage.

My flights were booked for a three-stage journey: Manchester Ringway to London Heathrow on the regular shuttle service, then Heathrow to Warsaw and Warsaw to Beirut on LOT Polish Airlines. I was eagerly anticipating meeting up with one of the Polish mature students whom I had met at the IFES Conference at Oak Hall College in the summer of 1977. I had kept in touch with Nina by letter and arranged to meet her at the airport. As I was due to arrive in Warsaw at 2.15 pm local time, departing for Beirut at 1.30 am the following day, there would be time to spend a few hours together in Warsaw. My mother had helped me to pack a small hamper of 'goodies' that were not available in Poland at that time, including some homemade cakes. I had previously paid for a transit visa at the Polish Embassy in Beirut that was neatly stamped in my passport.

Dad drove as steadily as he could to Ringway, but we were held up time and again with broken-down vehicles and snow ploughs blocking the roads. At last, the airport was in sight, and I made my way as quickly as I could to book my cases through to Beirut. I then discovered that I was just too late to board the 8.20 am shuttle to Heathrow and my luggage was already on its way! Dad came with me to the airport desk and helped me to reroute my journey from Heathrow to Warsaw via Brussels, as it was now clear that I would miss the 10.50 am Heathrow to Warsaw flight. I was deeply disappointed, but thankful for the airline staff and Dad's help in paying the extra fee. We also asked the staff to cable a message to the airport to inform my friend Nina of the new expected arrival time of 9 pm. Thankfully, there was a seat on the next shuttle, and I arrived at Heathrow Terminal 1 late morning to the message that my cases had been offloaded at Terminal 2 – and would I please go and collect them? A little later, I bought a postcard of a tranquil-looking scene of Tower Bridge from the Thames and proceeded to pen the following in tiny writing:

12.40 pm, Terminal 1

Dearest Dad and Mum,

I'm sitting, at long last, with a ham sandwich and cup of coffee from the Buffet, and an orange Club biscuit from Mum, having collected my cases from Terminal 2, taken them through Customs (!), pushed it all back in the trolley back to Terminal 1 and rebooked it in for the next three flights! I feel a bit confused, but basically (the ham sandwich will help!) this postcard does depict the <u>peace</u> and the thankfulness that does indeed reign in my heart. <u>Thank you so much, Dad</u> – only the Lord knows why this had to happen, so I'm trusting Him. I want to ring you again, but I just can't speak at the moment. Trust this will serve instead. All will be well. Love and thank you. W

The flight to Brussels was short and smooth, with time for another sandwich in the airport transit lounge before it was time to board the Warsaw flight, which landed in pitch dark at 9 pm local time. The snow lay thick on the ground, like pack ice, and the air was decidedly frosty. I had snoozed (intentionally) on the flight because I was keen to spend at least a little time with Nina – but would she have received the message about the delay? Clutching my hand luggage with the precious hamper, I hurriedly made my way out of Arrivals using my Polish transit visa to access the main concourse. Anxiously, I scanned every face to see if Nina were waiting for me. I pleaded with the airport staff for any news of her but to no avail. Disappointment followed disappointment, as time passed and there was no sign of my friend. As I wandered round the concourse, memories of *Dr Zhivago*[1] came flooding back – men in long heavy coats and Cossack-style hats and women in dark woollen clothing with huge fur

---

[1] 1965 David Lean film based on the novel by Boris Pasternak set in Russia during the first half of the twentieth century

collars and hats. All seemed to have hard, sad and emotionless faces. The concourse was illuminated by bare lightbulbs that emphasised the darkness as passengers scurried about. As my hopes of meeting Nina gradually diminished, I sat on a bench trying to read and pray, pausing from time to time to check the decreasing number of faces as time wore on and the concourse emptied of passengers. *"How long, LORD? Will you forget me for ever? How long will you hide your face from me?"*[2]

As midnight passed, I made my way back into the Departure lounge. It was with a mixture of relief and sadness that I responded to the hollow sound of the flight call at around 1 am, weeping in my heart. I shall never forget the short walk from the airport building onto the tarmac, watching my breath form droplets in the freezing air. It was minus fourteen degrees centigrade as we boarded the plane and I sank into my window seat and the relative warmth of the aircraft. It was now eighteen hours since I had left home with my father, and I was still many miles from my destination. I was soon in a deep sleep, only to be abruptly disturbed in the early hours as we were informed that the aircraft would be landing at Istanbul airport for a short stop – and would all passengers prepare to disembark? I could hardly believe my ears and cried to the Lord for strength to move. Within minutes, a second announcement came over the speakers to the effect that ongoing passengers could remain in their seats and we would be departing for Beirut very soon. *"But I trust in your unfailing love; my heart rejoices in your salvation. I will sing the Lord's praise for he has been good to me."*[3] With a heart full of gratitude, I dozed again until woken with breakfast around 7 am. "The sun was rising and it was beautiful," I wrote home later, "and we landed on time in Beirut at 7.30 am, almost twenty-four hours since we left home on Tuesday, Dad." From then on, all went smoothly as I collected my luggage and walked through Customs. I was so thankful to spot Afaf along with Pastor and Mrs Taylor from the Alliance Church waiting at the barrier to welcome me back. The rest of that day was a blur as I went with Afaf to her home in Beirut and collapsed on her bed!

For the next few days, there were phone calls and visitors, and gradually my involvement at both Eastwood College and the Alliance Church began to take shape. Afaf helped me move into the sixth-floor flat near the Bristol Hotel, and there was a beautiful bunch of carnations from Alison in my room. Antoine and Mary from LIVF visited with roses, and

[2] Psalm 13:1
[3] Psalm 13:5,6

Joy and Sami invited me for a welcome meal along with Pastor and Mrs Taylor. It was such a precious time. Hazel came to speak about the school and encouraged me to come to Kafarshima as soon as possible. She would have liked me to be at school every day for a couple of hours, but eventually we agreed I would work at Eastwood for two full days a week, Mondays and

View of the Bristol Hotel from the flat balcony, June 1980.

Thursdays, taking Assemblies and administering the department.

My first day at school was non-stop! Amine picked me up at 8 am, and I was reminded of the sheer volume of traffic and the hazards of Beirut driving. It was a joy to meet the staff and go round the classrooms. There were now six classes in the department of over one hundred and sixty children and ten staff, some of whom were quite new to me. Hazel had organised a welcome lunch in her fifth-floor flat, and I was delighted to catch up with the teachers whom I knew and be introduced to the new ones and hear their concerns. Parents, too, were asking for progress reports and meetings, so I could see there was plenty to be attended to. "I'm so grateful," I wrote home, "that Hazel has accepted that I will not actually take classes, because I do believe this will give me more time for personal chats with the staff in their free periods and times of prayer and Bible study with them." I was amazed at how the numbers had increased throughout the school. Even though there was no permanent political solution in Lebanon, it did seem as though life was more relaxed and more roads were open, though I was aware of the occasional explosion and burst of shooting.

My first Sunday at the Alliance Church was a lovely time of worship, followed by a welcome meal at a local restaurant. Pastor and Mrs Taylor were keen that I should ease my way gradually into church work, for which I was grateful as it soon became clear that my two days a week at the school would be very busy. I knew that I would need time to adjust to regulating my energy levels and to be patient with myself. "Praise God," I wrote home, "that He's helping me to pace myself, though it isn't easy. I

Esther Oud, summer 1980.

get tired very quickly, feel fine for a while and then quite suddenly lose my stamina."

Initially, I committed to teaching Sunday school at the church with the little ones and attending the weekly prayer meeting on Wednesday evenings. After a few weeks, I was able to help Mrs Taylor with the weekly women's meeting at the church, which we eventually moved to the sitting room of the flat, as its location was convenient for most of the ladies. In the light of the uncertain political situation, Mrs Taylor's devotional Bible studies were wonderfully faith-building and greatly appreciated. I cherish a letter I received from one of the ladies later in the year:

My name is Esther. I found Jesus Christ in your apartment. I'm sure you remember me now. Wendy, I'm a servant for our Lord now. I walk with Him, I live with Him and I'll serve Him till the end of my life because He saved me. Praise the Lord.

With love from your sister, Esther.

Another lady, who with her family was emigrating from Lebanon because of the insecurities, gave me a bookmark on which she wrote:

Dear Wendy,

Thanks so much for all you did and meant to me. May the Lord keep you safely in Lebanon and use you greatly there. May He keep your family too in His peace. Hope to see you sometime in the future!

Much love from Elisheva.

The Taylors encouraged me to register for colloquial Arabic classes at Beirut University College (BUC), which was only a seven-minute walk from the flat. I was keen to improve my spoken Arabic and glad I had been able to continue studying the language whilst at home the previous year. "I believe I can afford it at long last with the help of the money from All Saints," I wrote home. Alison too was studying Arabic, in order to get to know some of the students. As Amine was paying me a part-time salary that was adequate for my daily needs, I was planning to save the rest of the All Saints' monies for purchasing a car when the time was right. "My Arabic classes started this week," I wrote on Monday, February 25th, when there was a strike in East Beirut and all the schools were closed for the day. "It's just so exciting. I go from 10.45 to 11.45 am on Wednesdays and Fridays, and already

My Sunday school class at the Alliance church, June 1980.

I've learnt how to conjugate regular verbs and weak verbs in the present and past tenses!" My teacher was the pastor's wife from the Presbyterian church. "She's a dear soul and a real believer," I wrote home, "and has taught many of the Alliance missionaries in the past."

It was about this time that I received an airmail letter from Brenda, the headmistress of the comprehensive school in Wallasey where I had taught previously. Her wise words and the Scripture verse she shared were a huge encouragement to me as I sought to make the most of the energy I had and the variety of school and church work as well as the language learning that lay ahead. She wrote:

I have been thinking of you so much this week and praying. I am sure that the Lord will enable you to do whatever He has prepared for you in Lebanon. If it's not exactly the same as before, don't be discouraged. When I started something new and different once, He gave me a verse that has always been a great help, 'Therefore, since through God's mercy we have this ministry, we do not lose heart.'[4]

On many occasions, I returned to this word from Scripture as a clear reminder that, in His mercy, God would indeed equip me with all I needed for each day's commitments. As I wrote home, "The Arabic lessons mean that I now have one definite purpose for each weekday: Monday, school; Tuesday, women's meeting at the Alliance; Wednesday, Arabic lesson and church prayer meeting at 5 pm; Thursday, school; and Friday, Arabic lesson." I was also working towards joining Afaf at the LIVF centre in Beirut for students' lunch on Wednesdays and Bible study on Friday

[4] 2 Corinthians 4:1

afternoons. "Do keep on praying I'll have more patience with myself," I wrote home, "and a 'sound mind' in the face of so many pressures." As Paul wrote to Timothy, "...*I put thee in remembrance that thou stir up the gift of God, which is in thee by the putting on of my hands. For God hath not given us the spirit of fear; but of power, and of love, and of a sound mind.*"[5]

My two days a week at Eastwood were challenging and emotionally exhausting. I knew I could continue to rely upon the hard work and good will of the teachers I had worked with in the past, but now I was keen to train the two new kindergarten teachers and spent time preparing teaching schedules for them to follow. "It's a joy to be planning the Assemblies again," I wrote home. "Did I tell you we now have two Assemblies in the department every day – one for the threes and fours and the other for the fives and sixes – about seventy-five to eighty children in each?" More than one hundred and sixty children had proved too large a number, especially as we continued to celebrate birthdays in Assembly and encourage individual children to contribute to the worship. I often witnessed the Bible story gripping everyone, children and adults alike, and rejoiced in the power of God's Word. What a privilege it was to share it in school and with my Sunday school class at the Alliance Church.

In addition to teacher training and taking Assemblies, I was also helping with report-writing and organising parents' meetings, but this was clearly taking its toll on my limited supply of emotional and physical energy. I often found myself in a tearful and overanxious state, and was thankful for those at school, at church and LIVF friends who would pause to listen and pray with me. "I love it when I'm here at school," I wrote home, "but it's when I get home that the extreme exhaustion and heart-pounding sets in and really gets me down." I was due for routine blood tests mid March, and the results were satisfactory with the liver functioning normally. "Praise God," I wrote home. "I knew He had completely healed, but it has been so easy to get depressed because of my still very limited stamina. I pray the Lord will lay it on someone's heart to take my place when the time comes."

Dr Manoogian did, however, suggest that I should take a mild tranquilliser for a few months as I sought to steer an even course through all the demands of anxious parents and unruly children. "You are recovering from the aftereffects of the hepatitis, and you must pace yourself," he cautioned. "Don't be ashamed of resting when you need to."

[5] 2 Timothy 1:6,7 (AV)

I often found the Psalms to be a source of strength and comfort. *"My flesh and my heart may fail, but God is the strength of my heart and my portion for ever."*[6]

Pastor and Mrs Taylor were very gracious in their acceptance of my need to take time to rest, and I appreciated their understanding. I had joined the international Alliance Church in Beirut not long after my arrival in Lebanon. As Hazel was a regular attender at the 11 am English service, she had encouraged Margaret, Kirstene and me to go along with her and meet her English-speaking friends. There were many from the United States, including Pastor Harry Taylor and his wife Miriam. This was not the first time I had worshipped with American Christians, and I had come to appreciate their openness and big-hearted friendliness. Many worked with other mission agencies, basing themselves in Beirut and reaching out to other Middle Eastern countries.

My first experience of missionaries from the US was during my second trip to Morocco in 1972. I had been invited to meet an American family who lived and worked on a farm situated west of Tangier along the Atlantic coast. I recall being overwhelmed by their hospitality. "Well, hello Wendy. You are just so welcome. Come right in and make yourself real comfortable." This family offered the seclusion of their farmhouse, its land and outbuildings, not only to weary mission workers but also to groups of believers who would not otherwise have been able to meet openly and worship together. I found Pastor and Mrs Taylor to be similarly open-hearted and was warming to the opportunity of working alongside them in the coming months, as energy allowed. Mrs Taylor, in particular, took full advantage of the emphasis upon offering hospitality and visiting which is so important in Arabic culture.

Like Hazel, the Taylors had been working as missionaries for many years. Having met at Bible college in the States and married in 1935, their first assignment with the Christian and Missionary Alliance (C&MA) was in 1938. Miriam had grown up as the eldest daughter of missionary parents who worked in Palestine with the mission. She studied at the mission school in Jerusalem until she was sixteen years old. Most of her lessons were in Arabic, and Miriam was adept at learning the language. After some three years pastoring a church in Virginia, the Taylors' first mission assignment overseas, however, was not to an Arabic-speaking country but to Cambodia. Arriving with their two-year-old son in a country about to

6   Psalm 73:26

be overrun by the Japanese at the outset of World War II, it was not long before expediency demanded that they evacuate to the Philippines, especially as Miriam was pregnant with their second child. Even before their baby was born, they received the news that the Japanese had bombed Pearl Harbour, and within hours the islands were being overrun. There was simply no time to evacuate again, and miraculously their daughter was born safely on Christmas Day 1941. It was not long before all American and British missionaries were rounded up and interned in a large military camp where they were held as Japanese prisoners of war in appalling conditions. They were finally released in February 1945. Two years of recuperation followed for the Taylor family in the States, during which time their third child was born. Undaunted, in 1947, they returned to Cambodia and worked there for eighteen years. They set up a Bible school to train pastors, took prison services and distributed Cambodian New Testaments and Christian literature. There was much opposition from the government and from communist rebel bands who roamed the countryside.

Eventually, in 1965, all American citizens were deported from Cambodia, and the Taylors were redirected by the C&MA to the Middle East a year later. At last, Miriam could use her knowledge of Arabic. Mission churches had been planted in Syria, Jordan and Lebanon over many years and had need of an administrator. Pastor Taylor was happy to preach through interpreters in the Arabic-speaking churches throughout the region but had a deep desire to pastor a local congregation. He firmly believed that he and Miriam had been led at this stage of their lives to start an international church in Beirut and reach out from there.

By the time I joined the church, it was well established and was about to plant an Arabic-speaking fellowship in Karentina, near Beirut docks. This group would be pastored by Sami, father of Anna, one of my first pupils at Eastwood, and husband of Joy, who taught in the pre-school in those early days. It was Sami who had arranged for my miraculous flight home in December 1975 at the height of the Civil War, and I was so grateful for their hospitality and open home for me throughout my years in Lebanon.

The Taylors were nearing retirement from working overseas and yet still had energy for preaching and personal work amongst people of many different nationalities residing in Beirut. Harry was deeply committed to one-to-one Bible study with anyone who was searching for the truth of the gospel of Jesus Christ. His preaching was always rooted in Biblical truth. Influenced by the writings of A. W. Tozer, he often referred to the deeper Christian life amidst the busyness and risky living of war-torn Lebanon. Tozer was an American preacher whose teaching always focussed on our merciful God's undeserved love revealed in the person of Jesus Christ, our Saviour and Lord. I warmed to this emphasis upon knowing God personally and consciously, waiting and watching for His loving provision and being thankful for the gift of each day. *"We wait in hope for the LORD; he is our help and our shield. ... May your unfailing love be with us, LORD, even as we put our hope in you."*[7] How I trusted that my spiritual life would deepen and that my faith would be strengthened! I truly desired periods of quiet with the Lord as I came to terms with the need to pace myself in recovery from the hepatitis. *"Be still, and know that I am God..."*[8]

As time went by, it was becoming increasingly obvious that I needed to acquire a small car. This would enable me to drive independently to Eastwood on Mondays and Thursdays, as well as to make short journeys in and around Beirut when it was safe to do so. I had approached Edmond, Amine's brother, who worked with his father at their garage in Furn el Chebbak near the Green Line that separated East and West Beirut. If Edmond were willing to sell me a car, accept a small down payment and allow me to pay the balance by monthly instalments, I figured the All Saints gift of a hundred pounds per month would suffice. I asked my parents to pray for God's provision of the right car and that the monthly donations would continue until December 1980! "Edmond encouraged me to go and see a 1971 1400cc Renault 12," I wrote home, "which had been brought in from Belgium. It is slightly rusty around the headlamps but not too bashed about otherwise, and certainly not rusting in the bodywork above the tyres." Nada, who was sharing with us in the flat, came with me, and we drove round the block. This was the first time I had driven since my return to Lebanon; the gear change was smooth and I was delighted. Edmond could not have been more helpful, as he offered to check out the car mechanically and fit four new tyres. It would be ready for me the following week, along with the paperwork and contract for payment. "We made out the monthly payments in absolute faith, as far as I was concerned," I wrote home, "that All Saints would be prepared to support

7 Psalm 33:20,22
8 Psalm 46:10

Nada in Kafarshima.

me till December 1980 at one hundred pounds per month, and then the car will be paid for!"

I drove back to the flat in jubilation at my new freedom, and Afaf came to lunch, bearing mail from the UK that included a letter from the treasurer at All Saints, confirming that they would support me financially for the whole of 1980! I recalled with gratitude that moment in my farewell service in January when praying friends at the church had laid hands on me, asking for God to supply all my needs as I ventured back to Lebanon to serve Him. *"…my God will meet all your needs according to the riches of his glory in Christ Jesus."*[9]

Afaf and others had warned me about the high rate of stolen cars that were reported in the Arabic news bulletins. "It seems that between ten and fifteen cars are stolen in Beirut every night," I wrote, perhaps unwisely, to my parents. "I have to park on the road; there's nowhere else. Please do ask the church to pray that the Lord will really protect this car they're giving me." Being secondhand and somewhat worse for wear was a useful burglar deterrent in itself, and Afaf gave me a Krooklok, which I faithfully applied between the clutch and steering wheel every time I parked the car. I was now able to drive myself to school and back, and this proved to be a huge blessing. I could leave at 7.30 am and arrive in good time before the school buses offloaded their precious cargo and the children tumbled into their classrooms.

Travelling to school with Amine had given me insights into side roads and other detours from the main road south from Beirut to Kafarshima. These were useful escape routes when clashes and shooting were heard or people by the roadside were gesticulating that the road ahead was unsafe. One morning, as I made my way cautiously through the Beirut traffic, I realised that in spite of pumping furiously on the foot brake, I was gradually sliding towards the car ahead of me. Pulling on the handbrake, I graciously veered to the right into a petrol station. As I lifted the bonnet, I was horrified to find that the brake fluid had leaked and was non-existent! A helpful mechanic filled the container for me, and I set off again,

[9] Philippians 4:19

trusting the Lord for a safe journey to Kafarshima. Thankfully, Edmond was able to arrange for the brakes to be fixed whilst I was in school.

Not long before Easter, I arrived home and parked the Renault outside the entrance to the building. I duly applied the Krooklok, and hesitated as I considered the items on the back seat that I needed to take to school the following day. Finally, I decided to leave them covered over with an old sheet, locked the car

Afaf and Lina on sixth-floor balcony Alliance flat, Beirut, summer 1980.

and took the lift up to our sixth-floor flat. The following day, I discovered to my dismay that I had left the front passenger window completely open! Prayer for protection had certainly been answered, as not a single item had been disturbed.

Having earmarked the All Saints' gift entirely for purchase of the car, I was trusting the Lord for the finance to buy an air ticket for my flight home in the summer, and saving every penny! My part-time salary from Amine was sufficient for daily living expenses and little else, and I was to discover that living on the breadline would be a faith-testing experience. My aim was to garner enough mental and physical energy for the Arabic study and work with the church, and to avoid letting responsibilities at Eastwood spill over into the other days of the week. It was not always easy to make ends meet, and there were times when I was overwhelmed with people's generosity to me. Along with surprise financial gifts that came my way, friends were generous with their time, their prayers and their empathy with my health issues as I continued to recover from the hepatitis. Even Dr Manoogian refused to accept payment when I consulted him for medication to help me manage my anxiety and mental depression. "The Lord is really demanding that I live by faith in His ability to provide for me financially," I wrote home, "and also give me wisdom in using the money I do have."

It was towards the end of March that I received a letter from my parents in which they shared that my maternal grandmother, widowed the previous October, was failing in health and had been moved to a nursing home. She died on Good Friday, and though I was able to catch the line and speak with my brother Robin, which was a comfort, I longed to be able to fly home and be with the family. Knowing this would be impossible at that time, I wept on my own in the flat and became increasingly aware that I needed to be with God's people.

A friend had provided for Afaf and me, along with a group from LIVF, to spend a couple of nights midweek in a guest house run by some German nuns in Ainab, a mountain village on the western slopes of Mount Lebanon. The air was fresh as I drove myself up the twisty mountain roads and away from the hustle and bustle of Beirut. "Afaf and the others were so understanding," I wrote home, "and it was lovely to spend time together in such a quiet and peaceful place." As well as walking amidst the pine trees, we were able to sit together in the grounds and spend time with God's Word, which I found so reassuring. *"Make me to know thy ways, O LORD; teach me thy paths."*[10] *"Teach me thy way, O LORD; and lead me on a level path…"*[11] *"Commit your way to the LORD; trust in him and he will act."*[12] As I prayed these scriptures, I knew that the time had come to resign from Eastwood at the end of the school year and focus upon my work with the Alliance Church in Beirut. It was as if the burden of balancing the demands of school alongside my desire to serve the church was being lifted. "I praise God every time I realise the meaning and power behind people's prayer for me and Lebanon," I wrote home, "but fighting post-hepatitis depression and battling to get some sort of pattern into my life in this chaotic country with its constant political uncertainties is quite an experience."

The following Monday, before school reopened for the summer term, I had lunch with Hazel. To my great relief, I found that she, and later Amine, was understanding and accepting of my decision. "The Lord has given me a wonderful peace that He is guiding continually," I wrote home, "even in the darkest places." I concluded the letter, "I hope to be able to go to Eastwood tomorrow, but there was fighting around the road I usually take to school today! So I shan't go unless absolutely sure the road is safe."

One day, not long after Easter, I received a message from an LIVF friend that a Mr and Mrs Dbyan, a Druze couple with four teenage

[10] Psalm 25:4 (RSV)
[11] Psalm 27:11 (RSV)
[12] Psalm 37:5 (RSV)

children, were searching for a mother-tongue English speaker to teach them English and provide oral practice. Mrs Dbyan was French-educated and at an intermediate stage, and her husband was a complete beginner. They would pay the going rate of twenty Lebanese lira per lesson and would like me to go twice a week! Would I be interested? I most certainly was – and so thankful for this financial provision. The Dbyans lived in a large apartment in Beirut, and after an hour-long formal lesson with each of them, I was invited to stay for a meal on the balcony and continue conversing in English around the table with the whole family. Mrs Dbyan was a superb Lebanese cook, and one of her specialities was *kibbeh nayé*. *Kibbeh* is the national dish of Lebanon and Syria, and I had grown to enjoy Madame Khoury's *kibbeh*, a mixture of *burghal*[13], grated onion and minced lamb pounded to a paste, either baked in the oven or deep-fried in oval-shaped balls. Eaten raw, *kibbeh nayé* is served as an appetiser with young cos lettuce leaves, a squeeze of lemon and a drizzle of olive oil. I am ashamed to say I would roll the smallest portion of *kibbeh nayé* around in my mouth and then surreptitiously hide it under a lettuce leaf on my plate.

My twice-weekly lessons with the Dbyans were an unexpected joy, and I felt so blessed, especially so when they introduced me to a young teacher from their school called Ibtisam, a complete beginner, who would come to the house and became my third adult pupil. Her name means 'smiling' and she too was a joy to teach. "Teaching these three has been a good experience and far less physically tiring than school work," I wrote to my parents. *"No good thing does the* LORD *withhold from those who walk uprightly."*[14] I was now in a position to be generous and hospitable and enjoy having friends for meals in the flat. "The Taylors came for a meal last Tuesday evening, and we had a relaxed time together," I wrote home at the end of May, having booked my air ticket for my flight home on Friday, June 20th via Budapest and Heathrow. "They really want me back to work full time with the church, but only when I know I'm really fit. So we wait on the Lord for His timing." *"Be still before the* LORD, *and wait patiently for him…"*[15]

The final couple of weeks were full of packing and farewells. Afaf and her mother had continued to offer me hospitality, especially on Sundays when I would drive to their home after church and Sunday school. I

[13] fine cracked wheat
[14] Psalm 84:11b (RSV)
[15] Psalm 37:7a (RSV)

thanked my Arabic teacher, prayed with the ladies who came to the flat for Bible study and fellowship, said goodbye to LIVF friends at the Centre and to the Dbyans, and enjoyed farewell meals with the Taylors and others from the church. My final day at school was memorable, and I was so thankful that Heather had agreed to lead the department in the future. The kindergarten had organised a *haffleh*[16] for me, followed by Assembly and a lovely gift from the staff as we shared lunch together. I cherish this gift – a gold pendant in the shape of a small cedar tree with a chain. I wrote to my parents, "To everything there is a season, and certainly the season for my work at Eastwood has definitely come to an end. The Lord knows what both their future and mine hold, and I'm content to rest in the awareness of that." I was fully anticipating my return to Beirut in September 1980 in better physical health in order to work full time with the Alliance Church. But that was not to be.

Just as my journey back to Lebanon was fraught with hold-ups and disappointments, I was to discover that though the liver was completely healed and free from infection, the transition back to normal life was to be far from easy. There was no doubt that these were increasingly unsettled and dangerous days, and many expatriates were preparing to leave. 'Normal living' was a veneer that covered an uncertain and worrying future for Lebanon. The capital city and effectively the country were still divided politically, and kidnappings were on the rise. Yet though I did not return, other than for a brief visit early in 1981 to pack up my belongings, God never failed to keep the promise He had given me in November 1972: *"...I will be with you; I will not fail you or forsake you."*[17] His call was reiterated time and again, especially through the period of rehabilitation from the hepatitis. *"Abide in me, and I in you. ... for apart from me you can do nothing."*[18] I was convinced that God was in control and there was a purpose for my being in this country to which I had been called at that time. I am forever grateful to all those who drew alongside me during those bewildering six months and who prayed with me. I am grateful, too, for the comfort and presence of the Holy Spirit during times of intense anxiety and tearfulness. I am thankful for every opportunity to listen and pray with people whose lives had been shattered and whose cares were so great. I was in no doubt that the Lebanese people would always remain close to my heart whatever

[16] party
[17] Joshua 1:5b (RSV)
[18] John 15:4,5 (RSV)

298

happened in the years to come. It was the end of the beginning of a lifelong desire to serve God amongst Arabic-speaking peoples.

Epilogue

Lord, You've been good to me
All my life, all my life.
Your loving kindness never fails.
I will remember
All You have done.
Bring from my heart
Thanksgiving songs.[1]

I will be ever thankful for the opportunity God gave me to live and work in Lebanon during those tumultuous years for the country and her peoples. This period of my life was just the beginning of a lifelong love of the Lebanese and Arabic-speaking peoples. The call to love and share Christ has never wavered. With the passage of the years of war in Lebanon and the multiple displacements from different homes and places of refuge, the families of the children I taught are doubtless now scattered around the world. Only eternity will reveal their heart responses to the message of Jesus and God's love for each one that we shared in school each day.

As I settled back in England during the 1980s while the strife raged on in Lebanon, the post-hepatitis depression began to lift. My father helped me to buy a little terraced house in Cheltenham near to where I had previously spent four years teacher training. This was familiar territory, and it was a joy to welcome visitors from Lebanon, especially during the summer months. Nerissa, whom I had taught in my first Junior 1 class and daughter of Jill, one of the Eastwood teachers, became my lodger for two years as she studied for A levels at the local grammar school. By 1986, I was teaching again at a primary school in Gloucester with a high percentage of Asian children who were learning Arabic at the local mosque. With the help of Alan and Irene, a local couple who had prayed for MECO[2] partners for many years, a Middle East prayer group was started, which was a support to me too as I visited the homes of Muslim

---

[1] Graham Kendrick. Copyright ©2001 Make Way Music. www.grahamkendrick.co.uk. International copyright secured. All rights reserved. Used by permission.

[2] Middle East Christian Outreach, now SIM Middle East

families in the city. I longed to return to Lebanon, but the political situation was still volatile, with violence and kidnappings widely reported.

In 1990, I met Ian, who had returned from a three-year work assignment in the United States. We soon found we had many common interests and aspirations, not least the desire to work abroad! On his first Sunday back at church, he was asked to read from the Old Testament. *"'For I know the plans I have for you,' declares the LORD, 'plans to prosper you and not to harm you, plans to give you hope and a future.'"*[3] I knew God was once again speaking very directly to me through His Word, and had a deep inner conviction that this man would be part of God's good plan for me. By this time, my parents were living in a flat in Cheltenham, and my father's health was failing as Alzheimer's and Lewy body dementia took its toll. Ian and I married in October 1992; I was forty-five.

In 1997, after my father's death, Ian and I were able to visit Lebanon together. I was not prepared for a country recovering from sixteen years of civil war and trying to rebuild. Emotionally, the whole experience was draining as we listened to one story after another – homelessness, forced displacement from one part of the country to another, emigration overseas and missing family members. Buried memories on my part were kindled and I was deeply troubled. How could I contemplate returning to Lebanon with such inner disquiet? Furthermore, how could I bring to mind the violence and tragedy of living through the early years of the Civil War in order to debrief the trauma so many years later?

My husband Ian was at that time in the process of preparing for work in the international Office of SAT-7 in Nicosia, Cyprus as their Personnel Officer. He had registered for a year's 'Professionals in Mission' course at Redcliffe College, the same institution where I had studied in 1978, now located in nearby Gloucester. To my amazement, I was offered free counselling at the college in order to debrief the memories long buried and so be prepared for a return to the Arab world. My writing now is in part the result of those sessions, as I started to read the letters from Lebanon I had written to my parents and which my mother had kept, all in their original envelopes. The repressed memories were brought into the daylight, and tears were shed in the safe space that my counsellor offered. Writing became my catharsis as I started to piece together the details and line up my patchy memories with the facts, my feelings and my faith, and put pen to paper. This was how my story began, as I sought to remember

3 Jeremiah 29:11

how I was led to fulfil my desire to serve Arab peoples. It was an immensely healing process.

By the autumn of 2000, we were living and working with SAT-7 in Nicosia. This was followed by five weeks of language study in Beirut the following summer. It was a privilege to visit friends, share memories, listen sensitively to their struggles and afflictions, and pray together. Though my widowed mother had initially been enthusiastic about our work in Cyprus and even came to visit us, it was becoming clear that she needed more support. This coincided early in 2003 with Ian's move to Middle East Concern (MEC) as their Research Officer. We were able to visit Lebanon for Easter that year and then to move back to our home in Cheltenham. Ian continued his work with MEC, making regular sorties to the office in Nicosia. As I readjusted once more to life in England, I was able to pick up the writing and, slowly but surely, this book has come into being. Together, Ian and I have spoken at numerous meetings about the issues facing believers in the Middle East when they seek to make their faith known and God's utter faithfulness to those who choose to follow Jesus. I have cherished my visits to Lebanon in recent years and especially when we were invited to attend the fortieth anniversary celebrations at Eastwood College in Kafarshima in 2013.

"Be strong and courageous. Do not be afraid; do not be discouraged, for the LORD your God will be with you wherever you go."[4] God's promise to me has never wavered, but rather deepened in meaning through times of despair and danger as I faced the civil disruption and its consequences, my own health issues and the challenges of readjusting to life in the UK. I continue to remember all the way that God has led me down the years. The journey has been strewn with rich experiences of life, meeting and working with people of many nationalities, languages and cultures. I know that the One who called me to Lebanon will never forsake His people and I will always hold them in my heart. Jesus said, *"In this world you will have trouble. But take heart! I have overcome the world."*[5]

---

[4] Joshua 1:9
[5] John 16:33b

Appendix

In March 2003, I was invited to speak at the World Day of Prayer service that was held in Our Lady of Grace Cathedral in Nicosia, Cyprus. The service had been written by the Christian women of Lebanon, some of whom I knew from my days living and working in the country during the 1970s. The theme of the service was 'Holy Spirit, fill us'. I include my notes here as a testimony to the courage and resilience of these women.

A READING

"In the sixth month … God sent the angel Gabriel to Nazareth, a town in Galilee, to a virgin pledged to be married to a man named Joseph, a descendant of David. The virgin's name was Mary. The angel went to her and said, 'Greetings, you who are highly favoured! The Lord is with you.' Mary was greatly troubled at his words and wondered what kind of greeting this might be."[1]

A PRAYER

"Holy Spirit, come amongst us now. As we ponder these verses of Scripture when the angel appeared to Mary, give us receptive hearts, allowing the Spirit to take the written Word and apply it as the living Word to our inner beings."

I do thank the World Day of Prayer committee for inviting me to lead the meditation at this service. I lived and worked in Lebanon from 1973 to 1980. I taught in a Christian school about ten kilometres south of Beirut in a village called Kafarshima, alongside Lebanese teachers who cared deeply for the children in our charge. I have listened and prayed, laughed and wept with many Lebanese friends as they have sought to come to terms with forces at work in politics and in history – even in Civil War – and to understand that there is a God of justice in control of these processes, a God who is intimately involved in human pain and suffering.

As I meditated upon these words from Luke 1 that we've just heard in Greek, I was moved by the words said to Mary and her response to the surprise visit from the angel. She was *"highly favoured"* and yet *"greatly*

[1]   Luke 1:26-29 (NIV, 1980 edition)

troubled" as she wondered what his words meant. It occurred to me that she remained that way more or less for the rest of her life. I don't believe that she is alone in this; so many of the Christians I meet are very aware of the blessings of God. I recall Georgette, a former colleague of mine in the school who is about to retire. She and her family lost everything in Damour in the early stages of the Civil War in Lebanon. We met her recently. "God has arranged everything in my life," she said, and her heart was full of praise.

Our Lebanese Christian friends who have written this service are only too aware of the blessings of God's provision, His protection and His empowering, but they are also deeply troubled by the pain and problems of this life. That doesn't mean that they have failed – far from it. It means that, like Mary, they have given up the struggle to grasp happiness (as the world sees it). They have settled instead, as Mary did, for the joy of a relationship with Jesus, being with Him, following Him, sometimes into the light and sometimes into apparent darkness. Mary wept for sorrow at the foot of the Cross and for joy when He came back to life. Jesus said we would have troubles in this life, but He also said, *"...take heart! I have overcome the world."*[2]

So may we be willing and obedient, as Mary was, to offer ourselves afresh and to say with the Christian women of Lebanon, "Holy Spirit, fill us."

[2] John 16:33

What Shall I Read Next?

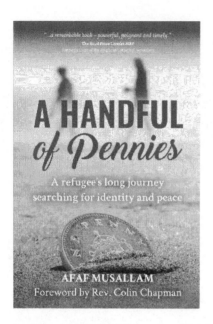

A Handful of Pennies

A refugee's long journey searching for identity and peace

Afaf Musallam

ISBN 978-1-78815-983-8

Available from your local bookshop or scan the QR code below:

In *Letters from Lebanon*, Wendy frequently mentioned her friend Afaf and the kindness shown to her by the Musallams. In *A Handful of Pennies*, Afaf tells her own story.

Born in Haifa, Palestine, Afaf shares her story of becoming a refugee as a child. Soon the whole family settles in Lebanon. Life there is beautiful, but only until religious tensions escalate quickly and the country becomes divided with fierce daily fighting. Her life continues through waves of peace and war, making many necessary choices for her safety and future.

Journey with Afaf as she battles with fear, identity and the guilt of having to leave her elderly mother behind. Through it all, she recognises a God who provides and cares about the very details of her life, leading her to experience true peace, purpose and identity wherever she finds herself.